OBSERVING DEVELOPMENT OF THE YOUNG CHILD

Janice J. Beaty

Elmira College

Charles E. Merrill Publishing Company
A Bell & Howell Company
Columbus   Toronto   London   Sydney

Published by Charles E. Merrill Publishing Company
A Bell & Howell Company
Columbus, Ohio 43216

Text Designer: Susan King
Cover Designer: Cathy Watterson
Production Editor: Susan King
This book was set in Serifa Roman, Serifa Light Roman, Serifa Italic, and Serifa Light Italic

Photo Credits: cover, Vivienne della Grotta; p. 4, Larry Hamill; pp. 36, 61, 77, 186, Ben Chandler; pp. 2, 34, 47, 58, 86, 103, 110, 118, 128, 133, 152, 160, 161, 170, 183, 194, 196, 212, 220, 242, 245, 260, 278, 282, 302, Lloyd Lemmerman; p. 94, Andrew Brunk; pp. 121, 143, 222, 253, 268, 284, 304, Janice Beaty; p. 230, Janet Gagnon.

Library of Congress Catalog Card Number: 85-43083
International Standard Book Number: 0-675-20408-9
Printed in the United States of America

2   3   4   5   6   7   8   9   10—92   91   90   89   88   87   86

To my mother and father

PREFACE

This textbook presents a unique system for observing and recording the development of young children ages two- to six-years-old in an early childhood classroom setting. The text is designed to be used by college students preparing to be teachers in nursery schools, day-care centers, Head Start classes, prekindergarten programs, and kindergarten classrooms. The book also can be used by teachers and assistant teachers in such programs who want to learn more about children in order to make plans for individuals.

The text focuses on observation of the six major aspects of child development: emotional, social, motor, cognitive, language, and creative. Each of these aspects is further divided into two specific areas, which include: self-identity; emotional development; social play; prosocial behavior; large motor development; small motor development; cognitive development of classification and seriation skills; cognitive development of number, time, space, and memory skills; spoken language; written language; art skills; and imagination.

These areas of child development are outlined in a *Child Skills Checklist,* which includes specific, observable child behaviors in the sequence in which they occur. Each of twelve chapters discusses one of these areas, giving ideas for classroom activities if the child being observed has not yet accomplished the items of development. The most recent child development research in each area is presented as background for the *Checklist* items as they are discussed.

The text may serve college students as a guide for observing and recording the development of young children in their student teaching and course work. The book is especially well suited to be a supplementary text for child development courses. It also can be used by in-service teachers and assistants who are upgrading their skills in observing children, as well as learning to plan for individuals based on developmental needs. And, for early childhood teachers and assistants who are working toward their national Child Development Associate (CDA) credentials, this text may serve as a companion volume to the author's *Skills for Preschool Teachers* (Columbus, Ohio: Charles E. Merrill Publishing Company, 1984), which is designed around the CDA Functional Areas.

Unique aspects of *Observing Development of the Young Child* include the latest information on the development of human emotions from babyhood through kindergarten, a new look at moral development in young children (called "prosocial behavior"), a discussion of written language as a natural development rather than as something that has to be taught to children, and a section on the development of the imagination as an important aspect of creativity.

Students and teachers using this detailed system of observing child development should come away with a broader, deeper appreciation of the uniqueness and complexity of the young child. In addition, they should gain confidence and knowledge as they discover specific methods to support and promote individual growth.

ACKNOWLEDGEMENTS

I would like to thank Bonny Helm, CDA field supervisor at Elmira College, for her many hours of reviewing the manuscript and sharing her expertise. Thanks also go to Faith Gray, director of Steppingstone Nursery School, for allowing my students to observe her program in order to field-test the *Child Skills Checklist*; to both Faith and Head Start teacher Sandy Shepard, for allowing me to photograph their children; to Elmira College students in my class "Studies in Early Childhood: Observing and Recording," for being "guinea pigs" in the development of this text (especially Elaine Harvey, Dolores Polvent, Mary Thibadeau, and Robin Whitaker who allowed me to use their observations); to Karen McCormick, teacher in the Bradford County (Penn.) Day Care Program, for an in-depth review of the *Checklist*; to Sandra Novick, director of the Macfeat Nursery School at Winthrop College, Rock Hill, South Carolina, for allowing me to field-test the *Checklist* there; to Linda Pratt, director of the Elmira College Reading Program, for her insightful critique of the manuscript; and to the many parents who allowed their children to be featured in the photographs. Finally, I would like to thank the reviewers of this text: Mary S. Link of Miami University, Nancy B. Benham of The Pennsylvania State University, Rosalind Charlesworth of Louisiana State University, Elisa Klein of Ohio State University, Judith Reitsch of Eastern Washington University, and Kathleen Lentz of the University of Houston.

Janice Beaty

CONTENTS

 Observation of Development

A

ll children go through a sequence of development that can be observed. From large to small motor coordination, from simple ideas to complex thinking, from two-word utterances to lengthy sentences, from scribbles to representational drawings . . . all children everywhere seem to proceed through a step-by-step sequence of development that can be traced by an observer who knows what to look for.

This textbook gives students of child development and teachers of young children a method for observing and recording this natural development. The text focuses on children ages two to six as they work and play in the environment of the early childhood classroom.

Rather than focusing on children's behavior in general, this method will help observers to determine specifically where each child stands developmentally in the areas of emotional, social, physical, cognitive, language, and creative development.

The purpose of observing children's development in this manner is twofold: 1) for students of child development to gain an in-depth understanding of children and their sequences of growth, and 2) for teachers of young children to become aware of each child's growth, in order to support individual development and to give special help where developmental lags are apparent.

Many textbooks of this nature focus on the teaching of observational skills and strategies. These factors are particularly important for researchers and child psychologists. While this text will not neglect such skills and strategies, its primary purpose is to teach non-specialist observers to understand children through the gathering and interpreting of objective data about children's development. The *Child Skills Checklist* at the conclusion of this chapter will assist the observer in focusing on particular aspects and sequences of development. Each of the following chapters will expand on one aspect of that development as outlined in the checklist:

Emotional
    1. Self-Identity
    2. Emotional Development
Social
    3. Social Play
    4. Prosocial Behavior
Physical
    5. Large Motor Development
    6. Small Motor Development
Cognitive
    7. Cognitive Development (Classification and Seriation)
    8. Cognitive Development (Number, Time, Space, Memory)
Language
    9. Spoken Language
    10. Written Language

All children go through a sequence of development that can be observed.

Creative
  11. Art Skills
  12. Imagination

Each chapter treats one of these twelve areas of development, and each area contains eight or nine items based on recognized developmental sequences of children's growth, where possible, that have been field tested in actual settings. Not every detail of development is included. However, the eight or nine representative items make the observations inclusive enough to be meaningful, but not so detailed as to be cumbersome. Each area of the checklist and its eight or nine representative items give the observer a sense of what to look for and why. For items the observer does not check as apparent when observing a child, there is a section of ideas following each item that should be useful in planning for individual help.

Observational assignments at the end of each chapter will include not only use of the *Child Skills Checklist* for individuals and groups of children, but also use of anecdotal records, running records, specimen records, time sampling, event sampling, and rating scales.

WHY TO OBSERVE YOUNG CHILDREN

People have been observing infants and young children, informally at least, ever since children have been around. Parents want to know what their children are doing, how they are coming along, and how they compare with siblings or the children next door. Grandparents and relatives want to know what clever new things the young child is doing or saying. Teachers would like to find out why their students behave the way they do or why they aren't doing what they should be. Psychologists often observe troubled children in a natural setting to determine their problems and prescribe help. Pediatricians need to observe children in a clinical setting to assess health problems. Researchers observe young children in both natural and clinical settings in order to test hypotheses about development and to formulate new theories.

Systematic observation of children (that is, observation using a particular system) is different from informal observation, which is really little more than watching. In systematic observation, there is a specific purpose for gathering the information about the children, as well as a particular method for collecting and recording it. For teachers and students who wish to learn more about the youngsters they work with, the following may be among their own particular reasons for systematic observing and recording.

1. To make an initial assessment of the child's abilities.
2. To determine a child's areas of strength, and areas needing strengthening.
3. To make individual plans based on observed needs.
4. To conduct an ongoing check on the child's progress.
5. To learn more about child development in particular areas.
6. To resolve a particular problem involving the child.
7. To use in reporting to parents, or specialists in health, speech, mental health.
8. To gather information for the child's folder, for use in guidance and placement.

WHAT TO LOOK FOR

What kinds of children's actions are important for observers to watch and record? In each of the six principal areas of child development, there are particular behaviors that observers should look for and record. Under "emotional development," for instance, the observer needs to pay special attention to nonverbal cues: What facial expressions are exhibited? What do the eyes look like—the eyebrows, the mouth? Are the eyes staring, downcast, slit, closed? Are the eyebrows raised, lowered, straight? Is the mouth in a pout, a smile, a scowl? What about the posture? Is it ramrod straight, slumped, swaggering, slouched? What kinds of gestures are made with the hands, arms, feet? Are the hands to the sides, fists clenched, arms swinging free, feet together? Does the child walk with a swing, a shuffle, a skip?

Under "social development," the observer should be aware of how children interact and get along with one another. Is she alone or a part of the group? Is he a leader or a follower? Popular with the others or often excluded? What roles does he play when pretending? How does she respond to sharing or taking turns? Is he cooperative and helpful? How?

Under "physical development," the observer needs to watch how the child walks, runs, climbs, jumps, balances. Does he have eye-hand coordination in using tools, making puzzles, painting? Can she dress herself and tie her shoes? These questions need to be answered with more than a "yes" or "no." In all observations, the observer needs to be recording detailed evidence to tell "how." When she walks, the child may amble, stroll, skip, strut, clump, shuffle, stumble, trudge, tiptoe. What happens with her legs and feet when she "clumps"?

In "cognitive development," it is obvious the observer cannot look inside the mind of the child but must rely on classroom responses and reactions that demonstrate reasoning ability, problem solving, and memory. Even language ability is intertwined with cognitive development as, in fact, are all developmental aspects. No single aspect of development truly stands alone but should be considered brush strokes on the intricate picture of the whole child being drawn by the observer.

"Language development" can be observed by listening closely to the child and recording on paper or tape. Does the child initiate conversations, or is he a listener? Can he speak complete sentences? Are they understandable? Can he print his own name? Does he recognize names of others?

What about "creativity"? Is the child manipulating the medium by swishing paint around the paper, or can she represent people and buildings? How far does her pretending go? Must she have a physical prop in order to play a role or will her imagination do?

We need, then, to look for and be aware of physical gestures, movements, and features, as well as verbal and nonverbal communication, and interaction with people and materials.

METHODS FOR OBSERVING AND RECORDING

Systematic observation always implies recording. Not only must the observer have a particular reason to look at the child and know what he should be looking for, but he also needs a method for recording the information gathered. A number of useful methods have been developed over the years by observers of young children. The following will be included for discussion and use in this text: anecdotal records, running records, specimen records, time sampling, event sampling, and the use of observation tools such as rating scales and checklists.

Anecdotal Records

Anecdotal records are brief narrative accounts describing an incident of a child's behavior that is important to the writer. Anecdotes describe what happened in a factual, objective manner, telling how it happened, when and where it happened, and what was said and done. Sometimes, they include reasons for the child's behavior, but "why" is better kept in the commentary part of the record. These accounts are most often written after the incident has occurred, by someone who witnessed it informally, rather than while it was occurring by someone who was formally observing and recording.

Anecdotal records have long been made by teachers, physicians, psychologists, social workers, even parents who record when their babies first walk and talk. Sometimes these latter records are referred to as "baby biographies."

Although they are brief, describing only one incident at a time, they are cumulative. A series of them over a period of time can be extremely useful in providing rich details about the person being observed. Other advantages for using anecdotal records include

1. The observer needs no special training in order to record.
2. The observation is open-ended. The recorder writes anything and everything witnessed and is not restricted to one kind of behavior or one type of recording.
3. The observer can catch an unexpected incident, no matter when it occurs, for it will be recorded later.
4. The observer can look for and record significant behavior and ignore the rest.

As in all observational methods, there are disadvantages, too. Observers need to decide why they are observing, what they want to find out, and which method will be most useful. Some of the disadvantages of the anecdotal records method are

1. It does not give a complete picture because it records only incidents of interest to the observer.
2. It depends too much on the memory of the observer. Witnesses to events are notoriously poor on details.
3. Incidents may be taken out of context and thus interpreted incorrectly or used in a biased manner.
4. It is difficult to code or analyze narrative records like this; thus, the method may not prove useful in a scientific study.

Such records can be more useful if recorded on a vertically divided page with the anecdote on the left side and a space for comments on the right, or the page can be divided horizontally with the anecdote at the top and commentary at the bottom. (See example on next page.)

This anecdote tells what happened in an objective manner. Especially good are the direct quotes. The anecdote could have included more details about the child's facial expression, tone of voice, and gestures. The reader does not get the feeling of whether the boy was enjoying himself as a helper, trying to ingratiate himself with another child who was not paying much attention, or trying desperately to gain the attention of the other boy. Sometimes, such details are missing from anecdotes because they have not been written down until the end of the day or even later, and by then, are forgotten.

The comments contain several inferences and conclusions based on insufficient evidence. Obviously, this observer has spent some time watching

---

Anecdotal Record

Child's Name: *Stevie*   Age: *4*   Date: *2/23*
Observer: *Anne*   Place: *S. Nursery*   Time: *9:00–10:00*

Incident

Stevie went over to the block corner and asked two boys, Ron and Tanner, if he could help them build. They told him it was okay. As they were building, Stevie accidently knocked some blocks down. "I can put it back up," he said, and handed the blocks to Ron. For awhile he watched Ron build and then said, "I found a smokestack, Ron," and handed him a cylinder block. Ron told him where to put it, and Stevie then began getting cylinders off the shelf and handing them to Ron and Tanner to place. Finally he started placing his own cylinders around the perimeter of the building. The teacher asked him if he wanted to finger paint, but he replied, "I'm not gonna finger paint unless Ron finger paints."

Comment

Stevie is often involved in a lot of dramatic play with several other boys. He especially likes to be near or playing with Ron. Stevie seems to look up to him. Whatever rules Ron sets in the play, Stevie follows. Once engaged in play, he likes to continue, and will usually not let another child or even the teacher distract him.

Stevie, indicated by her comments, "Stevie is often involved" and "Once engaged in play he likes to continue and will usually not." She would need an accumulation of such anecdotes in order to make valid statements of this nature based on evidence. If this were one page of many about Stevie, the comments would perhaps be more accurate.

The observer infers that Stevie "likes to be near or playing with Ron" although there is not sufficient evidence here to make that definite inference. Perhaps she should have said, "Whatever rules Ron sets in the play, Stevie follows," if Stevie actually placed a cylinder block where directed. However, this was only hinted at and not stated. Particular words are very important in objective recording. Her conclusion about not letting another child or even the teacher distract him is only partially accurate, since we have no evidence about another child.

If you were writing the comment about this particular record, what things might you infer from the incident? Can you make any conclusions based on this information alone, or is it too limited? Are there things you might want to look for in the future when observing this boy that you should include in the commentary?

It is also helpful to indicate the purpose of the particular observation. Most observation forms do not provide a space for this item, but it will certainly add to the usefulness of the observation if it is included. In this case, the observer was looking for evidence of involvement in social play for this child.

Running Records

Another popular type of observing and recording method is the running record. It is a detailed narrative of behavior, recorded in a sequential manner as it happens. The observer writes down everything that occurs over a period of time, which may be as short as several minutes or from time to time during a full day. It is different from the anecdotal record because it includes all behavior and not just selected incidents, and it records behavior as it occurs, instead of later.

As with all factual recording, the observer must be careful not to use descriptive words or phrases that are judgmental. For instance, if the observer sees the child "acting grumpy this morning," he needs to avoid this judgment and instead record the actual details that explain what happened such as: "Jonathan would not respond to the teacher's greeting at first, and when he did, he muttered 'good morning,' in a low voice with his head bent down."

The running record has a number of advantages for persons interested in child development.

1. It is a rich, complete, and comprehensive record not limited to particular incidents.
2. It is open-ended, allowing the observer to record everything he or she sees, and not restricting the observations to a particular kind of behavior.
3. It does not require that the observer has special skills and therefore is particularly useful to the classroom teacher.

There are also several disadvantages to using this method, once again depending on the purpose for gathering the information.

1. It is very time-consuming, and it is difficult for observers to find periods of uninterrupted time.
2. It is difficult to record everything for any length of time without missing important details.
3. It works best when observing an individual, but it is very inefficient and difficult when observing a group.
4. Observers must keep themselves apart from the children which is sometimes difficult if they are the teacher.

Running records are more useful if recorded on a form where the observer can make comments later. (See example.)

It is difficult for the observer to record every word of all that is said and every facet of all that occurs when children are busily playing together. This observer has caught the essence. The dialogue is especially well recorded. His inferences and conclusions are carefully kept on the commentary side of the record. Although we cannot make the same conclusion about Katy being more comfortable playing with only one child at a time based on this evidence, the

Running Record

Child's Name: *Katy*   Age: *4*   Date: *2/9*
Observer: *Rob*   Place: *S. Nursery*   Time: *9:00–10:00*

Observation	Comments
Katy is playing by herself with plastic blocks, making guns. She walks into another room: "Lisa, would you play with me, I'm tired of playing by myself." They walk into other room to slide and climbing area.	*Clips blocks together to make gun, then copies it to make one for Lisa. Cleverly done. Intricate. Shows creativity. (Does teacher allow guns?)*
K: "I am Wonder Woman."	
L: "So am I."	
K: "No, there is only one Wonder Woman. You are Robin."	*Seems to be the leader here as in other activities I have observed. Lisa is the friend she most often plays with.*
L: "Robin needs a Batman because Batman and Robin are friends."	
All this takes place under slide and climber. Lisa shoots block gun which Katy has given to her. Katy falls on floor.	
L: (to teacher) "We're playing superfriends, and Wonder Woman keeps falling down."	
Katy opens eyes, gets up and says: "Let's get out our bat mobile and go help the world." She runs to other room and back making noises like a car.	*Katy switches roles here. She shows good concentration and spends much time on one play episode.*
L: "Wonder Woman is died. She fell out of the car." She falls down.	
K: "It's only a game, wake up Lisa. You be Wonder Woman, I'll be_____."	*She can distinguish reality from fantasy.*
L: "Let's play house now."	

Katy begins sliding down the slide.

K: "We have a lot of superfriends to do." She says this while sliding. "Robin is coming after you!" she shouts to Lisa, running from the slide and into the other room.

Lisa has gone into the housekeeping area and says to Katy: "Katy, here is your doll's dress." (Lost yesterday).

John joins the girls.

L: "I'm Wonder Woman."

K: "I'm Robin."

J: "I'm Batman. Where is the bat mobile?"

K: "It's in here." They run into the other room, and Katy points under the slide telling John what the bat mobile can do. Then all run to the other room and back again. Then Katy says: "John we are not playing superfriends any more."

Shows good large motor coordination. Spends much time every day like this running and skipping around room. Seems to know she is good at this and spends a lot of time doing it.

Seems to be more comfortable playing with only one child at a time.

observer had been gathering this evidence for several weeks and perhaps felt he could. Such an explanation should then be included here. It also would be helpful to record the time that the various incidents occurred in order to know how much time had elapsed on the gun play, the slide play, and the running back and forth.

Specimen Records

Specimen records, or *specimen descriptions*, as they are sometimes called, are similar to running records but more detailed and precise. They are most often used by researchers who want a full and complete description of behavior; whereas, running records are used especially by teachers in a more informal way. The observer is definitely not a part of classroom activities with the specimen records method and must keep aloof from the children.

Like the running records, specimen records are narrative descriptions of behavior or events as they happen, but descriptions usually based on predetermined criteria such as the time of day, the person, and the setting (Irwin, p. 103). The amount of detail to be recorded depends upon the purpose for the observation. Enough detail should appear to give the reader a sense of how everything being described actually happened. Can it be dramatized? Does the description tell how the children moved, what their facial expressions and gestures were, and not only what they said but also how they said it? It is better to record too much detail than not enough. Here is an extraction from one:

> *Mark's friend Rob is playing in the play grocery store taking empty food boxes off the shelves, so Mark watches him for a moment, begins to take the boxes off the shelves and places them in a toy shopping cart. Two girls proceed over to where Mark is, and they knock his boxes over (which were teetering because there were so many in the cart). Mark then opens his eyes wide, grits his teeth, and places his hands on his hips, saying, "You guys, why do you knock it down like that?" Meanwhile, the girls appear little affected by his question and walk off. Meanwhile, his friend Rob is still taking the boxes off the shelves, and he says to Mark, "We are stealing stuff." So Mark joins the act, hiding the boxes in the rear by the playhouse. It appears that no one pays any attention to their act of "stealing," so Mark loses interest.*

Can you dramatize this specimen record? It neither tells us exactly how the girls take action, nor what Mark does to show his loss of interest; but otherwise, it is rich in detail.

Specimen records are later coded by researchers to elicit findings regarding kinds of behavior, lengths of incidents, interaction patterns, or other information relevant to the purpose of the observation. Advantages and disadvantages of this particular method are the same as for the running record.

Objective Recording of Narrative Data

Objectively recording the narrative data gained from observing young children—a process required with anecdotal, running, and specimen records—is not a simple task. We are used to observing what happens around us and making simultaneous interpretations about it. In objective recording, we must separate these two roles and guard against confusing them. What we record must be the objective facts only, no judgments, inferences, or conclusions. Perhaps if we think of ourselves as witnesses at a trial, it becomes more evident to us what information is acceptable and what is not.

If we see a child come into the room in the morning, for instance, refuse to greet the teacher, walk over to a table and sit down, push away another child who tries to join him, and shake his head in refusal when the teacher suggests an activity, how can we record it? An anecdotal record might read like this:

> *Jonathan walked into the room this morning as if he were mad at the world. He would not look up at the teacher or respond to her greeting. He sort of slumped as he walked across the room and plunked himself down in a chair at one of the activity tables. Richie tried to join him but was pushed away. The teacher went over and asked if he wanted to help mix play dough, but he shook his head no.*

This record is rich enough in detail for us to visualize it, but is it factually objective? No. The words, "as if he were mad at the world," are a conclusion based on insufficient evidence. The recorder might better have described his entrance objectively.

> *Jonathan walked into the room this morning frowning. He lowered his head when the teacher greeted him, and did not respond.*

This behavior was unusual for Jonathan. Later the teacher found out that he was not "mad at the world," but sad because his pet cat had been killed by a car the night before. We realize then that frowning looks, lowered head, and refusal to speak or participate may be the result of other emotions than anger. It is up to us to sift out our inferences and judgments, then, and make sure we record only the facts.

The following are judgmental phrases and sentences sometimes found in observation records. Should they ever be there? If not, what could you substitute for them?

> He was a good boy today.
> Marcie was mad at Patty.
> shouted angrily
> showed his strength
> lost his temper
> got upset
> would never talk like that

Other observer errors include 1) omitting some of the facts, 2) recording things that did not happen, and 3) recording things out of order. Here is the "Jonathan incident" again with some of these errors. Can you find them?

> *Jonathan walks in the classroom this morning. He doesn't look at the teacher but goes straight to a seat at one of the tables. The teacher wants him to help mix play dough, but he refuses. Richie comes over to play with him, but he pushes him away.*

Omitted facts include

1. Has frowning look on face.
2. Does not respond to teacher's greeting.
3. Walks across room with shoulders slumped.
4. Drop himself down into seat at activity table.
5. Shakes his head no when teacher asks him to help mix play dough.

Added facts include

1. Richie comes over "to play with him"

A fact recorded out of order is

1. Richie tries to join him before teacher asks him to help mix play dough.

Such errors can creep into an observation almost without the recorder's awareness. You need to practice with at least two observers recording the same incident, and then comparing results. If you find discrepancies between the records, check carefully that you have followed the following guidelines for objective recording:

Guidelines for Objective Recording

1. Record only the facts.
2. Record every detail without omitting anything.
3. Do not interpret as you observe.
4. Do not record anything you do not see.
5. Use words that describe but do not judge or interpret.
6. Record the facts in the order they occur.

Time Sampling

In the time sampling method, the observer records the frequency of a behavior's occurrence over time. The behavior must be overt and frequent (at least once every fifteen minutes) to be a candidate for sampling (Irwin, p. 149). For example, talking, hitting, and crying are such behaviors, but problem solving is not.

Time sampling thus involves observing specified behavior of an individual or group, and recording the presence or absence of this behavior during short time intervals of uniform length. The observer must prepare ahead of time, determining what specific behavior he will look for, what the time interval will be, and how he will record the presence or absence of the behavior.

For example, in order to help an aggressive child named Jamie change his ways, the teacher wants to know how frequently Jamie's negative behavior occurs. First, Jamie's aggressive behavior must be specifically defined. It includes

hitting
pushing
kicking
holding another against his will
taking another child's toy

These particular behaviors are usually determined by previous formal or informal observations made to discover exactly what the observer needs to be concerned with in her sampling. Jamie, for instance, did not use words aggressively. Another child might have expressed aggression quite differently, and the observer would sample that.

Next the decision is made about what time intervals to use. It may be decided to sample the child's behavior for five minute intervals during the first half hour of the morning for a week. The teacher already knows that this seems to be the most difficult time for him.

The teacher then must decide what and how to record on the sheet, which is blocked into time intervals. Often, a time sampling observer simply records "1" after the interval if the behavior occurs, and "0" if it doesn't. This method is called "duration recording" and is concerned with the presence or absence of the behavior (Bell, p. 65).

Check marks or tally marks can also be used if the teacher wants to know how many times the behavior occurred, rather than its presence or absence. This strategy is called "event recording" and is concerned with the frequency of the behavioral event.

Furthermore, the teacher may be more concerned with specific categories of aggression rather than just aggression in general. In that case, each of the categories can be given a code.

h = hitting
p = pushing
k = kicking
hd = holding
t = taking

The teacher will be doing "event recording" of specific categories rather than frequency of occurrence. The observation form can be set up like any of the following examples or in the teacher's own manner, depending on the information desired. The observation for Jamie's first half hour of one morning could look like any of those in Figure 1.

Time Intervals

		1	2	3	4	5	6
Duration Recording (presence or absence)		1	1	1	0	0	0
Event Recording (frequency)		ЖЖ	III	I	0	0	0
Event Recording (presence or absence)		h,p	h,p,t	h	0	0	0

FIGURE 1. *Event recording of specific categories*

From this the teacher might conclude that Jamie's aggressive actions on this morning occurred mainly during the first fifteen minutes and involved mostly hitting and pushing the other children. If this turned out to be the pattern for the rest of the week, the teacher might want to plan an interesting transition activity for him to do by himself as soon as he arrived. Once he had made the transition from home to school by getting involved in an activity, he might then be able to interact with the other children nonaggressively. Future observations would help the teacher to determine whether the intervention strategy had been successful.

Time sampling is thus a useful method for observing children for some of the following reasons:

1. It takes less time and effort than narrative recording.
2. It is more objective and controlled because the behavior is specified and limited.
3. It allows an observer to collect data on a number of children or a number of behaviors at once.
4. It provides useful information on intervals and frequencies of behavior.
5. It provides quantitative results useful for statistical analysis.

There are of course certain disadvantages as well.

1. It is not an open method and therefore may miss much important behavior.
2. It does not describe the behavior, causes, or results, because it is more concerned with time (when or how frequently the behavior occurs).
3. It does not keep units of behavior intact, because its principal concern is the time interval, not the behavior.
4. It takes the behavior out of its context and therefore may be biased.
5. It is limited to observable behaviors that occur frequently.

Event Sampling

Event sampling is another method in which the observer waits for and then records a specific preselected behavior. Event sampling is used to study the conditions under which particular behaviors occur or their frequency of occurrence. It may be important to learn what triggers a particular kind of behavior—biting, for instance—in order to find ways to control it. Or, the observer may want to find out how many times a certain behavior occurs. Time sampling would be used if time intervals or time of day were the important factor. But, if the behavior occurs at odd times or infrequently, then event sampling is more appropriate.

The observer must first define the event or "unit of behavior." Then, the setting in which it is likely to occur must be determined. The observer takes the most advantageous position to observe the behavior, waits for it to occur, and records it.

Recording can be done in several ways, depending upon the purpose for the observation. If the observer is studying causes or results of certain behaviors, then the so-called "ABC analysis" is especially useful (Bell, p. 73). It is a narrative description of the entire event, breaking it down into three parts: A = antecedent event, B = behavior, C = consequent event. Each time the event occurs, it is recorded; for an example, see the following event sampling for Darrell.

If subsequent observations of Darrell show the same sort of sequence as in the event sampling presented, the teacher could interpret this to mean that Darrell does not initiate the kicking, but rather responds to interference with his activities in this inappropriate and harmful manner. Intervention strategies may need to be different with this boy. The teacher wants to help him learn an acceptable way to vent his frustration. In addition, he needs help in getting along with other children and in feeling accepted in the classroom. Until these issues are resolved, he may have to keep his shoes off in the classroom to prevent injury. This in itself may reduce his kicking, since his own toes will learn how it hurts to kick.

Event Sampling

Name: *Darrell*   Age: *3½*
Center: *Head Start*   Date: *10/5*
Observer: *Sue S.*   Time: *9:00–12:00*
Behavior: *Kicking: striking out at other children or teacher with right foot,
hard enough to make children cry.*

Time	Antecedent Event	Behavior	Consequent Event
9:13	*Darrell is playing alone in block corner; Rob comes in and puts block on Darrell's building*	*Darrell looks at Rob with frown; stands; pushes at Rob; Rob pushes back; Darrell kicks Rob on leg*	*Rob cries and runs to teacher*
10:05	*On playground; Darrell is waiting turn in line with others to go on slide; Sally tries to cut in*	*Darrell kicks Sally hard on leg;* *Darrell kicks teacher*	*Sally cries; teacher comes and takes Darrell away by arm to talk to him*

If frequency of occurrence is the main concern, the observer can record with tally marks rather than narrative description. This procedure tends to be more useful for research than for practical classroom applications.

The advantages for using event sampling are

1. It keeps the event or behavior intact, making analysis easier.
2. It is more objective than some methods, because the behavior has been defined ahead of time.
3. It is especially helpful in examining infrequent or rarely occurring behaviors.

Event sampling has several disadvantages as well, depending on the purpose for the observation.

1. It takes the event out of context and thus may lose other happenings that are important to the interpretation.
2. It is a closed method that looks only for specified behavior and must ignore other important behavior.
3. It misses the richness of the many details that anecdotes, specimen records, or running records provide.

TOOLS FOR OBSERVATION

Rating Scales

Rating scales are tools that indicate the degree to which a person possesses a certain trait or behavior. Each behavior is rated on a continuum that goes from the lowest to the highest level (or vice versa) and is marked off at certain points along the scale. The observer must make a judgment about where the child's behavior lies on the scale. As an observation tool, rating scales work best where particular degrees of behavior are well-defined or well understood by the observer, and where there is a distinct difference between the behavior at the various points on the scale.

These tools are useful in diagnosing a child on a wide range of behavior at one time. The observer watches the child and checks off or circles a point on the scale to indicate the child's current position in regard to behaviors or abilities. Such scales are simple to make: simply state the behavior, draw a line, then mark off a number of points or intervals along the line. Five intervals are often used so that there is a middle, neutral, position and two intervals on either side of it.

Rating scales may be used on their own, implemented with other observation methods as a part of the procedure, or filled in later from data gathered through specimen or running records. As with the other methods, there are several advantages to using rating scales.

1. They are easy to design and less time-consuming to use.
2. They provide a convenient method for observing a large number of traits at one time.
3. They make it possible to measure difficult-to-quantify traits such as "shyness."
4. They can be used by non-specialist observers.
5. They are easier to score and quantify than most other methods.

The disadvantages also need to be considered before the observer decides to use a rating scale.

1. Rating scales utilize a closed method. They examine specified traits and may overlook other important behavior.
2. They feature the negative as well as the positive side of each trait.
3. Clearly differentiating between each point on the scale is sometimes difficult, both for the designer and the observer.
4. It is difficult to eliminate observer bias when judgments must be made quickly on so many different traits.

Graphic Scales

Here is a rating scale for only one behavior. Many similar behaviors could be listed on this same scale.

Graphic Scale

Shares toys: _____

      Always   Often   Sometimes   Seldom   Never

Such scales are called "graphic scales" and can be drawn either horizontally as shown here or vertically. Many traits can be listed on one sheet. Graphic scales may be easier to construct than to use. The observer must know children well, be able to interpret their behavior, and be able to make an objective judgment within a limited period of time.

Numerical Scales

Other rating scales may be "numerical" in form.

Numerical Scale

Attention Span

1. *Rarely finishes task, moves rapidly from one to another.*
2. *Usually needs encouragement to stay with task until complete.*
3. *Can usually remain with task appropriate to age level until it is finished.*
4. *Can stay with a chosen activity for very long periods, even returning next day.*

Curiosity

1. *Shows little or no interest in anything new.*
2. *Can be intrigued by really exciting things, but often uninterested.*
3. *Actively explores any new things in the room.*
4. *Interested in new ideas, words, and relationships as well as things.*

NOTE: From Hodgden, p. 119.

Two items—attention span and curiosity—are shown here, but altogether, there are twelve total items on this scale.

Raters observe children for as long as it takes to check off a number for each item, or raters can observe on a daily basis and then average their scores. The numbers on the above scale were also represented by words.

1 = Definitely needs help
2 = Could use help
3 = Adequate
4 = Strength

Semantic Differential

A third type of rating scale sometimes used with children is the "semantic differential," sometimes called the "Osgood scale," because it was developed by Charles Osgood (Irwin, p. 209). It uses a seven-point scale with adjectives of opposite meanings (bipolar) at either end.

Happy └──┴──┴──┴──┴──┴──┘ Sad

Friendly └──┴──┴──┴──┴──┴──┘ Hostile

A number of traits should, of course, be included in order to develop a comprehensive profile of the child.

Forced Choice

A fourth type of rating scale is the "forced choice" scale, where observers must choose one out of the several ranges of behavior listed for each trait (Hodgden, p. 67).

Ball Catching

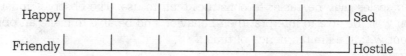

Fearful	Usually misses	Often misses	No accommodation	Uses body	Hands only
___	___	___	___	___	___

A different kind of observer error can affect the use of rating scales. Contrary to other types of observation, the use of this tool calls for the observer to make an on-the-spot judgment. It is extremely difficult for such an observer to be totally unbiased and objective. Other things already known about the child or his family, or outside influences completely unrelated to the situation being observed, may influence the observer. For example, one observer persistently gave lower ratings to an overweight child. When asked about it later, the observer admitted a prejudice against overweight children because he had been one himself.

To guard against these tendencies, the observer should rate all of the different children being observed on the same trait before going on to another trait. To check objectivity, a second rater could observe the same child and compare results.

Checklists

Checklists are lists of specific traits or behaviors arranged in a logical order for the observer to indicate the presence or absence of each. They are especially useful for types of behaviors or traits that can easily and clearly be specified. We tend to see what we look for; thus, a checklist can prove to be a valuable tool when many different items need to be observed. A survey or inventory of a situation can be done more efficiently, for instance, with a checklist than with almost any other observation tool. If the observer needs to know whether a child displays the specified behavior or not, a checklist is the instrument of choice to use.

Both checklists and rating scales often include large numbers of traits or behaviors. The difference in the two is not necessarily in their appearance, but rather in their use. An observer using a checklist merely checks off the presence of the trait (a blank denotes absence). The observer using a rating scale must make a judgment about the degree to which the trait is present.

Checklists can be used in a number of ways. A different checklist, for instance, can be used for each child in the class, or all of the children's names can be included on the same checklist along with the checklist items. The items can simply be checked off, or the date or time when they first appear can be entered. A different checklist can be used for each observation, or a single checklist can serve in a cumulative manner for the same child all year if dates are recorded for each item. Checklists are also helpful to several people observing at once.

Information gained from anecdotal records, specimen and running records can be transferred to checklists for ease in interpretation. It is much simpler to scan a list of checked behaviors than to read through long paragraphs of wordy description when attempting to interpret observational evidence.

It is obvious that checklists need to be prepared carefully. The items listed should be specified very clearly in objective, not judgmental, terms. The items should be easily understood by the users; thus, it makes sense to put them through a pretest before actual use as an observation tool. All checklist items should be positive in nature, unlike rating scale items where a range of behavior from positive to negative is necessary. Items an observer does not check are left blank, indicating absence of the particular behavior. If the observer does not have the opportunity to observe for certain behaviors, these items should not be left blank, but marked with some symbol, e.g., ''N,'' meaning no opportunity to observe. Some suggestions for developing checklist items include

1. Items should be short, descriptive, understandable.
2. They should be parallel in construction (i.e., word order and verb tense the same for each).
3. They should be objective and non-judgmental (e.g. not ''jumps high'' but ''jumps over a one-foot object'').
4. They should be positive in nature.
5. They should not be repeated elsewhere in the checklist.
6. They should be representative of children's behavior and not include every behavior.

Overall, the format of the checklist should allow the observer to scan the items at a glance. The *Child Skills Checklist* which follows at the end of this chapter is an example of an observation tool which looks at twelve important areas of child development, breaking down each into eight specific items. Each item is brief, representative of an important aspect of development, parallel in construction (beginning with a verb), and positive in nature. Together, the items form the profile of a whole child as he or she works and plays in the environment of an early childhood classroom.

Advantages for using checklists of this nature are

1. They are easy, quick, and efficient to use.
2. They can be used with ease by the non-specialist observer.
3. They can be used in the presence of the child or later from remembered behaviors.
4. Several observers can gather the same information to check for reliability.
5. These checklists help to focus observation on many behaviors at one time.
6. They are especially useful for curriculum planning for individuals.

At the same time, there are disadvantages of using checklists. The observer must weigh advantages against disadvantages, always keeping in mind his purpose for observing. Checklist disadvantages include

1. They are "closed" in nature, looking at particular behaviors and not everything that occurs. Thus, they may miss behaviors of importance.
2. They are limited to "presence" or "absence" of behavior.
3. They lack information about quality of behavior (how), duration (how long), and description.

USE OF THE CHILD SKILLS CHECKLIST

The *Child Skills Checklist*, around which this book is written, is as much a learning device for the observer as it is a planning tool for helping the child. With sequences of child development as its focus, it presents the areas of emotional, social, physical, cognitive, language, and creative development by dividing each of these aspects into two major categories, and then subdividing each category into eight representative items of development.

Language, for example, is divided into spoken and written language. The observer then learns some representative behaviors in the sequence of language development which can be seen in the early childhood classroom. These classroom representative behaviors will differ somewhat from a developmental sequence which might be observed in the home. This is because emotional and social stresses are different at school.

Learning for the Observer

As a learning device for the observer, the *checklist* is best used one section at a time. To understand the sequence of language development as it appears in the early childhood classroom, for instance, the observer should plan to use the Spoken Language section of the *checklist* in observing one or two children for enough time to see if all eight items are present. The observer should not only check off the items as they appear, but also record evidence for each item. This can be written next to the item on the checklist or, better still, on a separate sheet to which the items have been transferred. An example of this follows.

Child Skills Checklist
Spoken Language

Child's Name: *Sheila, 4*   Date: *9/22*   Time: *9:00–12:00*

Observer: *Connie R.*   Center: *Head Start*

_____ Speaks confidently in classroom.
> *Talks under breath saying things like "I'm going to the store, I'm going to the store," in dramatic play, but doesn't talk much to others.*

✓ Speech is clear to adults.
> *If I listen closely I can understand.*

✓ Speaks in expanded sentences.
> *When she talks to herself or to teacher, she speaks in complete sentences. Example: "We eated pizza for supper last night."*

_____ Takes part in conversations with other children.
> *Almost never.*

✓ Asks questions with proper word order.
> *She asked the teacher several times: "When are we going home?"*

✓ Makes negative responses with proper word order.
> *Said, "I can't find my mitten."*

_____ Uses past tense verbs correctly.
> *"I getted my dog back."*   *"We eated pizza . . ."*

N Plays with rhyming words.
> *No opportunity to observe this item.*

The observer should then read the chapter on Spoken Language, paying special attention to the items that were not checked. She will learn that Sheila may not be talking much yet to the other children because she is not yet confident enough in the classroom at the beginning of the year. She does have the ability—this has been noted in her talking to the teacher. Some of the suggested "Helpful Ideas" in the chapter may assist this child.

Once the observer is confident about each of the *checklist* areas and items, the entire *checklist* can be used with one child to gain a complete overview. Comparison of one child with another using the *checklist* for each is another helpful learning activity in the study of child development.

Planning for the Child

As a planning device for the children in the center, the *checklist* can be used in different ways. For an overview of children's strengths and needs in language, for instance, the observer should list all of the children's names on one sheet along with the eight *checklist* items for observation, as shown in the following example.

Spoken Language

	Speaks with conf.	Speech is clear	Speaks in sent.	Talks in conv.	Asks quest. correc.	Neg. sent. correc.	Past tense correc.	Plays with words
Sheila S.								
Bobby								
Sandra								
Linda								
Keith								

With this list, the observer can check off at a glance the children who have performed the various behaviors. Blanks show up as needs for individual children.

Using the *checklist* to screen like this helps to locate the children needing special assistance in language. Once they have been identified, it is possible to do a more in-depth observation using anecdotal or running records to gather more detailed data on their language behavior such as the actual words spoken. An observational method such as event sampling could be especially helpful with the nonverbal child to identify the antecedent and consequent behaviors displayed during the spoken language opportunities he has not responded to.

Once the observational data have been gathered and interpreted, plans for individual children can then be made. "Helpful Ideas" are listed at the end of the discussion for each *checklist* item. Then, after intervention strategies have been carried out, ongoing observation using the *checklist* can serve as a follow-up to see whether the child needs additional help.

Another method, which some observers prefer when using the *checklists*, is to observe a child, making a detailed running record of his behavior. Afterwards, this data can be transferred to the *checklist* by checking off the behaviors noted and indicating the evidence observed for each. Then, plans can be made for an individual child based on strengths and needs in a particular area as shown on the *checklist*.

The method most often followed, that of using the entire *checklist* to observe one child at a time, is discussed in detail in Chapter 14, "Observation of the Whole Child."

INTERPRETATION OF DATA

Once you have observed a child and recorded data about him or her through anecdotal, running, or specimen records—through time or event sampling—through using rating scales or checklists—the next step is to interpret the information.

It is a fascinating process, learning to know and understand a child. Objective observing and recording helps make possible a deeper understanding than could a lifetime of merely being around children. We need to step back from children and look impartially and objectively. Only then do we truly see who these children are, and how we can help them reach their highest potential.

Interpreting the information you have acquired from your observations takes knowledge and skill. You need to know a great deal about child development, both from reading and studying about children and from having actual experience with them, before you can make valid inferences and conclusions based on observations.

This textbook is organized to help you gain such knowledge. Using the *Child Skills Checklist* will focus your attention on important child behaviors in each aspect of the development of real children. Reading the chapters that feature each aspect will help you to acquire knowledge of the particular area. Interpretations of the data you acquire will then be more meaningful to you and helpful to the child as you apply them in your individual planning.

Inferences

The first step in interpreting the data you have gathered about the child is to read the information through carefully, making inferences where possible, based on the behavior you have observed. An inference is a statement considered to be true— tentatively at least—because it is founded upon a previous statement believed to be true. In other words, it is a possible explanation for the previous statement. You actually must have seen and recorded objectively the behavior upon which you base your inference.

Looking back at the "Stevie" observations recorded in the anecdotal records section of this chapter, we might consider making the inferences in the following chart.

Incident	Valid Inference	Faulty Inference
Stevie went to block corner and asked Ron and Tanner if he could help them build. They said OK.	Stevie knows how to join others who are engaged.	Stevie likes to be near Ron and Tanner. Stevie is a friend of Ron and Tanner.
Stevie accidently knocked some blocks down. "I can put it back up," he said, and handed blocks to Ron.	Stevie knows how to handle such accidents.	Stevie is clumsy.

Incident	Valid Inference	Faulty Inference
He watched Ron build and then said," I found a smoke stack, Ron," and handed him a cylinder block. Ron told him where to put it, and Stevie began getting cylinder blocks off shelf and handing them to Ron and Tanner to place.	*Stevie seems to be agreeable in his play with Ron and Tanner.*	*Stevie is a follower rather than a leader. Stevie seems to look up to Ron.*
Finally, he started placing his own cylinders around the perimeter of the building.	*Stevie knows how to do blockbuilding on his own.*	
The teacher asked him if he wanted to finger paint, but he replied, "I'm not gonna finger paint unless Ron finger paints."	*Stevie prefers to play with Ron.*	*Once engaged in play, he will not let another child or the teacher distract him.*

After reading carefully the first "unit of behavior" involving Stevie going to the block corner, asking to play, and being told it was okay, we need to ask ourselves what we can infer, if anything, from this. Do the words tell us that Stevie seems to know how to join other children when they are engaged in playing? Yes. Then this is a valid inference. Do the words tell us that he likes to be near Ron? No. Then, we cannot infer this from this particular observation. We do not have enough information on it. Perhaps later observations will accumulate this evidence. What about Stevie being a friend of Ron and Tanner? No. There is no evidence of this. Just because someone wants to play with someone else is not evidence that they are friends. If this play situation should occur again and again, we might make such an inference.

Can we infer from the second unit of behavior that Stevie is clumsy? No. The observer records that it was an accident. This, of course, is judgmental in itself and would be better stated if the observer had described what had happened: "Stevie got too close to the building and bumped against it without seeming to be aware this would happen, and several blocks fell down." Does Stevie show that he knows how to handle such a situation? Yes. Then, this is a valid inference.

Looking at the third unit of behavior, we see that Stevie seems to know how to play with the others as a newcomer would with children that are already engaged. He does not take over the play or intrude aggressively. Does this mean he is a follower rather than a leader? We don't know. We do not have enough information on this yet to make such an inference. What about Stevie looking up to Ron? Again, we do not have enough information to infer this.

The final behavior seems to indicate a rather strong interest on Stevie's part to stay and play with Ron. Can we infer that once engaged in play, he will not let another child or the teacher distract him? Not on the information gathered thus far. This may be the case, but we do not have enough evidence yet.

Try making inferences from an anecdotal or running record you have made. One thing you will learn from such an exercise is the importance of recording with rich detail. You need to learn this skill through practice. There is always something more you can add to an objective record—facial expressions, gestures, reactions of other children. These elements may be the keys to the inferences you are trying to elicit about a child.

The principal stumbling block in making inferences based on recorded observational data is that we try to read more into the data than is actually there. We are used to making judgments continuously about people and situations in our lives. Often, they are faulty judgments based on insufficient information, or misinterpreted information. Do not allow yourself to be misled like this when you have the written data on child observations before you. Look at the data, and ask yourself the question: "Is there evidence to support my inference?" If there is, then you can make it.

Conclusions

The final step in your interpretation of recorded data about children is to make whatever conclusions you can. A conclusion in this case is a reasoned judgment based on accumulated observational evidence. As with inferences, you cannot make such a judgment unless you can show sufficient evidence. Read through your observational data. Based on what you have recorded, what can you conclude about the child? We can conclude very little from the Stevie anecdote alone. We cannot even say that he knows how to join others, or that he can handle such accidents, or that he can be agreeable in his play—unless future observations show this. It may be that he only plays well with Ron and Tanner.

Observing, recording, and interpreting in this careful, objective manner should help you to sort out what children are really like. You may be surprised by what you find out.

SELECTION OF A METHOD FOR OBSERVING AND RECORDING

Table 1 compares the seven methods for observing and recording young children discussed in this chapter. Each method has advantages and disadvantages which an observer needs to consider before choosing a particular method. The final choice is often based on the purpose of the observation.

A checklist was chosen as the basis for this book because of the unique ability of a checklist to give an observer a good overview of child development. It is a teaching tool as well as an observational tool. The *Child Skills Checklist* at the

TABLE 1. Methods for observing and recording

Method	Purpose	Advantages	Disadvantages
Anecdotal Record: A narrative of descriptive paragraphs, recorded *after behavior occurs.*	To detail specific behavior for child's record, for case conferences, to plan for individuals	Open-ended; rich in details; no special observer training	Depends on observer's memory; behavior taken out of context; difficult to code or analyze for research
Running Record: A narrative written in sequence over a specified time, recorded *while behavior is occurring.*	To discover cause and effects of behavior; for case conferences; to plan for individual	Open-ended; comprehensive; no special observer training	Time-consuming; difficult to use for more than one child at a time; time-consuming to code and analyze for research
Specimen Record: A detailed narrative written in sequence over a specified time, recorded *while behavior is occurring.*	To discover cause and effects of behavior; for child development research	Open-ended; comprehensive and complete; rich in details	Time-consuming to record; time-consuming to code or analyze for research; difficult to observe more than one child at a time
Time Sampling: Tallies or symbols showing the presence or absence of specified behavior during short time periods, recorded *while behavior is occurring.*	For behavior modification baseline data; for child development research	Objective and controlled; not time-consuming; efficient for observing more than one child at a time; provides quantitative data for research	Closed; limited to observable behaviors that occur frequently; no description of behavior; takes behavior out of context
Event Sampling: A brief narrative of conditions preceding and following specified behavior, recorded *while behavior is occurring.*	For behavior modification input; for child development research	Objective; helpful for in-depth diagnosis of infrequent behavior	Closed; takes event out of context; limited to specified behaviors
Rating Scale: A scale of traits or behaviors with check marks, recorded *before, during, and after behavior occurs.*	To judge degree to which child behaves or possesses certain traits; to diagnose behavior or traits; to plan for individuals	Not time-consuming; easy to design; efficient for observing more than one child at a time for many traits; useful for several observers watching same child	Closed; subjective; limited to specified traits or behaviors
Checklist: A list of behaviors with check marks, recorded *before, during, and after behavior occurs.*	To determine presence or absence of specified behaviors; to plan for individuals; to give observer an overview of child's development or progress	Efficient for observing more than one child at a time for many behaviors; useful for an individual over a period of time; a good survey or inventory tool; useful for several observers at once; no special training needed	Closed; limited to specified behaviors; no information on quality of behavior

end of this chapter thus will assist the observer not only in gathering information on specific children, but also in learning the sequences of child growth in the areas of emotional, social, physical, cognitive, language, and creative development.

PLANNING FOR CHILDREN BASED ON OBSERVATIONS

The ultimate reason for observing and recording is not just to learn what children are like, but to help them grow and develop. That is why they have come to your classroom. You can assist them in this goal if you have learned to know from your observations their strengths and their areas needing strengthening.

The chapters to follow in this text can serve as guidelines for you in evaluating children's strengths and needs, and then help in planning for activities to help individuals or small groups of children with similar needs. After discussion related to each *checklist* item, there is a section of ideas for activities entitled, "If You Have Not Checked This Item: Some Helpful Ideas." These ideas should prove useful not only for assisting children in areas of their needs, but also in providing the stimulus for your own ideas for activities.

Chapter 14, "Observation of the Whole Child," brings together the twelve separate *checklist* areas and applies them to a single child. Observers learn how to use the *checklist* in a classroom situation, how to interpret the results, and finally, how to convert checkmarks into an individual *learning prescription*. Once you have learned where one child stands developmentally, then you can make similar plans for each of the children in your own program.

Child Skills Checklist

Name:_____   Observer:_____

Program:_____   Date:_____

Directions: Put a √ for items you see child perform regularly.
Put *N* for items where there is no opportunity to observe.
Put + for items where child has progressed to advanced level.
Leave all other items blank.

1. Self-Identity

_____ Separates from parents without difficulty

_____ Does not cling to adults excessively

_____ Makes eye contact with adults

_____ Makes activity choices without teacher's help

_____ Seeks other children to play with

_____ Plays roles confidently in dramatic play

_____ Stands up for own rights

_____ Displays enthusiasm in regard to doing things for self

2. Emotional Development

_____ Allows self to be comforted during stressful time

_____ Eats, sleeps, toilets without fuss away from home

_____ Handles sudden changes/startling situations with control

_____ Can express anger in words rather than actions

_____ Allows aggressive behavior to be redirected

_____ Does not withdraw from others excessively

_____ Shows interest/attention in classroom activities

_____ Smiles, seems happy much of the time

3. Social Play

_____ Plays by self with or without objects

_____ Plays by self constructing or creating something

_____ Plays by self in pretending-type activity

_____ Plays parallel to others with or without objects

_____ Plays parallel to others constructing or creating something

_____ Plays parallel to others in pretending-type activity

_____ Plays with a group with or without objects

_____ Plays with a group constructing or creating something

_____ Plays with a group in pretending-type activity

4. Prosocial Behavior

_____ Shows concern for someone in distress

_____ Shows delight for someone experiencing pleasure

_____ Shares something with another

_____ Gives something of his/her own to another

_____ Takes turns with toys or activities

_____ Waits for turn without a fuss

_____ Helps another do a task

_____ Helps another in need

5. Large Motor Development

_____ Walks down steps alternating feet

_____ Runs with control over speed and direction

_____ Jumps over obstacle, landing on two feet

_____ Hops forward on one foot

_____ Pedals and steers tricycle

_____ Climbs up and down climbing equipment with ease

_____ Throws object overhand to target

_____ Catches thrown object with hands

6. Small Motor Development

_____ Shows hand preference (which is _____)

_____ Turns with hand easily (knobs, lids, eggbeaters)

_____ Pours liquid into glass without spilling

_____ Unfastens and fastens zippers, buttons, Velcro tabs

_____ Picks up and inserts objects with ease

_____ Uses drawing/writing tools with control

_____ Uses scissors with control

_____ Pounds in nails with control

7. Cognitive Development: Classification and Seriation

_____ Recognizes basic geometric shapes

_____ Recognizes colors

_____ Recognizes differences in size

_____ Sorts objects by appearance

_____ Discriminates things that are alike from those that are different

_____ Puts parts together to make a whole

_____ Arranges events in sequence from first to last

_____ Arranges objects in series according to a certain rule

8. Cognitive Development: Number, Time, Space, Memory

_____ Counts by rote to ten

_____ Counts objects to ten

_____ Knows the daily schedule in sequence

_____ Knows what happened yesterday

_____ Can build a block enclosure

_____ Can locate an object behind or beside something

_____ Recalls words to song, chant

_____ Can recollect and act on a series of directions

9. Spoken Language

_____ Speaks confidently in the classroom

_____ Speaks clearly enough for adults to understand

_____ Speaks in expanded sentences

_____ Takes part in conversations with other children

_____ Asks questions with proper word order

_____ Makes negative responses with proper word order

_____ Uses past tense verbs correctly

_____ Plays with rhyming words

10. Written Language

_____ Pretends to write by making scribbles in horizontal lines

_____ Includes features of real letters in scribbling

_____ Identifies own written name

_____ Identifies classroom labels

_____ Knows some alphabet letters
_____ Makes real letters
_____ Prints letters of name
_____ Prints name correctly in linear manner

11. Art Skills

_____ Makes random marks or covers paper with color
_____ Scribbles on paper
_____ Forms basic shapes
_____ Makes mandalas
_____ Makes suns
_____ Draws human as circle with arms and legs attached
_____ Draws animals, trees
_____ Makes pictorial drawings

12. Imagination

_____ Pretends by replaying familiar routines
_____ Needs particular props to do pretend play
_____ Assigns roles or takes assigned roles
_____ May switch roles without warning
_____ Uses language for creating and sustaining plot
_____ Uses exciting, danger-packed themes
_____ Takes on characteristics and actions related to role
_____ Uses elaborate and creative themes, ideas, details

Permission is granted by the publisher to reproduce this checklist for evaluation and record keeping.

REFERENCES CITED

Bell, Donald, and Roberta M. Low. *Observing and Recording Children's Behavior.* Richland, Wash.: Performance Associates, 1977.

Hodgden, Laurel, et al. *School Before Six: A Diagnostic Approach.* St. Louis: CEMREL, 1974.

Irwin, D. Michelle, and M. Margaret Bushnell. *Observational Strategies for Child Study.* New York: Holt, Rinehart, and Winston, 1980.

OTHER SOURCES

Cartwright, Carol A., and G. Phillip Cartwright. *Developing Observation Skills.* New York: McGraw-Hill, 1984.

Cohen, Dorothy H., and Virginia Stern with Nancy Balaban. *Observing & Recording the Behavior of Young Children.* New York: Teachers College Press, 1983.

Richarz, Ann Sherrill. *Understanding Children through Observation.* St. Paul: West Publishing, 1980.

Touliatos, John, and Norma H. Compton. *Approaches to Child Study.* Minneapolis: Burgess, 1983.

LEARNING ACTIVITIES

1. Have two different observers use the *Child Skills Checklist* to observe the same child during the same time period for three days. Compare results. How similar were the observations? In what areas were there differences? In what ways can you improve future observing and recording?

2. Make an anecdotal record of a child after you have observed him/her for an hour. At the same time, have another observer make an on-the-spot running record. Compare the two. Which showed more detail? Which was more accurate? Which would be more helpful to you in understanding the child or planning for him? Why?

3. Have two different observers make a running record of the same child for 30 minutes. Compare the results. Which, if any, of the errors mentioned under "Methods for Observing and Recording," p. 6, turned up? How can you guard against these errors in the future?

4. Make an anecdotal record on a child after you have observed him/her for an hour. What inferences can you make about this child? What specific evidence is each inference based on? Can you make any conclusions? Why or why not?

5. Construct a graphic rating scale on five social behaviors of children, and use it to observe three children in your class. Discuss your results. Did you have any problems making judgments? How can you use the information gained?

2 Self-Identity

Self-Identity Checklist

- ☐ Separates from parents without difficulty
- ☐ Does not cling to adults excessively
- ☐ Makes eye contact with adults
- ☐ Makes activity choices without teacher's help
- ☐ Seeks other children to play with
- ☐ Plays roles confidently in dramatic play
- ☐ Stands up for own rights
- ☐ Displays enthusiasm in regard to doing things for self

F rom the moment of birth, the young human being engages in the dynamic process of becoming himself or herself. The child continually develops into a whole person with a temperament, personality, and value system—with a physical, cognitive, language, social, emotional, and creative makeup that is uniquely his or her own. It is a totally engrossing process that will take a lifetime to complete, but its early stages are perhaps its most crucial, for they set the pattern for all that is to follow.

This chapter will discuss some of the developmental sequences that are observable in children three-to-five years old as these children strive to develop in the setting of the child development center or classroom. Although each child carries a unique package of genetic traits and home influences, the caregivers met and the care received at the center nevertheless will have a strong bearing on the child's future development.

Each item of the *Child Skills Checklist* will be discussed separately in this and the chapters to follow. Each *checklist* item is positive in nature and should be checked if the observer sees the child performing in the manner described. Suggestions for helping and supporting the child's development in the unchecked items will follow the discussion of the item.

☐ SEPARATES FROM PARENTS WITHOUT DIFFICULTY

Initial Attachment

Most studies of young children agree that a key ingredient to successful development is a strong initial attachment to a primary caregiver, usually the mother. Without such an attachment, babies may seriously lag in their development and, in some cases, even die. It seems a great paradox, then, to suggest that for successful development to continue, the young human must learn at the same time to separate from the parent. But, such is the case. This separation should occur first in the home—not only with the child, but also with the parents, who must encourage the infant to become independent of them, and who also must let go of the infant.

35

A key ingredient to the young child's emotional development is a strong initial attachment to a primary caregiver, usually the mother.

Many current attachment/separation studies are based on the work of John Bowlby (1969) and Mary Ainsworth (1978), whose work also reflects Jean Piaget's theories of cognitive development.

The first separation of the child from the mother is of course the physical one that occurs at birth. Some psychologists believe that much of life thereafter is a striving of the developing being to achieve once again that perfect state of oneness with another human (Kaplan, p. 43).

But, in the first few months of life, the baby hardly recognizes itself as a separate being apart from its mother or primary caregiver. When it cries, the caregiver feeds or changes it. When it gurgles or coos, the caregiver holds it close or smiles. Little by little, as visual memory develops—and "person permanence" occurs—the infant comes to recognize this primary caregiver as being different from everyone else. The child then strives to be near to this caregiver or to bring this person close as often as possible. "Person permanence" means that the infant has developed the ability to hold the memory of the person in its mind when the person is out of sight (Damon, p. 34).

It is necessary, therefore, that this primary caregiver be a consistent one. The formation of a strong attachment becomes complicated if the infant has too many primary caregivers. If the mother works during the day, for example, she should make arrangements to turn over the secondary caregiving responsibilities to one consistent person while she is away. She still can function as a primary caregiver when she returns from work, if this is the role she has chosen. If she has turned over the role of primary caregiver to the father or to another person from the beginning, then this should be the consistent person whom the infant can turn to at the end of the day. The baby who has developed "person permanence" will welcome this person happily when he or she returns.

This is the beginning of the strong initial attachment which is necessary on the part of both infant and caregiver in order for later separation to occur successfully. Such an attachment leads to a sense of security and trust on the part of the infant. The lack of such an attachment often interferes with the child's building trust in future relationships. In fact, the failure to thrive in infancy is frequently the result of the breakdown of this initial attachment relationship (Seagull, p. 8).

Both the primary caregiver and the infant play a part in building this initial attachment. The adult must respond promptly and in an appropriate manner to the infant's cries—time after time. For example, the adult should feed the infant and not spank it when it cries out of hunger. Some adults don't. On the other hand, the infant should also respond appropriately to the caregiver's actions. For example, the infant needs to stop crying when the adult cares for its needs, or to show delight when the adult plays with or cuddles it. Some babies don't.

It is difficult for the initial attachment to be strong when the actions of one, the other or both are not satisfactory over a period of time. It takes most of the infant's first year to develop the relationship with a caregiver, in fact (Damon, p. 29). But, without such an attachment, it is difficult for the infant to develop trust in anyone else, and it becomes doubly difficult for the infant or developing child to separate from the caregiver. After all, if it cannot trust its primary caregiver, how can it risk trusting anyone? The attachment between the infant and primary caregiver, in fact, serves as a model for future human relationships.

Initial Separation

The initial separation of the infant from its primary caregiver begins when it first recognizes it is separate from that person. This develops within the first six months of life as the baby recognizes there is a difference between itself and the caregiver—and later, between itself and others. At this time, its first memories—visual in nature—are occurring. Some psychologists call this the "psychological birth" of the baby (Kaplan, p. 121). It is the first glimmering of self-identity.

Toward the end of the first year, as the infant learns to move about by creeping and finally by its first unsteady steps, an interesting pattern of interaction with the caregiver often emerges. The youngster uses the caregiver as a base from which to explore its environment. It moves out a bit and comes back, moves further and returns, moves out again and this time may only look back to make eye contact that will give it the reassurance to continue its exploration.

During this same period or sometimes before, "separation anxiety" also emerges; that is, the infant sets up a strong protest of crying or clinging if the caregiver attempts to leave. This pattern of distress also is exhibited when a stranger appears, making it obvious the baby recognizes the difference between the caregiver and others.

Thus self-identity develops as the toddler ventures out and scurries back, clings and pushes away, holds on and lets go. But, the stronger the initial attachment, the more secure the developing child should feel each time he or she lets go.

In addition, the young human learns who he is by the way other people respond to him (how others seem to be affected by whatever he does). Hopefully, this response is mainly positive, so that by the time he enters nursery school, day care or Head Start, he already will be feeling good about himself. Table 2 summarizes the child's attachment/separation milestones.

TABLE 2. Attachment/separation milestones in child development

Attachment

Preattachment . . . . Birth through first eight to twelve weeks
Responds to people but cannot distinguish one from the other; does not recognize self as separate from primary caregiver.

Person permanence . . . . First months
Learns to distinguish primary caregiver from others

Attachment to caregiver . . . . First months to second or third year
Seeks proximity to caregiver; shows "separation anxiety" when caregiver leaves; shows "stranger anxiety"—most common at seven months—when stranger appears

Partnership . . . . Second or third year on
Comes to understand caregiver's point of view and adjusts own behavior accordingly

Separation

Physical separation from mother . . . . Birth

Psychological birth . . . . First six months
Recognizes self as separate from mother

Exploration of physical environment . . . . Last months of first year to second, third years
Explores first by creeping, then walking; uses caregiver as base in exploring and returning

Strengthening of self-identity . . . . Second, third years on
Gets stronger recognition of self-identity as child and parent let go of one another for more frequent and longer periods of time

NOTE: Includes information from Damon, p. 33

School Separation

No matter how good the young child feels about him or herself, the initial school separation from a parent is often difficult. At three years old, the sense of self is still a bit shaky. Although the child has an identity at home and can hold onto an image of the caregiver even when the caregiver is not present, at school the child is in a strange environment as well. To complicate matters, the parent/caregiver may be experiencing "separation anxiety" too, and the child often senses this.

Each child handles the situation in his or her own way. One may be used to the home of a loving babysitter and will take this new "playroom" in stride. Another may cling to mother and scream whenever the mother attempts to leave. The child used to playing with others may quickly join the group in the block building corner. A shyer child may need the teacher's urging to join in. One fussing, crying child may stop as soon as mother leaves. Another may withdraw into himself and sit in a corner sucking his thumb.

You as a classroom worker hope the children will become adjusted to this separation within a few days or weeks. Most of them will. One or two may not. How can you help them develop a strong enough sense of self that they also feel free to let go of their primary caregiver?

If You Have Not Checked This Item: Some Helpful Ideas

One or more of the children in your center may have unchecked self-identity *checklist* items. Because you are aware that each item represents a step in the developmental sequence of young children, you may be able to lend children support at the outset by arranging your schedule or setting up your classroom ahead of time to address their problems. Here are some ideas that may help preschoolers separate from their parents with less difficulty.

- *Make an Early Initial Contact with Parent/Caregiver and Child*

If the child and the parent have met you ahead of time, they may feel less reluctant to separate on the day school begins. For the child, it is better if this meeting takes place close to the time of school opening rather than the spring before. Memories of a brief visit several months before school begins have little meaning for the young child. An immediate follow-up is more effective. If you visit the child's home, you might take a camera with you, recording the occasion and later using the visit photos in the classroom to help the child make an easier transition from home to school.

- *Try Staggered Enrollment*

Rather than having all of the children in your class begin school on the same day at the same time, you might consider having half of them begin on the first day, and half the second—or half in the morning and the rest in the afternoon. This will allow staff members to devote more time to the individual children and their parents. In addition, the first day may not be so overwhelming for the children if only half of the class is present at once.

- *Create a Simple Initial Environment*

The more complex the classroom environment, the more overwhelming it is for certain children. You might plan to have the classroom arranged with fewer activity areas and less material on the shelves for the first weeks. As the children settle in and become more secure, you can add activities and materials as needed.

- *Use Transition Materials*

Children can make the transition from home to school—can separate more easily from their parents—if there are familiar materials to bridge the gap. Water is one such material. A water table or basin with an eggbeater, funnel, and squeeze bottles may take a child's mind off a parent long enough to get happily involved in the center. Toy trucks and dolls often have the same effect. Have a special set of little toys you can allow children to take home with them at the end of the day and return again in the morning to make the transition less difficult.

- *Utilize Parent/Caregiver Visits*

Allow the parents to stay as long as necessary on the first days, or to come visit from time to time. The shy child may use her parent as a base for exploration in the classroom, venturing away from the parent and returning just as she did as a toddler at home. If the separation is a difficult one, have the caregiver return early to pick up the youngster. Little by little, the children should be able to stay longer without their parents.

- *Show and Foster Acceptance of the Child*

Up until now, the child's self-identity has evolved from the reactions of his family to him. Now that he is in your classroom, you, your co-workers and the other children will be adding details to the child's interior picture of himself. These details need to be positive, happy ones. You need to support this process first of all by accepting the child and his family unconditionally. Show your acceptance both verbally and nonverbally. Smile at him frequently. Greet him personally every day. Demonstrate that you enjoy being near him and having him near you. You are the behavior model for the other children as well. If they see that you accept a child no matter what, they will be more likely to do the same.

☐ DOES NOT CLING TO ADULTS EXCESSIVELY

The next developmental step for the children in your classroom is to build up enough confidence to become involved on their own with the other children and the activities available. Those with a strong sense of self may have no difficulty with becoming involved. Others may not be ready during the first days or weeks. A few may not be ready at all.

Psychologists use the term "significant others" in referring to the particular people who have the most important influence on our lives (Seagull, p. 13). For the young child, this usually means the immediate family. Once a child enters your classroom, however, you and your co-workers also will become significant others. This means that your reactions toward the child will have an effect on what she thinks about herself. This may reinforce the view of self learned at home, or it may modify that view. If the responses to her are generally positive, then her feelings about herself as a good person are strengthened. The opposite, of course, is also true.

The development of a self-identity is thus a subtle but lengthy process. No one knows for sure how long the process takes—probably much of a person's life. The early childhood years are the most crucial because they set the course. That is why it is so important for the young self in its most sensitive, formative period to receive positive responses from the adults around it.

Many children develop a similar kind of attachment to one or more of the adults in the early childhood classroom as they did to their primary caregiver at home. The child needs a consistent caregiver here as well, in order to develop trust in this new environment. It is thus important that the staff of an early childhood center is present consistently throughout the year—not merely dropping in and dropping out.

If the teacher must leave, she should try to have the replacement teacher visit the classroom several times before she departs so the children may get to know the replacement. The transition thus will be more gradual and hopefully more acceptable to the children. Otherwise, for certain children, changing teachers will be nearly as traumatic as changing primary caregivers.

The child who looks to the teacher as a caregiver may cling to the classroom adult. He or she may not have the necessary trust in the world, or may not have developed a strong enough sense of self yet to let go in a strange, new environment. Three-year-olds, especially, may relate much more comfortably to adults than to other children. After all, much of their life thus far may have been spent in a one-to-one relationship with an adult. A classroom of fifteen to twenty children may be totally overwhelming. How can you help such a child?

If You Have Not Checked This Item: Some Helpful Ideas

- *Display Acceptance*

You must accept the child's clinging behavior, knowing that it is a normal step in the developmental sequence. But, you also need to know ways to encourage and support this child when he is ready to move out. If he feels that you accept his presence near you and will not force him to do something he is not ready to do, then he is much more likely to move out on his own. Forcing a clinging child away from you before he is ready to go may only make him cling more tightly.

- *Have the Child Follow an Adult's Lead*

The child who clings to or "shadows" an adult may follow the adult's lead as well. You could lead her to a table and sit down with her to make a puzzle. If she becomes involved with it on her own, you might try moving to another group of children. Or you could try playing a role in the dramatic play area and inviting the child to accompany you on some pretend errand, or to help you accomplish some pretend task. If the child accepts your efforts to involve her, you can freely leave the activity. If she does not, she may not be ready yet to move out on her own.

- *Observe the Child*

You may be able to tell when the time is right by your observations of this child. Does he spend a great deal of time observing the other children? Is this looking behavior done from the "protection" of your side, or does he stand in a "safe" spot and watch? If his eyes seem to be more engaged in following the activities of the others rather than keeping track of you, it may be time to help him become involved with them.

- *Ask the Child to Help an Adult or Another Child*

The clinging child will sometimes allow herself to become involved in classroom activities as the adult's helper. Ask her to help you get out the paints or the puzzles . . . to dress a doll in the housekeeping area . . . to feed the guinea pig . . . to deliver a message next door. Little by little, she may venture away from you and then return just as she did with her primary caregiver at home. You might ask a second child to join you as a helper. The two of them could then do the same tasks, at which point you could try leaving them on their own.

- *Follow Up on the Child's Interest*

One of the most successful techniques for involving the clinging child in classroom activities is to discover what interests him. Your conversations with him may give you a clue. If he is nonverbal, your observations of the things that attract his attention may suggest an activity he could pursue by himself and then later with another child when he feels enough at ease. You might leaf through a magazine with him and ask him to point to the pictures of the things he likes. He or you could cut these out, and he could paste them in a scrapbook to get started. Or you could use the information you gain about his interests to involve him more directly with similar classroom activities.

If none of these ideas works you should continue to be patient about his clinging. Do not push. When he feels secure enough in the classroom, he will venture out on his own. The child who never feels secure enough is probably still not mature enough to handle a classroom situation. If he still continues to cling after several weeks in your program, you may want to discuss with the parent the possibility of keeping him at home for another year, or placing him in a home-type program with fewer children.

☐ MAKES EYE CONTACT WITH ADULTS

Nonverbal cues are among the most important signals people send out about their feelings. Facial expressions, head position, muscle tension, body carriage . . . all reveal a person's state of mind regarding himself and those around him. All of us read these expressions subconsciously. Our subconscious minds process this intake and help our conscious minds to make decisions about the people we interact with. We feel people are friendly, hostile, frightened, unsure as a result of this constant subconscious processing of visual stimuli.

As teachers of young children, we need to read nonverbal cues consciously as well, because of the important information these cues can give us about young children. In addition, we need to be aware of the importance of such information to young children. Because they are not fully verbal at ages three and four, young children depend heavily on nonverbal cues from us to make determinations about the people and situations they encounter.

We can say polite words to children and their parents, but if our face is tense and our eyes give out signals of distaste, the child picks up and responds to these. That is why we say children instinctively know which adults to trust. Children read nonverbal signals exceptionally well, partly because children are nonverbal themselves and partly because they are more visually oriented than most adults.

Eye signals are the most important. Eyes give messages of affection, love, happiness, contentment, and humor. They show pain, frustration, anger, fright, and despair. The way the eyes are partly or wholly open, the position of the eyebrows, the size of the pupils, the number of blinks, the length of a stare . . . all are indicative of a person's feeings. Words may not always tell the truth, but eyes do.

Earlier studies assumed that the size of the pupils of the eye remained constant if the level of light remained the same. Research subsequently has disproved this notion. What research discovered instead was that the pupils increase in size in the presence of pleasant things and become noticeably smaller if people and situations are disagreeable. Eyes also respond to more than visual cues. Laboratory tests have shown that eye pupils change size in response to voices. Loud, harsh, or scolding voices may cause the pupils to shrink. The size of eye pupils is, in fact, a reliable indicator of a person's feelings (Thompson, p. 90).

Eye contact between people is important. The first encounter with someone's eyes reveals much about the person's feelings concerning himself. Subsequent contact often tells a great deal of how that person feels about you. The first actual eye contact itself is a recognition that you exist in a person's world and that person exists in yours. If a person feels uncomfortable about himself or you, he often shifts his gaze. Hopefully, you will not need to do the same.

Preschool children are at an egocentric stage in their development when they enter your classroom. They see things only from their own points of view. If you asked one to hide so that you would not be able to see her, she might very well cover her own eyes. From her self-centered point of view, she believes that you cannot see her because she cannot see you. Children who are initially tense or frightened or uneasy in your presence may use this same subterfuge by refusing to make eye contact—if they do not look at you, surely you will not be able to see them—or if they do not look at you, maybe you won't really be there.

Certain cultures and ethnic groups also condition their children not to look adults directly in the eye because social norms say it is disrespectful. You need to decide whether your children avoid eye contact because of cultural conditioning or because they are truly uncomfortable with themselves or you. Eventually, you will need to have eye contact with all of your children in order for them to recognize the freedom and openness of this new environment—to understand they are worthy human beings in your sight.

When eye contact finally occurs, it often diffuses tense situations. If you can succeed in getting the shy or frightened child to make eye contact with you, you may be able to dispel his fears without saying a word. He will see in your eyes the friendliness, sense of humor, and enjoyment he can expect from your presence. But, you need to know that your eyes won't fake it. You must truly project to this young, developing child that you like him already, no matter what (because you really do).

Research shows that the more a person likes someone, the more he looks at him (Thompson, p. 91). This applies to teachers as well as children. It is therefore important that you do not pick favorites or reject any of the children in your care, because their sensitivity to nonverbal cues will soon tell them this. You will be looking more frequently at the children you like than at the children you do not like. As a professional, you cannot afford to pick favorites or dislike a child. Of course, it is human to like one person more than another. But, in your position as a child care worker, this is not permissible. You must make a concerted effort to correct your feelings if you find yourself responding like this.

If You Have Not Checked This Item: Some Helpful Ideas

- *Indicate Acceptance*

Many of the same ideas used to help the child who was not checked for the first two items also apply here. This child either is not sure of herself or has not developed basic trust in the people and world around her. Or she may have a disability of some sort. Autistic children seem to avoid eye contact. Some mentally retarded children have difficulty making eye contact with people outside the family.

To help any child develop a self-identity strong enough to make eye contact with strange adults, you, as the strange adult, must show you accept the child unconditionally. Use both verbal and nonverbal cues. Tell him how nice it is to have him in your center. Use his name frequently. Show delight when he accomplishes something, no matter how insignificant.

- *Make Eye Contact Yourself*

You are the model for behavior in your classroom. If you feel it is important for your children to behave in a certain way, then you need to do the same yourself. Make eye contact with the shy child at all times. When she finally has the confidence to return the look, she needs to see you smiling at her.

- *Be Patient*

Do not force the issue. You must remember that the child's avoidance of eye contact is not a negative action but a clue to you that he is still not confident enough in your presence to return the look. You need to do all in your power to help him develop that confidence. But, sometimes, the best thing to do is nothing. Have patience. Force will not help. You must have the confidence to know that his refusal to meet your eyes is nothing personal. When he finally feels at ease within himself and within your center, he will return your look.

All children at one time or another avoid looking at a caregiver. They may be embarrassed or ashamed or feeling foolish about something they have done. But, if they can see that you still accept them when they finally do confront your eyes, then the children will be able to return your look with confidence as they continue on their unique path of development.

☐ MAKES ACTIVITY CHOICES WITHOUT TEACHER'S HELP

One of the next observable indicators of a child's feelings about herself in your classroom is her willingness to make a choice on her own about the activity she wants to engage in. Once she feels confident enough to leave your side, she needs to explore the new environment and try out the various materials and activities on her own. Many children have a strong enough sense of self to go immediately to the activity areas upon first entering the room. Others use the adult who accompanies them as a base for their explorations, going into an area and coming back to the person, much as they did during their initial separation from their primary caregiver when they were infants. Some also use the teacher as this base.

Research seems to imply that having a secure base of attachment facilitates exploratory behavior on the part of two-year-olds in center-based day care (Fein, p. 88). Three-, four-, and five-year-olds also do better when they have this strong attachment. These attachment findings seem to indicate that, just as within the family, the child who is secure in his relationship with a caregiver will also be secure on his own. Thus, as previously mentioned, it is important to help a child build this relationship initially. It is also important to observe which children are able to become involved with activities independently—and which are not quite ready, possibly because the sense of self-identity in these children is not yet strong enough.

Your goal for children who do not participate independently in activities will be to help these children develop a sense of security with you and within the center. Once they develop this feeling of security, they take the next step toward self-identity: becoming involved in center activities on their own.

You may need to help the clinging child get started, as mentioned previously. But, then, you should withdraw. Children need to have every opportunity to express their self-identities on their own. They need to explore the center environment. They need to learn how to make their own choices.

It is so tempting for teachers to help children make decisions—and the children will listen. They even will ask for help. They are used to having adults tell them what to do. You must resist the temptation. Invite children to look for themselves. Then, support them in their exploration. It is so much simpler for you to make up their minds for them, you may argue. But, then, they will have lost the opportunity to take the next step in their development as a person. Give them this chance.

If You Have Not Checked This Item: Some Helpful Ideas

- *Provide an Explorable Environment*

For younger children, your environment needs to be simple with a few activity areas and a small number of items within each area. This applies especially to two- and three-year-olds. Some environments are just too complex for these children to be comfortable. Too many things are going on, and the children respond by refusing to explore or get involved. For this age group, you need to simplify your physical environment—at least at the beginning of the year. Later, the children will be ready for additional activities.

Four- and five-year-olds, on the other hand, need the stimulation of complexity, novelty, and variation. This age group tends to be less fearful of new things and more venturesome. For them, a more complex physical environment may encourage rather than discourage exploration.

- *Give Children Time*

Once children feel secure with you and your center, they should be able to make activity choices on their own if you give them enough time. Let them wander around at first during the free choice period. Don't force them into an activity before they are ready to go. Some children need more time than others. Others need to try out many things before they can settle on one.

- *Act as a Base for the Children's Exploration*

Sit or stand in an area of the room where children can see you—near, but not in any one activity area. Those who still need the security of an adult attachment can make eye contact, receive your smiles of support, and even come over for a moment or so before you encourage them to go off on their own again. The child who is still clinging can explore with her eyes. When she feels secure enough, she will join the others, knowing you are nearby.

☐ SEEKS OTHER CHILDREN TO PLAY WITH

Although this particular item seems to relate more to the child's social rather than emotional development, this activity actually indicates both. Seeking other children to play with is a part of the progression of the developing self as well as a step in the sequence of socialization.

As the preschool child moves away from the parent to stay by himself in the early childhood classroom, and then, as he moves away from the teacher to make activity choices on his own, his next step in the development of his self-identity should involve joining the other children in play. Yet, he often does not join the others—at least not right away. Depending on his previous experience—or lack of it—with peers, he may prefer to play on his own at first. In other words, other children do not replace a child's primary or secondary caregivers as objects of attachment. Finally seeking other children to play with definitely indicates the development of a stronger self-identity.

As the preschool child develops a stronger self-identity, he or she seeks other children to play with.

Children seem to recognize that other children are like themselves—having a dependence on adult caregivers. From their self-centered perspectives, in fact, children may see their peers as competitors for the attention of the caregivers as well as for the use of materials and activities.

Through socialization, children will be finding ways to get along with other children, as well as to share and take turns with materials—and even people—in your center. Through development of self-identity, the children will eventually be seeking contact with others like themselves.

Even as infants and toddlers, children recognize one another, and some engage in social behavior. But this contact is not of the same level, type, or intensity as interactions with adults. Infants' and toddlers' striving for attachment does not involve another child. While infants may look at, imitate, and even vocalize with peers, these activities are few and far between and are not sustained for long periods. With adults, on the other hand, and especially with their mothers, infants' interactions involve touching, holding, and hugging during more instances, for longer periods, and at more intense emotional levels than anything they do with peers. The most frequent initial contact between two infants, in fact, takes place around toys (Damon, p. 59).

By the time the young child enters your class, he or she in most instances has had a number of contacts with peers. Again, the interactions are not the same as with adults. Children look to the adult as a base of attachment. They look to their peers as a reflection of themselves. Those children with a strong sense of self will have less difficulty interacting with the other children in your center from the outset. Interaction behavior, therefore, indicates the development level of the self-identity.

Those who need help developing this sense of security within themselves may not seek to play with other children at first. As with the other areas of self-identity, you may need to help the children progress. Don't expect success to occur overnight in this particular area. Some children are just not ready for many days or weeks to make contact with peers. By looking at and treating each child in your center as an individual, you will begin to elicit clues about each that can help you support development in this crucial area. As before, you will need to use acceptance and patience whenever a child is slow in moving ahead.

If You Have Not Checked This Item: Some Helpful Ideas

- *Find a Friend*

For many young children who are used to dealing with a limited number of people at a time, a roomful of lively peers is overwhelming. You may need to help find a friend for the shy child who may be able to relate on a one-to-one basis with one other child before she can cope with a group. Choose someone who gets along with others, and ask the two to do an errand for you—perhaps mix paints or play dough, wash the doll clothes, or get out the cots for nap time. Or, you might ask the "friend" to show the shy child how to use the saw or how to record her voice on the tape recorder. Make the activities as personal as possible to attract the shy child's interest and get her to focus on the activity or material instead of her unsure feelings about herself. Once she successfully relates to one other child, she may begin to seek and play with others on her own.

- *Use Small Groups*

Young children relate better to peers when in small groups. You can arrange the physical environment of your classroom so that each of the activity areas accommodates only a certain number of children (say, no more than four). Methods to accomplish this include placing four chairs around a table; using masking tape on the floor to divide the block corner into four building areas; providing only four aprons for water play, two saws or hammers for woodworking, three pillows in the book area, etc. When you read to the children, read to two or three, rather than to the total group.

- *Employ Materials/Activities for Two or Three*

This idea is more often used in European programs to teach children to share, but you also can design or designate certain materials or activities in your classroom as always for use by two or three children together. Use of a saw, for instance, can be set up for three children: two to hold the wood, and one to saw. You might attach one of your wagons to a trike so that one child must pedal while one rides. Your job chart of daily chores (which children choose or are assigned to) could require that pairs or teams of children work together to do the jobs. Can you think of other team enterprises?

☐ PLAYS ROLES CONFIDENTLY IN DRAMATIC PLAY

Once the child has begun playing with others in your center, you need to be cognizant of another indicator of his developing self-identity. Is he able to take on and play a role in the pretend situations that abound in early childhood programs? Can he pretend to be father, brother or baby in the housekeeping corner? Is he a nurse, doctor or famous skater in the dressup area? Can he be a race car driver, helicopter pilot or crane operator on the playground? When a child can play a pretend role with confidence in your center, then he is presenting observable proof that his self-identity has taken on an even more mature aspect.

In order to play a pretend role, children need to be able to see things from a different point of view than their own. Their perspective, in other words, cannot be egocentric. We mentioned how young children cover their eyes and think you cannot see them because they cannot see you. That view is of course totally egocentric. At some point in time, however, three- and four-year-olds seem to be able to step out of themselves and pretend quite realistically to be someone else.

It is not clear whether this ability is stronger or appears sooner in some children because of opportunity, encouragement, and practice at home, or whether certain children are instinctively or temperamentally more imaginative. But, no matter what causes the behavior, it indicates to the observer of children that the child has reached a milestone in the development of self-identity.

A child's ability to play a role other than her own says a number of things to the observer, including

1. The child can distinguish reality from fantasy (i.e., she knows she is pretending.).
2. The child is able to symbolize things (i.e., she represents a real person or event in a make-believe manner.).
3. The child can see things from another person's perspective.
4. The child has a strong enough sense of self to step out of herself and be someone else.

Until all four of these statements are true for the young child, she is really unable to play make-believe roles.

Once she can perform this behavior, she suddenly is able to explore in a wholly new way. She can try out roles. She can see what it's like to be the mother, the older sister, the baby. She can dominate the situation. She can make her father or brother do what she wants them to. This ability is a heady discovery. Of course, in a group situation, she often is dominated or at least controlled to some extent by others and must remain in an assigned or assumed role. If she plays the role "wrong," then she will be reprimanded by those often strict conformists, her peers.

Adults in the early childhood classroom may wonder aloud: "Is this what we want our children to do? Isn't it wrong to encourage fantasizing like this?" Not at all, say child development specialists. This is a natural progression in the young child's development. This "fantasizing" is the way young children explore concepts about people and events in the world around them. While adults look askance at the "Walter-Mitty-type" who seems to live in a world of make-believe, it is not only natural but also imperative that children have the opportunity to use their imaginations playfully in exploring their own world. (See Chapter 13, Imagination.)

Besides, this playful use of the imagination is the next step developmentally for the young child in his creation of a strong self-identity. He started as a new human being so attached to his mother that he thought she was a part of him. Then, he made the separation in which he not only recognized he was separate from her, but also realized he could move out from her. Next, he developed confidence enough to come to a new environment and allow other adults to be his caregivers. From these adults, he moved out to explore his new environment and interact with his peers. Now, he has developed a strong enough sense of himself that he can try out being someone else.

A great deal of power surrounds gaining control over people and situations, even imaginary ones. Up until now, the young child has been virtually powerless in a world controlled by adults. But, when she plays a role in dramatic play, she is able to take a stand, be what she wants to be, and make things come out the way she wants them. Her self-identity is thus strengthened as she expands her horizons, gains control over ideas and feelings, and receives immediate feedback from the other players as to how her role affects them.

Also, in playing such pretend roles, the player gets to find out more about himself. The other children's reactions to his role and his own reactions to it help him realize his capabilities and understand his limits. He can explore gender roles more fully—what it's like to be female or male—for instance.

Children in our society are treated differently from the moment of birth, it seems, depending on their gender. Now the young pretender can try out being the mother, father, sister or brother in the family. Because children often play these familiar family roles in a very stereotyped, exaggerated manner—their own interpretation of the way real family members act—the players soon learn which roles are considered the "best" and how the others feel about mothers and fathers, boys and girls.

For a child who did not participate in dramatic play upon first entering your program, now doing so signifies a major step. It means she not only has a strong enough sense of self to try being someone else, but she also now has this unparalleled opportunity to practice her budding interpersonal and communication skills, thus strengthening her self-identity in a manner that was impossible before.

Again, a paradox exists: once she is able to be someone else, she becomes more of herself.

If You Have Not Checked This Item: Some Helpful Ideas

- *Provide Dramatic Play Material*

Have at least one area of your classroom set up for dramatic play. This section can be a family area with a child-size table, chairs, refrigerator, stove, and sink; a bedroom area with doll beds, dresser and mirror, and chest of drawers; a store with shelves of empty food containers and a toy cash register; or any other such setting. If you take your class on a field trip, you should consider setting up a similar pretend area in your room (for them to try out the roles they saw enacted on the trip): a doctor's office, a clinic, a laundromat, a barber or beauty shop. In addition to life-size settings and props, you need miniature toys to encourage role-playing as well. Little cars, trucks, people, animals, boats, and planes can be placed strategically, such as in the block corner, at the water table, and with the table blocks. A box full of dramatic play props can be taken out on the playground. Pictures of people in a variety of roles—from family members to community helpers—can be hung at children's eye level around the room to encourage the exploration of roles. Ask the children what types of roles they would like to try out, and have them help you to assemble the props. Books such as *Be What You Want To Be* are full of ideas for making your own props from discarded material.

- *Allow Time to Pretend*

Because the best dramatic play is spontaneous—even though you may have provided the props—you need to set aside a particular time during the day for free choice activities. Often, these activities are scheduled at the beginning of the day, but they can take place at any time. Allow enough time for children to become involved in their roles. The length of this time may vary from day to day depending upon the children's interests and yours, but free choice activities should be scheduled to occur at the same time every day so that the children can depend upon a set period for pretending and playing roles.

- *Play a Role Yourself*

Sometimes, the only way to help the non-participant to become involved is to play a role yourself. Obviously, if a child is not ready emotionally, your efforts may be wasted. But, some children who are ready to play a role may not know how to get started. In that case, you might pretend to be a mother and invite the child to go on a pretend errand with you, ending up in the dramatic play area where the other children are often delighted to see the teacher playing like they are. If the child accepts your lead and becomes involved with the others, you can gradually withdraw.

• *Be an Observer of Pretend Play*

It will help you immensely in your understanding of children if you take time out to observe and record the various children's engagement in pretend play. Station yourself unobtrusively in an area of the room where a particular child is playing, and jot down as many details as possible in a running record. Do this for several days if possible. Some things to look for can include

1. Theme of the play
2. Role the child is playing
3. Who else is playing, and what are their roles
4. Type of interaction with other children
5. Dialog
6. Length of time the child sustains the role

What can you conclude about the child from your observations? Have you learned anything that can help you plan your program differently so that other children will become involved more easily in dramatic play? Could you add props or suggestions to help the children sustain their play? Chapter 13, "Imagination," has additional suggestions.

☐ STANDS UP FOR OWN RIGHTS

In order for preschool children to stand up for their rights within the classroom, they need to have developed a strong enough self-identity to believe in themselves as individuals with a point of view worth other people's consideration. Thus far in their development of a self-identity, the children have been able to make the separation from their parents, not cling to the adult caregiver, establish eye contact with classroom adults, choose activities on their own, seek other children to play with, and try out roles confidently in dramatic play because they could see things from another person's point of view. Now, the children are progressing further by developing their own points of view, worthy of other children's consideration.

What are some of the classroom rights such a self-confident child might insist on? One is the right of possession. If a child is playing with a piece of equipment, he should be able to continue using it unless some previous turn-taking rule is in effect. Many childhood squabbles take place over objects, often because of children's egocentric perspectives. A child feels he should have a toy because he wants it. The fact that another child is playing with it does not count in his mind. The development of mutual respect is difficult among three- and four-year-olds because so many of them lack the ability to understand the other's perspective (Berndt, p. 255). The child who feels his right of possession is worth defending often will refuse to give in.

A child's choice of participation is another classroom right often established by day-care teachers. If a child opts to join or not join a particular activity, you and the other children need to honor her choice. Use enticements rather than force if you feel the child should be involved when she chooses not to be.

Completing independent projects his own way is a right self-confident children will defend. If a child is doing a painting, modeling clay, constructing a building, or dressing a doll on his own, he should be able to do the activity as he sees fit so long as he is not interfering with others. In a like manner, others should not be allowed to interfere with him. The child with the strong self-identity will continue in his own manner, disregarding or rejecting the attempts of others to impose their will.

Protection of property is another indication of self-confident children. Toys or games children have brought from home are often the focus of conflict. You need to provide a private space like a cubby for the storage of each child's possessions. Block buildings are also important to the children who have built them. The child who insists on saving his building may want help in making a sign informing others: "Please Leave Jeffrey's Building Standing."

Children may stand up for their own rights in a number of ways. They may physically prevent another child from doing something or making them do something. They may verbalize their position with the child. They may tell the teacher. Some of their actions may not even be acceptable in a classroom full of children. Use of power or aggression is of course not appropriate. You need to help such children find more acceptable means for making a point.

As you observe your children on this particular item, you look to see which ones do not allow another child to urge or force unwanted changes on them, and which ones do not back down, or give up a toy or a turn. At the same time, take note of children who always give up or give in to the demands of another. They also need your support in the strengthening of their self-confidence.

If You Have Not Checked This Item: Some Helpful Ideas

- *Model the Desired Behavior*

You need to model the behavior you want your children to follow. Stand firm on decisions you have made. Let your children know why. If you are "wishy-washy" or inconsistent in your treatment of them, they may have trouble standing firm themselves.

- *Allow Children Choices*

One way to help a child learn her rights can count is to give her a chance to make choices that are important to her. Let her choose a favorite activity to participate in or a toy to take home.

- *Stand Up for the Child*

When it is clear to you that a child's rights have been infringed upon by another child, you should take a stand supporting the child and at the same time, let the others know "why Karen can finish her painting now and Bobby can't," for example.

☐ DISPLAYS ENTHUSIASM IN REGARD TO DOING THINGS FOR SELF

The lifelong quest to develop an identity is, in the final analysis, a struggle for autonomy. If young children are successful in this quest, then they will be able and willing to behave independently in many ways. Louise J. Kaplan puts it well in her book, *Oneness and Separateness: From Infant to Individual,* when she says: "In the first three years of life every human being undergoes yet a second birth, in which he is born as a psychological being possessing selfhood and separate identity. The quality of self an infant achieves in those crucial three years will profoundly affect all of his subsequent existence." (p. 15)

Your observations will have helped you determine which children in your class are well on the road to developing strong self-identities and which ones are not. The most successful children will be those who can and want to do things for themselves. They will have achieved enough self-assurance about their own abilities to be able to try and eventually succeed in doing things on their own. Achieving this competence will then allow them a measure of independence from the adults around them.

What are some of the activities you may observe such children performing independently in your classroom? Here is a partial list:

Dressing and undressing	Painting with brush
Tying or fastening shoes	Mixing paints
Using own cubby	Getting out toys
Toileting	Putting toys away
Washing hands and face	Returning blocks to shelves
Brushing teeth	Dressing dolls
Setting table for eating	Handling hammer, saw
Pouring drink	Cutting with scissors
Dishing out food	Cutting with knife
Handling eating implements	Mixing dough
Eating	Using climbing equipment
Cleaning up after eating	Making puzzles

The adeptness level of three- and four-year-old children in these various activities depends on their own sense of self, the practice in developing self they have had at home or elsewhere, and the encouragement or discouragement the adults around them have offered. This author has noticed that children from low income families are often more adept at accomplishing many of the self-help skills than children from middle and upper income families. And I have inferred from this observation that children in low income families may have to do many self-help activities on their own and thus become more skilled sooner than their middle and upper income counterparts.

In the same manner, children who have always had things done for them by the adults around them, often give up the struggle for autonomy. You and your co-workers need to beware of the temptation to "help" the children in your care more than necessary. Children can do many more things for themselves than we realize. You need to allow time for children to learn to zip up jackets and pour their own drinks. Otherwise, you are denying them an unparalleled opportunity to develop their own independence.

The way adults behave toward children during these formative years indeed can make a difference in children's feelings about themselves and thus in the way they behave. Research regarding gender-stereotyping has found that mothers and fathers treat their young daughters differently from their sons when it comes to independent behavior. Parents allow and encourage boys to behave independently earlier than girls in areas such as using scissors without adult supervision, crossing the street alone, playing away from home, and riding the bus. When girls ask for help, they often get it, but boys more often receive a negative response. Boys are encouraged to manipulate objects and explore their environments, while girls more often are discouraged. Thus, it seems parents value independence in boys more than in girls (Brooks-Gunn, pp. 145–46).

This type of discriminating behavior of course may result in girls feeling less capable than boys, therefore attempting fewer things on their own. Or this behavior may cause girls—and therefore women—to become dependent on men and less willing to risk using their own capabilities.

You and your co-workers need to take special care that stereotyped attitudes about the roles of men and women do not color your behavior toward the boys and girls in your center. As in all areas of development, your goal should be to help each child become all he or she is capable of being. When each shows enthusiasm about doing things independently, then you know he or she is well on the way to developing a strong sense of self-identity.

If You Have Not Checked This Item: Some Helpful Ideas

- *Assess Your Center for "Independent" Possibilities*

What can children do on their own in your center? They achieve great satisfaction when accomplishing difficult tasks. Walk around your physical area, and make a list of things children can do. Some items which can go on your daily job chart and which individuals or teams can choose to do include

Feeding the rabbit	Taking own attendance
Cleaning the aquarium	Getting out playground equipment
Watering the plants	Sweeping the floor
Scraping carrots for snack	Sponging off the tables
Delivering mail to the office	Getting out cots for nap time

- *Encourage Performance of Self-Help Skills*

Teach children how to tie their shoes when their small motor coordination allows them this capability. Or have another child help them get started with buttons or zippers or Velcro tabs. Allow enough time for even the slowest child to perform this task on his own.

- *Help Children Get Started*

Sometimes, the first step is all a child needs to start her on the way to independence. Sit next to the child who tells you she can't make the puzzle, and put in a piece yourself. Then, ask her to look for the next one. Stay with her until she completes the puzzle if need be. Then, ask her to try it again on her own. Give her positive verbal support all the way, but refrain from helping this time.

- *Be Enthusiastic Yourself*

Enthusiasm always scores very high on lists of the competencies of successful teachers. You as a behavior model in your classroom always need to be enthusiastic and positive about everything you do. If children see you acting on your own with vigor, they will be encouraged to do likewise.

REFERENCES CITED

Berndt, Thomas J. "Fairness and Friendship," in Rubin, Kenneth W., and Hildy S. Ross (eds.). *Peer Relationships and Social Skills in Childhood*. New York: Springer-Verlag, 1982.

Brooks-Gunn, Jeanne, and Wendy Schempp Matthews. *He & She: How Children Develop their Sex-Role Identity*. Englewood Cliffs, N.J.: Prentice-Hall, 1979.

Damon, William. *Social and Personality Development: Infancy through Adolescence*. New York: W.W. Norton, 1983.

Fein, Greta, and Pamela M. Schwartz. "Developmental Theories in Early Education," in Spodek, Bernard (ed.), *Handbook of Research in Early Childhood Education*. New York: The Free Press, 1982.

Kaplan, Louise J. *Oneness and Separateness: From Infant to Individual*. New York: Simon and Schuster, 1978.

Seagull, Elizabeth A.W., and David J. Kallen. "Normal Social and Emotional Development of the Preschool-Age Child" in Enzer, Norbert B., with Kennith W. Goin (eds.). *Social and Emotional Development: The Preschooler*. New York: Walker and Co., 1978.

Thompson, James J. *Beyond Words: Nonverbal Communication in the Classroom*. New York: Citation Press, 1973.

OTHER SOURCES

Beaty, Janice J. *Skills for Preschool Teachers*. Columbus, Ohio: Charles E. Merrill Publishing Company, 1984.

Briggs, Dorothy Corkille. *Your Child's Self-Esteem*. Garden City, N.Y.: Doubleday & Company, 1970.

Fiarotta, Phyllis, and Noel Fiarotta. *Be What You Want to Be!* New York: Workman, 1977.

LEARNING ACTIVITIES

1. Observe all of the children in your classroom each morning of the first week of school, using the items in the self-identity checklist as a screening device. Note which children can separate without difficulty from their parents and which children cannot. Make a written plan for an activity which will help children overcome this initial anxiety. Discuss the plan with your supervisor, and then implement it. Discuss the results.

2. Choose a child who seems to have difficulty getting involved with other children or activities during the arrival period and free choice time, and observe him or her for three mornings during these periods. Make a running record of everything the child does or says. Check all possible self-identity checklist items, and write down the observable evidence on which you base each checkmark. How do you interpret the evidence you have collected? Can you make any conclusions yet about this child?

3. Meet with one or more parents of children in your classroom. Discuss how children develop their self-identities, and give the parents ideas that can be used at home to help strengthen their child's self-concept. Ask them for suggestions about how they would like you to work with their child.

4. Observe a child playing a role in dramatic play for three days. Keep a running record of everything the child does or says. Pay special attention to the things to look for discussed on page 49. Can you make any conclusions about the child's self-identity based on these observations?

5. Choose a child for whom you have checked: "Displays Enthusiasm in regard to doing things for self." Observe this child during the first half hour for three days. Which of the other items can you check for this child based on your observations? What is your evidence for each checkmark? What conclusions can you make about this child based on these observations?

3 Emotional Development

Emotional Development Checklist

☐ Allows self to be comforted during stressful time
☐ Eats, sleeps, toilets without fuss away from home
☐ Handles sudden changes/startling situations with control
☐ Can express anger in words rather than actions
☐ Allows aggressive behavior to be redirected
☐ Does not withdraw from others excessively
☐ Shows interest/attention in classroom activities
☐ Smiles, seems happy much of the time

T he emotional development of preschool children is somehow different from other developmental aspects. True, emotional growth happens simultaneously with physical, social, cognitive, language, and creative development and is interdependent upon them. But it seems as if the youngsters do not stay developed, or rather, that they must repeat the same sequences of emotional development over and over until they get it right . . . throughout life.

In some respects, this observation is true. Emotional development does have a physical and cognitive basis for expression, but once the basic human abilities are in place, emotions are much more situational in appearance.

If we agree that emotions are particular reactions to specific stimuli, then we would have to conclude that these reactions may not change much in a developmental sense during a person's lifetime. Many of us get red in the face when we are angry and cry when we are sad, both as infants and as adults. In other words, it is the situation—the stimulus—rather than the development of children that seems to govern their emotional responses.

Actually, emotional development is even more complex. Whereas physical and cognitive development seem to be based on "nature" and "nurture" and their interaction—that is, the genetic traits children inherit plus the environment in which they are raised—emotions have three internally interacting dimensions, including

1. The conscious feeling or emotional experience
2. The process in the brain and nervous system
3. The observable, expressive patterns or reactions
(Izard, p. 4)

Obviously, the brain and nervous system, because they are physical, can exhibit inherited traits. But, can emotions themselves be inherited and then developed through maturation and surroundings—just like the ability to think? Many psychologists have trouble accepting the idea that emotions are at all biological and based on maturity. However, scientists have to admit that certain emotional responses—separation anxiety, for instance—occur at about the same time and for the same reasons in infants and toddlers around the world. Similarly, other types of emotions seem to trigger universal "fight" or "flight" responses in adults.

Psychologists studying universal responses talk in terms of the functions of emotions (how emotions help the human species to adapt and survive). These scientists note that certain emotions triggering necessary survival responses in infants have outlived their usefulness when they occur in older children and adults. The acute distress felt by the infant and expressed in tears or screams when mother leaves the home, for example, has outlived its usefulness if it is a daily occurrence with a four-year-old when mother leaves him at the child care center. While such basic emotions seem to serve in helping preserve the self or the species, the higher emotions meet social purposes, and appropriate responses to these upper-level emotions must be learned.

Thus, we should focus on the response—not the emotion itself—when we speak of emotional development in preschool children. And, what most concerns us is not the development, but rather the control of the response. In the areas of physical and mental development, we want the young child to grow, mature, and extend his abilities to the utmost. With emotional development, we want the child to learn to make appropriate emotional responses, and especially to control negative responses. An emotionally disturbed child is often one who is out of control.

This chapter then looks at observable emotional responses of young children in eight different areas, which are followed by suggestions for improving the child's behavior if the particular item is not demonstrated. Each of the *checklist* items refers to a particular emotion. It should be noted, however, that the order in which the items are listed is not a developmental sequence, because sequence as such does not seem to be an important factor in emotional development.

Many psychologists recognize either eight or ten basic emotions and combinations of these, which are sometimes listed as: interest-excitement, enjoyment-joy, surprise-startle, distress-anguish, anger-rage, disgust-revulsion, contempt-scorn, fear-terror, shame/shyness-humiliation, and guilt-remorse (Izard, p. 46). The emotional responses of preschool children seem to be connected principally with the following seven emotions (plus one response): distress, fear, surprise, anger, aggression (a response), shame, interest, and joy.

In order to help children develop emotionally, the preschool teacher should be concerned with promoting positive emotions and helping the child to control negative emotions. Although techniques to accomplish this control may vary depending upon the emotion and the situation, the following four strategies could be used to control negative emotions:

1. Remove or reduce the cause of the emotion.
2. Diffuse the child's negative reaction by allowing him to "let it out" through crying, talking, or transferring his feelings into non-destructive actions.
3. Offer support, comfort, and ideas for self-control.
4. Model controlling behavior yourself.

Your goal for the child's emotional development should be the same as in the other aspects of her development: for her to gain self-control. In order to help her acquire this control, you first need to find out where she stands in her present development. Does she exhibit crying, whining, or complaining much of the time? Does she ever smile? Does she show anger or aggression toward others? The *Child Skills Checklist* for emotional development lists eight positive emotions typical of children ages three through five in early childhood programs. Observe the children in your class to determine which ones have accomplished the emotional self-control described in the checklist. Children who have not exhibited these checklist behaviors may benefit from the ideas and suggestions discussed in the remainder of the chapter.

☐ ALLOWS SELF TO BE COMFORTED DURING STRESSFUL TIME

Distress

Children who do not allow themselves to be comforted during stressful times often are exhibiting the negative emotion known as "distress."

At its lower extreme, distress may result from physical discomfort due to pain, extremes of temperature, or noise; whereas, at its upper level, distress may

Distress is not the most severe of the negative emotions; yet, adults should take it seriously in children.

take the form of anguish, grief, or depression due to the loss of a loved one. A basic cause of distress throughout life is physical or psychological separation, especially from a loved one. The child who perceives himself as having been abandoned by an adult, even when this is not true, experiences the same emotion as the child who has actually been abandoned.

Children express distress by crying, whining, showing a sad face, or sometimes, clinging to an adult caregiver. Children often feel uncomfortable, disappointed, lonely, sad, or rejected.

Yet, distress is not the most severe negative emotion found in children; therefore, adults do not always take it seriously. They should. Distress is an indication that all is not well with the child. Failure to reduce the distress or its causes over a period of time tends to break down the child's trust in adults. Furthermore, the child may not learn to become sympathetic to others who are uncomfortable, or she may not develop a very secure self-identity.

Every human being endures the initial distress of the birth experience, which is not only a physical discomfort but also a separation ordeal in the extreme. As such, birth is greeted with lusty crying by the distressed infant. Psychologists feel that distress, whenever it occurs, thus serves as a warning to others that something is wrong with the person and something should be done. Because it is concerned with separation, distress also seems to serve as a device to keep a group together (Izard, p. 293).

What are the principal causes of distress in the child care center? For many youngsters, the separation from their primary caregiver is the most stressful. Discomfort or pain from a physical cause, rejection by peers, dissatisfaction with performance, or a lack of skill are other causes of distress. A stressful situation in the family such as the birth of a new baby, a death, a move, or a divorce, also may be carried over into classroom behavior by the child who is disturbed by it.

The Teacher's Role

How can you help? Your principal role in the child's emotional development should be to help him master his feelings. You should not be the controlling device yourself, but instead, you should help the child find a way to control his feelings from within. An experienced adult may be tempted to take control of an emotional situation. Young children, in fact, look to you to solve the emotional problems which so often are overwhelming. You do children a disservice if you comply. Your role should be that of a facilitator, not a controller. Otherwise, without you, the child will be no better off the next time the emotional situation occurs. As with all other aspects of development, your overall goal for children should be their emotional independence (in other words, their emotional self-control).

Although the particular situation may determine your response, distress most often requires that you give comfort to the child first. She is upset and uncomfortable; she may be whining or crying. You can show your concern through comforting words and actions such as holding or hugging.

Requiring that he stop crying right away is not usually the way to approach helping a child master his emotions. Venting through tears is after all a catharsis. He may feel that you are not sympathetic to his plight if you insist he stop crying. He in fact may stop on his own when he hears your comforting words or feels your touch.

Once the child can verbalize, he can begin to take charge of his emotions. He may be able to tell you what happened or how he feels. This is the first step toward self-mastery of emotions. He even may be able to tell you what would make him feel better.

If the situation is too overwhelming for him to stop crying or to verbalize his feelings, your best strategy may be to redirect his attention when the time seems right. If he was injured on one leg, perhaps you can get him to show you the other leg. How does it look? How does he think it feels? Maybe together you can do something to make the injured leg feel like the uninjured one. Distress, then, often can be relieved when you 1.) Give comfort, and/or 2.) Redirect attention, and 3.) Help the child to verbalize.

As for mastering distress so that it will not happen again, this is probably not possible and certainly not appropriate. Distress may be relieved and perhaps controlled, but not completely mastered. Nor should we want it to be. Distress is a necessary symptom signaling that all is not well with the individual. In your child care program, you should hope to help relieve—not prevent—distress in a child. If you are successful, then a distraught child will allow herself to be comforted or redirected. But if her sense of self is not strong enough or if the distress is too overwhelming, she may not even allow this. What can you do to help such a child?

If You Have Not Checked This Item: Some Helpful Ideas

▪ *Hold and Rock the Child*

It's good to have an adult-size rocking chair in your center. Sometimes, the best help for a distraught child is to hold and rock him.

▪ *Have the Child Hold a Huggable Toy*

A child is often comforted by holding something soft. That is why toddlers carry "security blankets." Your center should have cuddly stuffed animals or similar toys available, not only for play but also for stressful situations. The child who does not allow you to comfort her may help herself by holding such a toy. Be sure the toy is washable for use by other children.

▪ *Use a Material with Soothing Properties*

Water play and finger painting are activities with soothing qualities. Distressed children can take out their frustrations by moving paint around a surface with their hands or by swishing water, thus transferring their negative energy in a harmless fashion.

■ *Let the Child Talk to a Puppet*

Again, verbalizing negative feelings is one of the best ways for defusing or controlling them. You could designate one of the puppets in your room as a "feelings" puppet and keep it in a special place for the times when children are feeling sad or upset. They can talk to the puppet about how they feel and ask the puppet how it feels. Your modeling use of this puppet when upsetting occasions arise will give the children a lead to follow.

■ *Read a Book*

Sometimes, distraught children will allow you to read a favorite book to them. You could keep particular books for them to look at individually during troubling times. Here are some books especially suitable for stressful situations

Feelings

Sometimes I Like to Cry by Elizabeth and Henry Stanton, Chicago: Albert Whitman & Company, 1978, is about a little boy Joey who smiles and laughs at his cat, frog, and brother, but sometimes cries when he cuts a finger, is not invited to a party, or experiences the death of his hamster.

Grownups Cry Too by Nancy Hazen, Chapel Hill, N.C.: Lollipop Power, 1978 (In English and Spanish) is narrated by a little boy and tells about the various stressful times in the boy's life when he and his parents cried.

Moving

Moving Gives Me a Stomach Ache by Heather McKend, Windsor, Ontario: Black Moss Press, 1980, reveals how a boy must pack his toys to move and tries to joke about it because he feels bad. Older children (ages five and six) would understand the humor better.

Moving Molly by Shirley Hughes, Englewood Cliffs, N.J.: Prentice-Hall, 1978, is a much more developed story than the previous one. This book tells about little city girl Molly who willingly moves to the country but is lonely until children move in next door.

Sad Day Glad Day by Vivian L. Thompson, New York: Scholastic Book Services, 1962, is about Kathy who reluctantly moves from a house to a city apartment and who accidently leaves her doll behind. But all is well when Kathy finds a doll left behind by the apartment's former tenant.

Death

The Tenth Good Thing About Barney by Judith Viorst, New York: Atheneum, 1971, is about a sad little boy whose cat, Barney, dies and whose mother tries to comfort him by having him think of ten good things to say about Barney when they bury him in the backyard.

My Grandson Lew by Charlotte Zolotow, New York: Harper & Row, 1974, is a touching story about six-year-old Lewis who misses his grandfather who had died earlier. In the book, Lewis shares memories of his grandfather with his mother.

Nana Upstairs & Nana Downstairs by Tomie de Paola, New York: G.P. Putnam's Sons, 1973, is the story of Tommy who makes visits to his grandmother and great-grandmother who live in the same house on different floors. When the great-grandmother dies, Tommy's mother comforts him by telling him that his great-grandmother will come back in his memory whenever he thinks about her.

☐ EATS, SLEEPS, TOILETS WITHOUT FUSS AWAY FROM HOME

Fear (Anxiety)

Children who have difficulty eating, going to sleep, or going to the toilet in your center generally behave this way because of tension. Most often produced by anxiety, tension is one of the most common expressions of fear.

Fear first appears as an emotion in the second half of an infant's first year of life, according to many psychologists. Somewhere between five and nine months of age, the baby begins to recognize an unfamiliar face and is afraid of it. Before this age, the baby's physical maturity and cognitive development have not progressed to the point where he can distinguish between friend and stranger. After this age, he recognizes unfamiliar faces as a possible threat . . . until he learns differently.

Thus, the emotion fear is caused by the presence of something threatening or the absence of safety and security (Izard, p. 356). Fear may result when the possibility of potential harm appears, when a strange person, object, or situation is confronted, or when specific fright-producing elements—such as heights, the dark, thunder storms, or particular animals such as dogs or snakes—are present. When children or others are afraid, they feel anxious and alarmed. They may tremble, cower, hide, run away, cling to someone, or cry, depending on their degree of fright. They often seek protection.

Fear is in some ways age-related. Young children are generally not afraid of heights, the dark, or animals much before age two. It seems children really don't know enough to be frightened before then. As they grow older, children add new fears to their repertory and drop some of the old ones. So fear, like distress, seems to serve as a warning signal for the human species; reduce the threat or seek protection. When this warning feeling persists but is no longer useful to the young human, you as a child care worker need to intervene.

We know of course that extreme fear can be paralyzing, but we need to realize that even lesser fears like anxiety produce tension of some sort, a tightening up of the body and mind. "It (anxiety) is the most constricting of all the emotions," declares psychologist Carroll E. Izard (Izard, p. 365). The anxious person has trouble relaxing or feeling at ease in tense situations or in unfamiliar settings which somehow pose a threat.

For the young child used to the security of her home, the early childhood classroom can be a tense setting in the beginning, no matter how relaxing and non-threatening you have tried to make it. The child views the setting as a threat for three reasons: 1) The setting is unfamiliar, 2) The child lacks initial trust in the setting and the people there, and 3) The child's mother or caregiver has left her.

Most children display some anxiety when they first experience an early childhood classroom. It is a natural reaction to being left in a strange place. But if they have a strong enough sense of self and trust in the world and people around them, the children soon should come to feel perfectly at ease in your center.

For children who do not achieve this sense of ease, you may need to provide special attention in order to help them overcome their anxiety. The routine functions of eating, sleeping, and toileting and how they are carried out can often provide the careful observer with clues concerning who is at ease in the classroom and who is not.

Because these routines are of such a personal nature and so closely connected with the home and primary caregiver, eating, sleeping, and toileting are deeply significant to the child. From his earliest memories, he is used to having his mother feed him or help him to feed himself. He expects his mother to tuck him in and kiss him goodnight. He is at ease in using the toilet—a rather formidable piece of equipment for a young child—in his own home, for he has learned the toilet will not flush him away.

Suddenly, he is thrust into a new and unfamiliar environment where these very personal processes are to be directed by strangers. Even the most secure and experienced young explorer may have moments of anxiety in the beginning. Anxiety produces tension in which muscles actually tighten up, and the tense person may not even be aware of what the muscles are doing. Unless the tense child is able to relax, he or she certainly may experience difficulty in eating, falling asleep, or using the toilet.

The anxious child in your classroom may not have difficulty with all three of these acts. One or the other may be more meaningful in her life at home and thus cause more problems for her away from home. Her difficulty possibly may have causes other than anxiety. A health problem, for instance, also could cause a disruption in her normal functioning. However, if a child exhibits persistent difficulty in eating, sleeping, or toileting at any time while in your care, the cause may be anxiety, and the child may need your help to overcome the negative effects of this emotion.

Eating

Eating is the act most closely connected with the child's mother. From babyhood, when he nursed at mother's breast or was held close to her while being bottle-fed, the child not only received life-sustaining nourishment but also comfort and love. It is not a surprise, then, that the child makes a connection between food and comfort. Later, as he is weaned from breast or bottle and learns to take solid food, he may perceive these as happy experiences or a battle of wills, depending on how the caregiver treats him. By the time he enters your center, the child has had at least three years of experience with the emotional nature of eating. You hope this has been positive. But, no matter what, you need to make sure eating is a positive experience for the child in your program.

Once you are aware of the emotional nature of eating and how a child's anxiety can interfere with eating habits, you will be better prepared to deal with children who refuse to eat.

Be sure at the outset that your meals take place in an atmosphere of friendliness and relaxation. Are classroom meals served family-style around small group tables? School cafeterias are too large, noisy, impersonal, and rushed for children this young. If you have been assigned to a cafeteria, talk with the supervisor in order to explain the eating needs of young children, and to see whether the food could be carried to your room instead.

Do you eat at the table with the children? It is important in family-style eating that a member of the staff sit at each table to converse informally with the children, answering their questions about the food and assisting them in their own pouring and serving. Help the children take a little of everything. If their portions are too large, they may not even want to begin. But, involving them with dishing out and passing their own food is a physical step which psychologically connects them with eating.

What about rules concerning food? Mealtime should be pleasant and relaxing. Too many rules about portions, second helpings, and dessert may create tension even in relaxed children. Is withholding of dessert used as a punishment for children who have misbehaved? No matter how food is used in the homes of your children, it should never be used in a punitive manner in your center. All of the food served, including dessert, should be nutritious, appealing, and available to all of the children all of the time.

Are you a good eating model yourself? "Practice what you preach" is a cliché worth repeating when it comes to eating. Your children should see that you: take a reasonable-sized portion of each food item, eat all your food, talk about how good it tastes, ask politely for seconds if this is appropriate, refrain from nagging, make positive comments about children who have cleaned up their plates, and drink all your own milk.

If You Have Not Checked This Item: Some Helpful Ideas

- *Refrain from Pressure*

Do not use force or pressure to get a reluctant child to eat. Force probably will not work anyway, but more importantly, it will certainly not reduce the anxiety and tension which may be the cause of a refusal to eat in the first place. All attempts to resolve the problem should be positive in nature, aimed at removing or reducing the cause of the negative emotion and helping the child to gain inner control over her reactions. Sometimes, patience alone is the only solution. When the child feels at ease in your program, she will eat.

- *Talk with Parents*

Ask parents what they expect of their child and what they hope the child will gain from your program. Talk about food habits and how the child eats at home. But, be aware that the child's basic problem may not be food, but anxiety and how the child reacts to it. Is the child under pressure at home? How does he react to pressure? How can you and the parents relieve him of this pressure?

- *Read a Book*

Perhaps a lighthearted approach will work. If you think the reluctant eater can deal with food in a playful manner, you might try reading to her one of the following books:

Gregory, the Terrible Eater by Mitchell Sharmat, New York: Scholastic Book Services, 1980, is the story of little goat Gregory who will not eat the goat food his mother serves (tin cans, rugs, and bottle caps) and only wants fruits, vegetables, and eggs . . . "Good stuff like that." When junk food becomes too much for him, he and his family finally reach a compromise.

Bread and Jam for Frances by Russel Hoban, New York: Scholastic Book Services, 1964, is the classic story of little girl badger Frances who only wants to eat bread and jam . . . until she finds out that is all her family will serve her.

Sleeping

If the children spend all day in your center, then you must provide them with a nap period in the afternoon. For some children, this is a welcome relief from the exuberant activities of the morning, and they welcome the chance to rest and promptly fall asleep. For others, sleep time is a period of tossing and turning, whispering and squirming, and disturbing other children and the teacher. Some children may have outgrown naptime. Others may be so wound up they need to relax before they can fall asleep. A few may be the anxious children we have been discussing: children who cannot fall asleep because of tension.

First of all, you need to prepare all of your children for nap time. They can help to get out the cots or mats. They can choose their own area of the room to sleep in. They should know when the lights are turned out or the curtains pulled that it is time to close their eyes. You might try playing dreamy music at a low volume on the record player. Or, you could read a story in a monotone or whispery voice. You might read a sleep story such as *Goodnight Moon*, or *Good Night Richard Rabbit*, or *Bedtime for Frances*. For some children, rubbing their backs helps them let go and fall asleep. But, if you rub the backs of some children, be sure to do it for all who want it. What if some children still do not fall asleep?

If You Have Not Checked This Item: Some Helpful Ideas

- *Use Nap Time Toys*

If after fifteen minutes or so, some of the children show no signs of falling asleep, you may decide to allow these children to play quietly on their cots with some sort of "nap time toy," perhaps a tiny car or doll from a basket you pass around to the nonsleepers. Because they do not move from their sleeping quarters, the nonsleepers still have the chance to go to sleep if they want. Some teachers may prefer to have a different area where nonsleepers can go to play quietly.

- *Reduce Tension*

If some children are still too anxious and tense to allow themselves to fall asleep, you may need to try a variety of methods for reducing tension. Can these children take a teddy bear to bed? Ask them how they can help themselves get sleepy. Will rocking help? What do they do at home? In the end, your acceptance of them as worthy human beings should eventually help them to relax and take a nap if their bodies have the need for it.

Toileting

Children's bathroom habits are as different from one child to another as their eating habits. Children will probably learn the most about what is expected of them in your center from their peers. But, you also need to be aware of what the children expect or need. Do you have a single classroom bathroom or a public-type bathroom with several stalls? Are the children used to being in a bathroom with other children? Can they handle their clothing, clean themselves, and wash their hands alone?

You may need to talk to newcomers in the beginning about what they can expect and what they are used to. You may need to go in the bathroom with them in the beginning to help them and get them used to the equipment. Would they feel better if another child accompanied them at first?

If parents tell you their children are not using the center facilities, or if children begin to have accidents in the classroom, you will want to talk with the youngsters as gently as possible. Because toilet training is controlled in some homes through the negative method of shaming, you need to be careful that your attention will not make a child feel ashamed.

Is a child too shy to use the bathroom with other children? You may need to accede to his feelings at first until he is used to your center and his peers.

If You Have Not Checked This Item: Some Helpful Ideas

- *Use Rewards*

A behavior-modification idea, rewards are always controversial, but for some children, they work. With rewards, an extrinsic prize solidifies an intrinsic behavior if the child plays her part. Try keeping a private chart which gets a check or a smiley face each time the child uses the toilet. Once a child is in the habit or has overcome her anxiety about using your facilities, the use of the chart should fade away.

- *Display Acceptance*

Use every strategy you know to show the child you accept him. Nonverbal cues such as smiles or hugs, as well as friendly words, special activities, and jobs or errands make a child feel accepted. Help him to be accepted by the other children as well. Once anxiety about your center and its inhabitants is lessened, a new child should not be so tense about using the bathroom facilities.

☐ HANDLES SUDDEN CHANGES/STARTLING SITUATIONS WITH CONTROL

Surprise (Startle)

Surprise is different from other emotions in that it lasts only for a moment, although its results may continue for some time with young children. A sudden or unexpected external event causes a reaction of surprise or startle. The event could be a loud noise such as an explosion or clap of thunder at one extreme, or the unexpected appearance of a person at the other extreme. A startled person's mind goes blank for an instant, and his muscles contract quickly. He may even jump if the incident is surprising enough. Depending upon the situation, the person may be shocked, bewildered, confused, embarrassed—or delighted—because of his reaction.

Although a startle reflex appears in babies a few hours after birth, the reflex does not seem to be the same as the emotion of surprise, which does not emerge in infants until the fifth to seventh month. By that time, enough cognitive development has occurred to enable the infant to form expectations (Izard, p. 283).

Because everything is new for the child, there will be many startling events in her young life. If most of her surprises are pleasant ones, she will come to view surprises positively. If the opposite is true, then surprises may cause the child to cry or exhibit defensive behavior.

Many mothers help to prepare their children for surprises (unintentionally, no doubt), by playing low-key surprise games such as peekaboo with the children. The surprise in peekaboo is always a pleasant one, of course: the revealing of mother's hidden face. If a child, however, is scolded or ridiculed too severely at home when he cries or makes a fuss over unexpected happenings, he may become fearful of anything different, whether or not it is sudden.

Research shows that most adults view surprise as pleasant. Experience has taught them this. Young children, on the other hand, do not necessarily show the same response. Perhaps because their experience is limited, or because the occurrence of sudden happenings leaves them overwhelmed, they tend not to greet unexpected things as adults do. Most young children, for instance, do not react happily to surprise birthday parties. Young children are more likely to cry or withdraw. It may take some time for the shock to wear off and for them to become their pleasant selves again. Sensitive adults will not impose such startling events on children, who enjoy pleasant anticipation—rather than startling surprise—with parties.

What about the children in your center? How do they respond to the unexpected? They need to be prepared for it in their lives, and they need to be able to control their responses. Like the other emotions, surprise/startle cannot be eliminated, nor should it be. It serves the useful function of preparing an individual to deal with an unexpected event. But, if an individual's reaction is of such alarm as to immobilize her, then you need to help her deal with surprise in a better way.

What are some startling events you might anticipate? Most centers have fire alarms which they may or may not be able to control. Ask your building supervisor if your children can have a chance to practice a fire drill with the alarm until they are able to do it with ease. Practicing with simulated emergency situations is one of the best ways to learn how to deal with them.

In addition to practice, your children can learn to handle sudden changes or surprising events by acting the way you do. You need to be calm and collected yourself, modeling the behavior you would like your children to emulate.

Some children go to pieces when they are startled. They may be the ones who have not developed a strong enough sense of self, or a sense of trust in the people around them. These children may cry, cling, or withdraw long after the event is past. How can you help them?

If You Have Not Checked This Item: Some Helpful Ideas

- *Read a Book about Startling Situations*

Children may be helped to overcome their negative responses if they hear how others like themselves deal with surprises. Books about startling situations should be read not only to a group of children, but also to individuals who have exhibited a poor emotional response to a surprise. Books with this theme include

Peek-a-Boo! by Janet & Allen Ahlberg. New York: The Viking Press, 1981. While this story seems to be directed to infants because it is about a baby in his crib, his high chair, his stroller, etc., it is much too complex for any babe-in-arms. A preschooler, instead, should enjoy shouting *Peekaboo* and looking through the dollar-sized hole in every other page to guess what complicated things the other members of the family are doing.

Maybe a Monster by Martha Alexander. New York: The Dial Press, 1968. Children enjoy small-format books like this one in which a little boy narrator builds a trap and a cage to catch a monster and becomes afraid as he thinks about it. The building and the suspense take up all but the ending of the book when the little boy is surprised to catch a rabbit.

Jim Meets the Thing by Miriam Cohen. New York: Greenwillow Books, 1981. Many young children are startled and frightened by the things they see on television. In this story, young Jim seems to be the only one in his class who is scared by the monster movie on TV the night before. But, when playing super heroes on the playground at lunch time, only Jim stays calm when a praying mantis bug suddenly lands on Danny.

Drummer Hoff by Barbara and Ed Emberly. Englewood Cliffs, N.J.: Prentice-Hall, 1967. If loud noises frighten your children, perhaps this book will help to diffuse their fear. A cumulative folktale-like story, this book tells about colorful playing-card soldiers who put an old cannon together piece by piece and then fire it off at the end.

Although some teachers have indicated that certain quiet children are frightened even by book experiences, you might ask the children themselves if hearing a book like *Drummer Hoff* will help them to get over their fear of loud noises. Let the children say the "ka-a-a-a-boooom!" at the end.

☐ CAN EXPRESS ANGER IN WORDS RATHER THAN ACTIONS

Anger

Anger is the negative emotion of most concern not only in the child care center, but also in society at large, perhaps because anger has the potential for so much destruction. We are very concerned that people learn to control their anger. Therefore, we begin teaching what to do—or rather what not to do—very early. We often are not very successful. There is, however, a positive, controlling approach that uses or diffuses anger so that children do not turn it against others or themselves.

First, we need to look at the emotion itself to understand what anger is, what causes it, and what purpose it serves. [Anger is the emotion or feeling that results when we are physically or psychologically restrained from doing something, frustrated in our attempts, interrupted, personally insulted, or forced to do something against our will.] We feel hurt, disappointed, and irritated. We frown, our face gets hot, our blood "boils," our muscles tense, our teeth clench, and our eyes stare. At anger's highest level, we feel rage which threatens to erupt in an explosive manner. At the other extreme, we feel hostility, a cold type of anger.

With anger comes a sense of physical power and greater self-assurance than with any other negative emotion (Izard, p. 331). The body, in fact, rallies its resources and readies to strike out against the cause of the anger. In primitive man, anger mobilized the body's energy quickly and was important for survival. In modern man, anger still appears, but its primary purpose has all but vanished.

Here we are, then, ready to turn this rush of physical energy against the "enemy." What should we do with it? This energy must be released or somehow diffused; otherwise, we will turn it against ourselves. Repressed anger has been implicated as one of the causes of skin diseases, ulcers, migraines, hypertension, and certain psychological disorders (Izard, p. 351).

Most parents teach their children from the start not to display anger. When they allow angry feelings to begin to show on their faces, children sense their parents' response of displeasure. Many children soon learn to conceal or disguise their expression of anger. Others let anger out in acts of aggression. Neither response is satisfactory. Yet, many of us carry these responses throughout life.

Instead, we need a positive approach that teaches children from the start what they should do (expression) rather than what they must not do (repression). Anger definitely calls for some sort of release, but children and adults need to "let off steam" harmlessly.

One of the most satisfactory methods used by many preschool teachers coaches children to verbalize their feelings [Verbalizing involves, not yelling or name-calling, but expressing in words how one feels about the thing causing anger. This approach has at least two advantages: It gives children an acceptable release for their strong feelings, and it puts the children in control. They—not adults—deal with the situation. And solving the problem on their own strengthens the children's sense of self.]

Strong feelings such as anger overwhelm and thus frighten young children. A method for learning control from the inside and not being controlled from the outside will help children in the future when adults are not around. The anger emotion calls for action. But, if children learn to speak out rather than strike out, they will not have to suffer guilt or remorse afterwards for an unacceptable act.

Expressing anger in words is not easy in the beginning. It does not come naturally for young children whose communication skills still are limited. It is even more difficult for the child caught up in the throes of an overwhelming emotion, who finds it simpler to strike out physically or shout or cry. Yet, three-, four-, and five-year-olds can learn the response of telling how they feel in words.

How do you teach them? First, you have to model this behavior yourself. When you become angry, tell the individual or the group how you feel and why you feel this way: "It makes me feel very upset to see you dropping the tape recorder on the floor like that! If you break it, no one can enjoy the music any more," or "Paul and Gregory, I am so angry to see you ganging up on Leslie again! Two against one is not fair!"

You also must convey to your children that their actions—not them as individuals—make you angry. You must show you still respect and like the children no matter how angry they get or how upset you feel over their actions. Show the children both verbally and nonverbally that you still accept them as good people.

You also must intervene at every occasion where the children display tempers, and you must help them to repeatedly express their feelings in words. "Shirley, tell Rachel how you feel when she takes your book," or "Von, don't hit Tony, tell him how you feel."

Make eye contact with the children. Help them to make eye contact with one another in order to help diffuse their anger. "Von, look Tony in the eyes, and tell him."

Teaching children to express anger in words is a time-consuming process. But then, so is all learning. If you believe children must gain inner control over their anger, and if you understand they must have some acceptable way to vent their feelings, then you may find it worthwhile to put in the time and effort necessary to divert anger's destructive energy into words. You will know you have been successful when the children begin telling one another: "Don't hit him Bobby, tell him!" What can you do for children who still need special help with "Can express anger in words rather than actions"?

If You Have Not Checked This Item: Some Helpful Ideas

- *Talk about Feelings*

Have a "feelings" corner in your room with pictures of people looking sad, angry and glad. Ask the child to tell you what he feels when he looks like that. Have a "feelings" hand puppet that each child can hold and talk to about his bad feelings.

▪ *Read a Book*

Read a "feelings" book to a child or small group at any time of the day (not necessarily only when tempers are short).

I Was So Mad by Norma Simon, Chicago: Albert Whitman & Company, 1974, has many different children who tell about what makes them mad, how they feel, and what they do about their feelings. They talk about being teased, picked on, or blamed; not being able to do something; having an activity interrupted or ruined; and being forced to do something they did not want to do. The story ends with the words and music to the song one father sings: "There Was a Man and He Was Mad." Your children can learn the song.

Uproar on Hollercat Hill by Jean Marzolla, New York: The Dial Press, 1980 is an exuberant story in rhyme about a family of cats whose happy times set tempers flaring when Poppa's drumsticks get broken and Momma's tractor runs wild. With things totally out of control, Momma finds cookies, Poppa gets tea, and everybody kisses and makes up.

☐ ALLOWS AGGRESSIVE BEHAVIOR TO BE REDIRECTED

Aggression

Aggression is not an emotion but the expression of one, the actions commonly taken by an individual as a result of anger or frustration. An individual using these hostile actions or angry words intends to harm, defeat or embarrass the person who caused the anger. Aggressive behavior in the classroom most commonly takes the form of hitting, throwing, name-calling, spitting, biting, kicking, pushing or pulling, physically forcing someone to do something, restraining someone, destroying property, and forcefully taking someone else's possessions or turn.

Young children who have not learned to control their negative emotions often resort to this aggressive behavior. Children who have been neglected or treated harshly sometimes use aggression to strike out at the world around them. Children who have had to fend for themselves among older peers without much adult guidance may have learned aggressiveness as a survival strategy. Other children with highly permissive parents may have learned certain aggressive acts to get their own way: hitting and name-calling, for instance.

Research tells us boys are more aggressive than girls. Since Helen Dawe's early observational study of the quarrels of preschool children in 1934, all findings everywhere have shown boys are more aggressive (Brooks-Gunn, p. 130). We can blame boys' aggression on genetics—physical development and hormones—but we also need to look at society's expectations for boys and girls. Society expects boys to be more aggressive than girls; thus, boys are allowed to be more aggressive. If aggressiveness were considered a feminine trait, then, no doubt, the findings would quickly change.

Is all aggressiveness among children bad? Not according to researcher Wendy Matthews who found in 1972 that among preschoolers in Paris, the most popular child in play groups of six was also the most aggressive both physically and verbally, whether or not the child was a boy or girl. Aggressive children were the leaders, using forceful behavior to keep their followers in line (Brooks-Gunn, p. 131). This type of forceful behavior, however, is not the same as aggression due to anger and frustration.

How, then, can a preschool teacher help children control their unwanted aggressive behavior? Putting negative feelings into words of course helps achieve inner control of anger. But, if their actions are already aggressive, then the children need to be redirected into a less destructive activity.

Children who strike out aggressively could be redirected to hit a ball of clay, hit a nail with a hammer, punch a pillow, kick a ball, hit a tetherball, throw a beanbag at a target, or use rhythm band instruments. Activities that will calm down overwrought children include finger painting, water play, working with play dough, mixing dough, and listening to music or a story.

If you have not checked the item "Allows aggressive behavior to be redirected," then you also might consider the following:

If You Have Not Checked This Item: Some Helpful Ideas

- *Sit the Child on Your Lap*

Sometimes, you physically must restrain a child from hurting someone else. Because you are bigger, you can hold the child so she cannot hit or kick until she calms down enough to control herself. Hold the child on your lap, restraining her from using her arms. If she kicks as well, you may need to remove her shoes. This child is totally out of control and needs your help to restore herself to normalcy. Do not lose control yourself. Children are afraid of their own overwhelming emotions, and they need you to remain calm and to prevent them from doing damage. Ask the child if she feels calm enough for you to let her get up. If she can't tell you, she is not ready yet.

- *Read a Book*

When the right time comes, some children who use aggression to solve problems may want to listen to a book about others who do the same.

The Grouchy Ladybug by Eric Carle, New York: Thomas Y. Crowell Company, 1977, is a time/counting book that tells about a ladybug who challenges one after another of the world's animals to a fight. When each agrees, the ladybug flies off telling each one it is not big enough. Finally, the whale, without knowing it, slaps some sense into the grouchy ladybug.

No Fighting, No Biting! by Else Holmelund Minark, New York: Harper & Row, 1958, is a classic book that contains four different stories. Some of the stories tell about two little children and their older cousin Joan who will not let the younger cousins sit with her while they continue to fight and pinch. The other stories focus on two little alligators who also fight and bite.

☐ DOES NOT WITHDRAW FROM OTHERS EXCESSIVELY

Shame (Shyness)

As you observe the children in your classroom at the beginning of the year, you may note certain ones seem to stay by themselves. They may stand apart or sit apart, even stay off in a corner. If you try to get them involved, they may lower or avert their eyes, turn their heads or even put a thumb in their mouths. They almost may seem to want to shrink into invisibleness. In fact, they may seem to exhibit all the indications of painful shyness.

Shyness is one of the least studied of the negative emotions. Yet, nearly all humans experience shyness at one time or another. Early childhood is a common time for such an occurrence. Shyness results from a heightened degree of self-awareness in which the individual feels exposed, helpless, incompetent, and somehow shameful about it all.

As with so many of our feelings about ourselves, shyness seems to come from a combination of inherited traits plus first-year experiences (Izard, p. 405). The earliest "shame" feelings that an infant experiences occur when he first recognizes the face of a stranger around the age of five to seven months. Previously, the infant has been fascinated with the human face, which has served as a stimulus for excitement and joy. He has wanted contact with it; he has needed some kind of interaction.

Then, something occurs within the cognitive development of the infant that allows him to discriminate one face from another. And suddenly, when a stranger appears, the infant realizes he is not looking at a familiar friendly countenance. He no longer responds joyfully, but instead, seems to realize his mistake and thus suffers his first embarrassment. He may cry, become red in the face, or try to get away. If the child has a series of negative experiences with strangers at this time, then he will learn that he is subject to shame whenever he meets a stranger (Izard, p. 395). Highly sensitive children exhibit such embarrassment whether or not their experiences have been negative.

In addition, something else is happening within the child. He is becoming aware of himself as a separate being. This has to happen before embarrassment—and therefore shyness—can occur. The shame (shyness) emotion is, after all, the feeling of exposure of self, of extreme self-consciousness; the person feels that all eyes are on him and that he is uncomfortably out of place. According to research, these feelings develop most frequently in large groups, in new situations, and with strangers (Izard, p. 399).

Is it any wonder, then, that certain children exhibit this emotion in your classroom, especially at the beginning of the year? These children may be sensitive. They may have been disciplined through shaming by their parents, or they may not have developed a strong enough sense of self to be comfortable among strangers. Shyness can emotionally cripple a child. It can prevent her from enjoying herself and others in your center. You need to find a way, using the utmost tact and sensitivity to help the shy child.

Some children, especially at the beginning of the year, may take their time in becoming involved with others.

Children have no reason to feel ashamed, but they often feel ashamed because they are not able to live up to their expectations of themselves. They look around at other people and see themselves as a shameful example of what they could be. To help them change this inaccurate perception, you need to show the children—in many ways—how good they really are: tell them verbally, show them nonverbally, and involve them actively in important duties and projects. You need to engage the children in activities that will help them discover their own worthiness. Never use shaming or ridicule as a method of discipline or scolding (e.g., ''Ronny, look what you did to the paints! How could you be so clumsy!'').

The shame emotion does have a use in human development. The emotion is very powerful, and it keeps us from acting shamefully among others so that we do not bring ridicule down on our heads. Rules for behavior (such as polite manners) result from the shame emotion. People who lack a sense of shame may commit such shameful acts as incest or child abuse. But, on the other hand, people who are overcome with an irrational sense of shame also may be emotionally crippled by it.

Some young children have this irrational feeling of shame. Because shame results from a real or perceived put-down of the self, and not just from an act the self has performed, the child may continue to feel that he is not a good person. If a child in your classroom seems to demonstrate this feeling by withdrawing from others excessively, you may need to make a concerted effort to correct the situation.

If You Have Not Checked This Item: Some Helpful Ideas

- *Focus on the Child's Strengths*

Because the shame/shyness emotion expresses the feeling that a child has not accepted herself, you can best help a shy child by finding ways for her to gain self-approval. Is she wearing a brightly colored dress? Maybe she could cut out pictures from a magazine of other dresses that are the same pretty color as hers. Or, have her look at her pretty hand. (She may be too sensitive to look at her face in a mirror at first.) Could she trace around her fingers, color the hand drawing, and cut it out?

- *Do Not Dwell on the Shyness*

Reading books such as *The Shy Little Girl* is not a good idea. The shy child is already painfully aware of how he feels. To point out these feelings by reading a book about them may only make them worse.

- *Pair the Child with Another Child*

If one other child accepts her, the shy child may find it easier to accept herself and become involved with others. You may need to take the initiative in this case, asking another child to work with the shy child on a puzzle, or to go on an errand for you together.

- *Talk with Parents*

Does the child exhibit this same behavior at home? Maybe not. Many children act completely differently at home than at school. This may mean that it is in your classroom where the child feels self-conscious and thus exhibits shyness. In that case, continue your activities to show acceptance and to help the child accept himself. But, if the parents admit that the child behaves the same at home, you may want to discuss tactfully the discipline methods they are using. If shaming or ridiculing are involved in the child's discipline, then perhaps the parents could learn another way. You might consider having a parent meeting where a speaker or film discusses this discipline issue.

☐ SHOWS INTEREST/ATTENTION IN CLASSROOM ACTIVITIES

Interest (Excitement)

Interest is the most frequent and pervasive positive emotion that human beings possess. Children show interest by directing their eyes toward an object or person that catches their attention and then by exploring it with their eyes and, if possible, their other senses. Interested people are alert, active, self-confident, and curious. Interest is the motivator for much of children's learning as well as for their development of intelligence and creativity. Thus, the growing child must be encouraged to exhibit interest, and that interest must be stimulated by the people, objects, and ideas in the environment.

Psychologists believe that change or novelty usually causes this basic emotion. Once someone is aroused by and curious about an object, he should be motivated to find out more about it. And as he finds out more about the object, he thus increases his knowledge, skill, and understanding. Interest, in other words, is the impulse to know, and the impulse sustains our attention in the things attracting our curiosity. Excitement is the most intense form of interest.

For an infant to perceive an object, she first must pay attention to it over a period of time. The interest emotion keeps her attention. Without this emotion, the infant may become passive, dull, and apathetic; she may have little movement. The final result may be developmental lags or even retardedness.

The interest emotion appears very early in an infant's life. Interest is evident in the attention shown to the human face; the eyes rivet to mother's face and turn to follow it. The eyes and mouth fascinatingly explore objects such as rattles, bottles, mobiles, and the infant's own fingers and toes. Later the infant shifts from external exploration to manipulation: What will objects do when kicked, thrown, or dropped?

When he throws his cereal dish on the floor, the child is not being naughty, only normal. He finds out about his world this way. Acts like this against physical objects obviously teach the child many additional things about the feelings of the people around him. If the family is strict or harsh or punitive about his actions, then such exploration motivated by interest will be inhibited. If the child is punished too many times, he may cease exploring altogether, which poses dire consequences for his future development. On the other hand, encouragement to explore, play with things, and be curious will stretch his mind, senses, and physical skills.

Poverty frequently interferes with the development of strong interests because the variety of objects or activities available in the child's environment is often limited. In some cases, parents also must spend most of their energy struggling to survive, and they may have little or no time to interact with their youngsters. The parents may, in fact, actively discourage their children from exploratory endeavors. If, in addition, negative emotions dominate the atmosphere, then interest quickly fades away.

Thus, you must know which children in your classroom have retained their native curiosity and which have not. The interest and attention children pay to classroom activities may give you a clue. But, you need to remember that interest is stimulated by novelty and change, so a truer test might be to set up a new activity area and observe which children notice it, who plays in it, and for how long. Because interests by now are very much individualized and personalized, what interests one child will not necessarily cause a flicker of attention in another. For this reason, you must provide a wide range of activities and materials for your group. Just remember to add something new once in awhile.

The basic interest emotion also affects attention span. Children first must be attracted to an activity through interest, which is activated by change or novelty. If they find the activity interesting, the children are likely to pay more attention to it; in other words, they will give their attention longer to the activity. Although we know that age and maturity have a great deal to do with how long a child's interest can be held (i.e., the older, the longer), we can increase the attention span by providing highly attractive materials and activities. Because children must attend in order to learn, the length of attention span is most important in every learning situation. Teachers thus need to know what kinds of things are attractive to children three, four, and five years old.

If You Have Not Checked This Item: Some Helpful Ideas

- *Focus on the Self*

Although children's interests vary widely, all humans, and especially egocentric youngsters, have a basic interest in themselves. Think of something new and different about the child who shows little interest in center activities. Make some kind of question, problem, or challenge that is intriguing and fun. Then, turn the child loose. For instance, have a *Slappy Shoe Contest* with a "winner" every day. He can start the contest by being your first "winner." Have him make a paper crown or design that he can tape to the top of his shoes. At some time during the day, have him slap out a rhythm with his shoe while you tape-record the sounds. Play the tape. Let other children try to copy it. Let him choose who will be the Mr. or Ms. Slappy Shoe "winner" tomorrow.

Is this novel enough? It may sound strange, but it is not when you remember how much children love shoes. Can you think of other things about the children—their clothing; their hair; their favorite foods, songs, or pets—that can be turned into a similar activity? Start with the children who seem to show little interest, and go from there.

- *Arouse the Curiosity*

Children love mysteries. Have a mystery guest (an adult dressed in a costume and mask) visit the classroom. Let children guess who it is. Or, bring a big stuffed animal in a bag, and let the children guess what it is. Give them hints about what it eats and the noises it makes. Maybe the slow-to-respond child would like to think of a name for the animal.

Read a book about a mystery. Steven Kellogg has written several small-sized picture books involving mysteries including

The Mystery of the Magic Green Ball by Steven Kellogg. New York: The Dial Press, 1978. This is the story of Timmy who loses his big green ball in the woods and the Mystery Gypsy Fortune Teller who finds the ball but will not give it back until Timmy uses some magic himself.

The Mystery of the Flying Orange Pumpkin by Steven Kellogg. New York: The Dial Press, 1980. A startling but hilarious escapade, this book tells about a pumpkin the children grow in a garden that comes to be owned by a scrooge-type character. When the "scrooge" refuses to let the children have their pumpkin for Halloween, three "ghosts" make it rise out of the field and fly away, and then they involve him in a party to get the pumpkin back.

The Mystery of the Missing Red Mitten by Steven Kellogg. New York: The Dial Press, 1974. Another small-sized book, this book is about a little girl who loses her mitten in the snow and, after a long search, finds it as the heart of the snowman she has built.

The Vanishing Pumpkin by Tony Johnston. New York: G. P. Putnam's Sons, 1983. This full-sized book tells about a 700-year-old woman and an 800-year-old man whose Halloween pumpkin has been stolen, and who must confront a ghoul, a rapscallion, a varmint, and a wizard before finding it. This book is just the thing to tickle the fancy of a bored child. Can she make up her own mystery afterwards and tell it to a tape recorder?

- *Start with Something Simple That the Children Like*

Do the children like apples? How many things can you do with an apple? The book *Apple Pigs* by Ruth Orbach. New York: Philomel Books, 1976, might get the children started in a classroom activity when they hear the zany story in rhyme about the family that was so overwhelmed with apples that they invited an entire zoo into their house to help consume the fruit. Directions are given for making "apple pigs."

☐ SMILES, SEEMS HAPPY MUCH OF THE TIME

Joy (Enjoyment)

Joy, the most positive emotion, is also the most elusive emotion. Seek it, and you may not find it. Try to experience it directly, and it may elude you. But live a normal life, and it will appear spontaneously. It does not occur on its own as much as it does as a by-product of something else: a pleasant experience, a happy thought, a good friendship. In other words, this emotion is indicative of a child feeling good about himself, others, and life in general. The absence of joy tells us the child is not feeling good about these things. We need to observe the children carefully to see where they stand in regard to this important indicator of inner feelings, and we need to take positive action if this emotion is missing.

Joy is the feeling of happiness that may precede or follow a pleasant experience: sensory pleasure such as a hug, a kiss, or a back rub; psychological pleasure such as the remembrance of good times; or the anticipation of seeing a loved one, or of having fun with friends. People express joy with smiles, laughter, "lit up" eyes, increased heartbeats, inner feelings of confidence, a sense of well-being, and a glow. The emotion itself is fleeting, but the good feeling it creates may color the child's actions and responses for many hours.

As with the other emotions, the capacity for joy is inherited; it is different for each individual (Izard, p. 239). The development of joy, however, depends greatly on how the mother or primary caregiver responds to joy in the infant. A person cannot teach another person to be happy, but she can influence the occurrence of happiness by creating a pleasant environment in the first place, and then responding positively when joy occurs.

A baby may smile during the first days of life. At first, the baby smiles in revery or dreams; then, the infant smiles during waking hours when a pleasant, high-pitched voice talks to it, and finally, by the fifth week, the child smiles at the sight of a friendly face coming close (Izard, p. 239). The first smile, in fact, is almost a spontaneous reflex coming two to twelve hours after birth. But, the elicited smile that comes as a result of a voice occurs soon afterwards within the first week. By the second or third month, the infant smiles spontaneously without seeing or hearing anyone, that is, if he has been responded to pleasantly by his caregivers. But the human face is the single most effective stimulus to smiling (Izard, p. 248).

Laughter has its own developmental sequence; it first occurs between five and nine weeks of age, usually in response to patty-cake-type games or tickling. Scientists believe the motor development of the child has some relationship to the development of laughter. But, both laughter and smiling can be stimulated by the same expressions of joy on the part of another.

Situations which discourage or prevent the emotion of joy from occurring include poor physical health, conditions of fatigue or boredom, harsh treatment or neglect, conditions of poverty which limit a child's possibilities, and the lack of joy on the part of caregivers.

Recognition of a familiar person, object, or situation helps stimulate or encourage the expression of joy. Whereas change and novelty seem to stimulate the emotion of interest, the familiarity and comfortableness of things set the stage for joy. Keep this knowledge in mind in your child care center. A little change is challenging. Too much change is overwhelming for the young child. He or she needs to depend on a stable schedule of daily events and a physical arrangement of materials that does not change too drastically overnight.

If You Have Not Checked This Item: Some Helpful Ideas

- *Talk to Parents*

Children who express no joy probably are not very happy. You need to converse with their parents in a sensitive manner, trying to elicit how the child reacts at home, whether any particular problems or pressures presently affect him, and what his basic personality is like. Is the child basically happy? What are his favorite things: foods, colors, toys, and activities? What makes him laugh? Perhaps you can use some of these favorites as a focus for an activity to make him feel good.

- *Read a Funny Book*

You cannot teach a child to be happy, but you can help him experience joy and therefore stimulate him to want more of it. Maybe a humorous book will tickle his funny bone enough to open his life to joy. The first two books that follow have words. The others are wordless, and the child must make up his own story. Read the books on a one-to-one basis with a child, or with no more than two or three others, if you want individual participation.

What Do You Do with a Kangaroo? by Mercer Mayer. New York: Scholastic Book Services, 1973. What do you do when a kangaroo, opossum, llama, raccoon, large baby moose, Bengal tiger, and camel invade your house and make themselves at home, one by one, whether you want them to or not? In this book, a little girl tries throwing them out but ends up with the whole menagerie in bed.

Squeeze a Sneeze by Bill Morrison. Boston: Houghton Mifflin, 1977. This book provides a hilarious rhyming game with words like pickle, tickle, and alley cat matched up with zany pictures to illustrate the nonsensical rhymes.

Ah-Choo by Mercer Mayer. New York: The Dial Press, 1976. An elephant sneezes, and that is where the trouble begins in this comical wordless picture book. The rhino policeman doesn't think it is very funny when Mr. Elephant sneezes down the jail and then ah-choos his way into his girlfriend's heart. The children will have to make up their own words to suit the pictures.

A Boy, a Dog and a Frog by Mercer Mayer. New York: The Dial Press, 1967. This is the classic picture story of the boy and dog who fail to catch the frog they want as a pet, so the frog catches them. This is the first of several books with the same characters.

- *Be a Joyful Person*

Children and others feel joy when they meet a person who feels they are delightful and wants to be around them. Make yourself that kind of person.

TABLE 3. Childhood emotions in the classroom

Emotion	Common Cause	Possible Results
Distress	Separation from loved one; abandonment	Crying; whining; clinging
Fear (anxiety)	Presence of threat; absence of safety	Tightening of muscles; refusal to eat, fall asleep, go to toilet
Surprise	Loud noise; unexpected appearance or event	Crying; withdrawing; clinging
Anger	Physical or psychological restraint; interruption; insult	Red face; loud words or screaming; physical aggression
*Aggression	Anger; frustration	Hitting; throwing; biting; kicking; pushing
Shame (shyness)	Heightened self-consciousness; exposure	Red face; crying; withdrawal
Interest (excitement)	Change; novelty	Looking at something; exploration with senses; wide eyes
Joy (enjoyment)	A pleasant experience; happy thoughts; friendship	Smiling; laughing; lighting up of eyes; talking happily

*NOTE: Not a true emotion

REFERENCES CITED

Izard, Carroll E. *Human Emotions*. New York: Plenum Press, 1977.

Brooks-Gunn, Jeanne, and Wendy Schempp Matthews. *He & She: How Children Develop Their Sex-Role Identity*. Englewood Cliffs, N.J.: Prentice-Hall, 1979.

OTHER SOURCES

Beaty, Janice J. *Skills for Preschool Teachers*. Columbus, Ohio: Charles E. Merrill Publishing Company, 1984.

Candland, Douglas K., et al. *Emotion*. Monterey, Calif.: Brooks/Cole Publishing, 1977.

Cherry, Clare. *Please Don't Sit On The Kids: Alternatives to Punitive Discipline*. Belmont, Calif.: Pitman Learning, 1983.

Enzer, Norbert B. (ed.), with Kennith W. Goin. *Social and Emotional Development: The Preschooler*. New York: Walker and Company, 1978.

Kvols-Riedler, Bill and Kathy. *Redirecting Children's Misbehavior: A Guide for Cooperation Between Children & Adults*. Boulder, Colo.: R.D.I.C. Publications, 1979.

CHILDREN'S BOOKS

Brown, Margaret Wise. *Goodnight Moon.* New York: Scholastic Book Services, 1947.

Hoban, Russel. *Bedtime for Frances.* New York: Harper & Row, 1960.

Kraus, Robert. *Good Night Richard Rabbit.* New York: Windmill Books, 1972.

LEARNING ACTIVITIES

1. Observe the children in your classroom for a week regarding the eight areas of emotional control. Which children exhibit behavior that seems to show emotional control? Which ones have not yet learned inner control? How can you help them? Write out and discuss a plan with your supervisor.

2. Choose a child who has trouble allowing his/her aggressive behavior to be redirected. Observe the child for three mornings, making a time sampling of behavior. Use a behavior modification idea as discussed in Chapter 1 to see if you can reduce the number of times this negative behavior occurs. What are the results of your follow-up observation?

3. Choose a child who has trouble either eating, sleeping, or toileting in your center. Observe him/her, making a running record on three different days. What other indications of tension do you find? What suggestions do you have for alleviating the tension?

4. Work with one of the children in your classroom who has difficulty expressing his/her anger in words. What actions can you take to help the child? Observe and record the results of your actions.

5. Choose a child for whom you have checked "Smiles, seems happy much of the time." Observe this child on three different days. Which of the other items can you check based on your observations? What is your evidence for each check mark? What conclusions can you make about this child based on these observations? Do you need any additional evidence in order to make conclusions?

4 Social Play

Social Play Checklist

- ☐ Plays by self with or without objects
- ☐ Plays by self constructing or creating something
- ☐ Plays by self in pretending-type activity
- ☐ Plays parallel to others with or without objects
- ☐ Plays parallel to others constructing or creating something
- ☐ Plays parallel to others in pretending-type activity
- ☐ Plays with a group with or without objects
- ☐ Plays with a group constructing or creating something
- ☐ Plays with a group in pretending-type activity

T he social development of the preschool child is revealed in how he or she gets along with peers. Often, we think of social actions as manners and politeness, but with the study of young children, social actions refer to how children learn to get along with their peers. This "getting along" rarely involves manners and usually is not very polite. Young children, in fact, frequently struggle to develop socialization.

They start out completely self-centered, which no doubt stems from a survival mechanism in infancy. Chapter 2 discussed how infants do not even recognize themselves as different from their primary caregiver in the beginning. Then, little by little, the infants begin to discover their own self-identities. By the time they arrive in your classroom, the children have begun to know themselves as individuals, but mainly in relation to their adult caregivers. If the children already have developed strong self-identities, then they should do well away from home. They will be able to let go of their primary caregiver more easily and will be more willing to try new things and to experience new people. If the children have siblings at home, they will have learned to respond and react to children as well.

Peers in the early childhood classroom, however, pose a different problem for the young child. Many, if not most, three- and four-year-olds simply have not developed the social skills for making friends or getting along with others. These children focus on themselves. Everything has been done for them up to this time. Even if a new baby has replaced them as the youngest in the family, they still struggle to be first in the eyes of their parents.

This egocentric point of view does not serve them well in the world at large because sooner or later, they must learn to deal with others and to be treated as part of a group. They may have been enrolled in your program to learn precisely this. The purpose of many preschools, especially nursery schools, is to provide primary socialization for preschoolers.

What do these preschoolers need to learn? If it is not concerned with politeness and manners, then what does "socialization" involve in the early childhood classroom? A few aspects include

1. Learning to make contact with another child
2. Learning to interact with peers, to give and take

87

3. Learning to get along with peers, to interact in harmony
4. Learning to make friends
5. Learning to take turns, to wait for a turn
6. Learning to share with others
7. Learning to show concern for others
8. Learning to show respect for others' rights

Their success in developing these skills, either on their own or with your help, may make the difference in how children get along for much of their lives to come.

This chapter is particularly concerned with the young child's ability to make contact, interact, and get along with peers. In order to determine where each of your children stands in the development of these skills, you need to be aware of behaviors which will indicate his or her level of development. Because all children engage in play—often together—and because play is an observable activity in the preschool classroom, we will focus on observing social play in this chapter.

EARLY RESEARCH

Many early childhood specialists have been interested in determining how children develop the skills to get along with one another. Social play has been the focus of such research since Martha Parten first looked at "Social Participation Among Preschool Children" in the late 1920s and published her findings in 1932. She found that social participation among preschoolers could be categorized, and that the categories correlated closely with age and maturity.

Altogether, she identified six behavior categories which since have served as a basis for determining children's social skills levels in several different fields of study. Her categories include

1. *Unoccupied behavior:* The child does not participate in the play around him. He stays in one spot, follows the teacher, or wanders around.
2. *Onlooker behavior:* The child spends much time watching what other children are doing and may even talk to them, but he does not join or interact with them physically.
3. *Solitary independent play:* The child engages in play activities, but he plays on his own and not with others or their toys.
4. *Parallel activity:* The child plays independently, but he plays next to other children and often uses their toys or materials.
5. *Associative play:* The child plays with other children using the same materials as—and even talking with—them, but he acts on his own and does not subordinate his interests to those of the group.
6. *Cooperative play:* The child plays in a group that has organized itself to do a particular thing, and whose members have taken different roles.
(Parten, pp. 248–51)

Since 1932, a number of other researchers have tried to replicate Parten's study with varying results. A great deal of new information about the development of young children has surfaced since then, especially through the work of Jean Piaget and the cognitive psychologists. Today, we acknowledge that these early play categories are indeed a valuable beginning point for gathering observational data about a young child's social development, but we also need to incorporate more up-to-date information.

RECENT STUDIES

Sara Smilansky's work, published in 1968, supported the notion originated by Piaget that a child's play was influenced by cognitive development. Since we now recognize that most development is interactive, this idea cannot be disregarded. Smilansky elaborated on the play categories described by Piaget and labeled them

1. *Functional play:* Doing simple, repetitive muscle movements with or without objects
2. *Constructive play:* Manipulating objects to construct or create something
3. *Dramatic play:* Pretending or using the imagination in play, role playing
4. *Games with rules:* Accepting prearranged rules and playing by them (Smilansky, pp. 5–7).

We view these categories as age-related, with functional play appearing first in infancy, and games with rules appearing last around age six or seven. Smilansky's work points out the importance of considering cognitive development when we look at the levels of children's play. But how does her work relate to Parten's familiar categories? Should we give them up?

Kenneth H. Rubin and his associates have been working on this problem since the mid-1970s. His studies have been successful in combining the Parten and Smilansky categories in observing the relationship between social and cognitive play. For example, he looks for "solitary play" in Smilansky's "functional," "constructive", and "dramatic" categories. The same three Smilansky categories also were studied for "parallel play" and "group play" (a combination of "associative" and "cooperative play"). Games with rules are played more frequently by children older than preschoolers and will not be considered here (Rubin, p. 18).

The results of Rubin's studies have done much to clarify the developmental levels of children's play in light of our new knowledge about children. A modified version of the Rubin-Parten play categories is used in the *Child Skills Checklist* and is discussed in this chapter as we consider observing the level of each child's social play in the preschool classroom. The social play checklist contains nine rather than eight items in order to include the important Rubin findings. (See Table 4.)

SOCIAL PLAY DEVELOPMENT

The development of social play is very much age-related, and it thus can be observed by the preschool child care worker in a particular sequence (as children

TABLE 4. Social play categories

	Solitary Play	Parallel Play	Group Play
Functional Play	Child plays by self with or without objects. (See pp. 91–92.)	Child plays parallel to others with or without objects. (See pp. 96–97.)	Child plays with a group with or without objects. (See pp. 100–102.)
Constructive Play	Child plays by self constructing or creating something. (See pp. 93–94.)	Child plays parallel to others constructing or creating something. (See pp. 97–98.)	Child plays with a group constructing or creating something. (See pp. 102–104.)
Dramatic Play	Child plays by self in pretending-type activity. (See pp. 94–96.)	Child plays parallel to others in pretending-type activity. (See pp. 98–100.)	Child plays with a group in pretending-type activity. (See pp. 104–107.)

progress from solitary play through parallel play to group play). Exceptions to the sequence will be discussed under each *checklist* item.

"Age-related development" signifies that the child's skill level depends upon his maturity; with social play, a child's skill level depends especially upon his cognitive, language, and emotional maturity. And, if a child is older, he probably has had more experience with social contacts.

Observers have noted that infants first begin to imitate one another in play toward the end of their first year. Early in their second year, they already are engaging in peer play whenever they have the opportunity (Smith, p. 132). Often, two-year-olds start engaging in peer play by playing alongside another toddler in a parallel manner. If they interact with an age mate, they only interact with one. Two-year-olds do not seem to be able to handle more than one playmate at a time. A threesome does not last long for children this age.

Then, as they become more mature and experienced, three-year-olds play with more than one other child at the same time. As they become less egocentric and more able to understand another child's point of view, three-year-olds have more success with social play. Using more mature language, listening to their play partners, and adjusting their behavior to the situation all support such play.

The trick for many children in your center, you will note, is to gain access to play that is already in progress. Sociologists call these maneuvers "access rituals." Children new to the group may try different strategies to get involved: 1) The youngest children may use nonverbal appeals such as smiles or gestures of interest as they stand nearby and watch, hoping a player will take note and invite or allow them in; 2) They may walk around and watch, or stand and watch, waiting for an opportunity to insert themselves; 3) They may engage in similar play parallel to the original players, hoping to join the original players by having the parallel play accepted; 4) The younger children may intrude in a disruptive manner, claiming that the space or the toys are their own; 5) Older preschoolers often use words, asking "Can I play?" or "What are you doing?" to gain access.

The most successful strategy for gaining access to ongoing play seems to be engaging in parallel play. The least successful strategy is being disruptive. (Smith, p. 130) Researchers have noted that parallel play among preschoolers decreases as group play increases. Still, parallel play seems to be the principal mode of social play for three- and four-year-olds in most centers.

☐ PLAYS BY SELF WITH OR WITHOUT OBJECTS

The first three *Checklist* items under "Social Play" relate to Parten's "solitary play" category. The young child engages in this type of play at first. Children, when they first come into your center, often will play by themselves. Part of this play characteristic results from the strangeness of the situation and a lack of self-confidence, but now, we recognize that the level of cognitive development also governs the ability to play with others. This development level is age-related and can be observed by the type of solitary play chosen. Thus, we not only need to look at solitary play alone, but also at the particular kind of solitary play the child engages in.

The first level of solitary play is the functional level, in which the child makes simple, often repetitive, movements, sometimes with an object, sometimes without. Most children begin at this level when they are unfamiliar with objects or situations. This manipulative kind of play helps the child to see what she or an object can do.

In block play, the functional level usually consists of picking up a block, putting it down, pounding with it, or filling and dumping containers. Very young children, such as two-year-olds, start here. Older children who are unused to playing with blocks also begin by manipulating them in this way. But, very quickly, the mature child progresses through the sequence and soon stacks towers, builds roads, and constructs buildings. This tells you that the child needs practice with the materials rather than cognitive maturity.

Observations also have revealed that children from low income families spend more time doing this first-level functional play. We can make several possible inferences: 1) These children indeed may be less socially and cognitively mature than their middle-class peers; 2) Children from low income families may have fewer play materials in their homes and thus may not have had an opportunity to learn to play with these things, or 3) The play materials in the program may be unfamiliar to these children who thus must spend more time in a solitary manner manipulating these materials to see how they work or what they can do. (Rubin, p. 19)

Whatever the case, we need to provide a wide range of learning materials, to encourage children to become involved with these materials on their own, and to give the children time to become involved.

If You Have Not Checked This Item: Some Helpful Ideas

All nine of the items under solitary, parallel, and group play are, of course, descriptive rather than judgmental. We are interested in observing individual children on each item to try to discover the child's level of social skills. Our observations may or may not reveal a child's development level. Thus, we must be careful not to judge a child negatively if we check or do not check a certain item. The items themselves are not negative nor positive. They merely describe behavior. What we infer from the checkmarks, or lack of them, will be more meaningful if we also write down the evidence on which we base the checkmarks.

If the child is beyond this stage of development and does not play by himself but participates in more mature solitary, parallel, or group play, then you should mark this first item with a + to indicate he has advanced beyond it. On the other hand, if you check no other items under "Social Play," then the child may be unoccupied: either standing alone, following the teacher, or wandering around aimlessly. In this case, you should leave the item blank.

• Help but Do Not Pressure the Child

You first must help—but not pressure—the child to become engaged with an activity on her own, and later, you must help the child to become involved with the other children. You might try sitting at a table with the child and helping her to get started with a puzzle, a pegboard or some other table game. Once the child is involved, you unobtrusively should extract yourself and let her complete the game on her own. Put another puzzle or game on the table beside the first so the child can continue her activity.

• Introduce Another Child

At another time when she seems to be working comfortably on her own, you might try to introduce another child to the activity.

• Leave the Child Alone in Some Instances

On the other hand, you may not have checked the "plays by self with or without objects" item because the child is an onlooker rather than a participant. Some children who are new to a program begin by watching. They even may talk to the participants in an activity but still not be engaged physically. Watching is often the first step toward group participation. If the child seems engaged, then it may be best to leave him alone. He may join the others once he is at ease in the center.

• Suggest Parallel Play

If, after some time has elapsed, the child still has not joined in with the others or even done much solitary playing, then you may want to suggest that she build a building next to Carolyn's or dress a doll like Susan's. Friendly support—not pressure—works best. And, for some children, patience on your part is the only answer.

☐ PLAYS BY SELF CONSTRUCTING OR CREATING SOMETHING

Constructing or creating something by oneself is quite different from playing alone with or without objects. In "constructing or creating," the child is engaged in making something. She may make a building, a painting, or a play dough creation; put together a puzzle; or read a book. She no longer merely manipulates objects. She purposefully uses the materials toward some end. Although working alone like this may indicate immature social skills on the part of some young children, a checkmark for this particular item has other meanings as well.

Of the nine items under "Social Play," this item is most frequently out of sequence with children. In other words, while the youngest children usually spend more time in solitary play, and the oldest children in parallel or group play, in some instances, older children again begin to do more solitary constructive play.

This sequential change makes sense when you think about it. Once children have developed their small motor skills and cognitive abilities to a certain point, they find it satisfying to do a creation or construction on their own. While two- and three-year-olds may not be able to control the medium well enough to paint a representational picture, many four- and five-year-olds can have this control and enjoy utilizing it.

Therefore, we should not worry or feel these four- and five-year-olds are "regressing" in their development. Instead, we should note whether the type of solitary play is manipulative, pretending, or constructive. If the play is constructive, then we should recognize that this is typical. A higher level of skill development in these children finally has made it possible for them to get satisfaction out of making something on their own. In this case, the *Checklist* item reflects less of social play and much more of cognitive, physical, and creative development.

Instead of discouraging such children from solitary, constructive play, we should provide them with many opportunities for expressing this creativity. The children will join in group play again when the time is right for them.

The kinds of materials available in the classroom also affect the levels of social play your children will engage in. Are your materials mainly for the use of one person at a time? Puzzles, stacking toys, sorting games, and easels are usually one-person materials. You also should provide group materials such as unit building blocks, hollow blocks, and dramatic play props as well as group play opportunities with water or sand.

Programs, such as Montessori's, have an approach that mainly features one-person problem-solving materials. These programs have a great deal more solitary constructive play going on and a corresponding lesser amount of group play than other programs.

If You Have Not Checked This Item: Some Helpful Ideas

You may not have checked this item, then, because the child has progressed beyond it to parallel and group activities. In that case, mark the item with a +. Note all nine items under "Social Play," however, before deciding what an unchecked item means. If you notice an unoccupied child or a child onlooker during your free choice/free play period, then you may want to entice him to play with a new or different game.

• *Find Out the Child's Particular Interests*

Try to find out the child's interests. If she likes animals, perhaps she would like to look at an animal book, cut out a new box for the guinea pig, or listen to a tape of animal sounds and make some of her own. If she talks about liking peanut butter and jelly sandwiches, maybe she would like to grind up peanuts to make her own peanut butter, or spread peanut butter on a peeled banana and roll it in graham cracker crumbs.

• *Ask the Child to Help You*

Ask the child to cut or tear out pictures of children, animals or cars for you from old magazines. The two of you could then paste the pictures on construction paper as a collage.

☐ PLAYS BY SELF IN PRETENDING-TYPE ACTIVITY

The third item in the solitary play series is not necessarily more advanced than the second item; as discussed previously, children sometimes return to constructive,

If a child is used to playing alone at home, she may play by herself at first in the preschool.

solitary play when their motor skills have improved. But, children who have not yet experienced parallel or group imaginative play may move toward these activities by first playing by themselves in a pretending-type activity.

"Plays by self in pretending-type activity" refers to the child who pretends as he or she plays alone. He may be moving a toy truck or race car along the floor and pretending to be the driver while making motor sounds and giving directions. She may be the nurse or doctor giving the baby doll a shot as she plays alone in the housekeeping corner. He may be building a garage for his car and talking to himself about what he is doing.

Most dramatic play in preschool programs occurs in group situations, as you might guess. But, some dramatic play seems to take place in solitary situations like the ones just described. Often, this solitary play is a temporary practice situation, or a holdover from home if the child is used to playing alone. The child soon will have opportunities to join others; or rather, they probably will be joining her if her pretending sounds interesting to them. Then, you will see whether she is ready yet for group play. She may not be. She may rebuff the joiner.

Some observers have found that the self-talk of solitary pretend players is less mature than that heard in group dramatic play. Perhaps the child still plays alone for this reason. Her language level may not equal group conversation levels. On the other hand, group language experiences may improve her own vocal production.

If you check this solitary dramatic play item for a child, then you should recognize that it is not a negative finding. Instead, this item is a step on the ladder of socialization. When the child is ready, he will take the next step.

If You Have Not Checked This Item: Some Helpful Ideas

As with solitary functional and constructive play, you should mark the item with a + if the child has progressed beyond the behavior. Most children do not go back to solitary dramatic play once they are engaged in group pretending.

You should concern yourself with children who are unoccupied or merely watching others. You should engage them in an activity eventually; you might try engaging them in solitary dramatic play. Not every child will agree to play this way; on the other hand, solitary dramatic play may be a helpful first step for some children who do not seem to know how to pretend.

- *Give the Child a Pretending Toy*

Give one of the children not engaged in play a hand puppet, and try to engage her in pretending. You may want to wear a hand puppet yourself to get her started. Try the same thing with a toy person, animal, or vehicle.

- *Give the Child a Wordless Picture Book*

When you give a child a wordless picture book, he first just may leaf through it looking at the pictures. You may need to make up a story as the two of you look at it together. Then, encourage the child to make up his own story. Many wordless books are available. If you are unfamiliar with them, ask your local librarian about them. Pages 83 and 292 discuss several of these books.

☐ PLAYS PARALLEL TO OTHERS WITH OR WITHOUT OBJECTS

A fascinating phenomenon, parallel play—if you are unfamiliar with it—almost must be seen to be believed. It often involves two children who seem to be playing together. But, as you get close enough to witness what is going on, you find that both are playing different games from different points of view. If the children use language, they seem to be talking to themselves rather than to each other.

This first level of parallel play involves functional actions: The children play near one another and merely manipulate objects or materials. The first level is the least mature of the three levels. You might observe it in two or more children at the water table, swishing their hands around, or picking up and dropping the water toys without much purpose to their actions. The same type of play might occur at the woodworking bench, the sand table, the housekeeping corner, and the block area.

Rather than build with blocks, two or more children only may take the blocks off the shelves, or push them around the floor aimlessly. This type of play, however, eventually can evolve into parallel constructive play when the children begin building or making something.

This first level of parallel play is seen more frequently among children from low income families than among those from middle income homes (Rubin, p. 18). Again, these children may be less mature or may have had less practice with the materials and the play situation.

All kinds of parallel play go on in the preschool setting, regardless of the children's backgrounds. More parallel play occurs with younger than older children. Parallel play, as previously mentioned, seems to enable young children to learn to play cooperatively with others in an early childhood center. This statement makes a great deal of sense when you consider that your center houses a large group of highly egocentric children who are strangers for the most part. They come together in a physical setting full of toys and activities just for them. How should they deal with this setting?

They begin by trying out things on their own. Then, they play side by side using the same materials individually. Finally, the children begin to cooperate, interchange ideas, and come together to play as a group with self-assigned roles and tasks.

If You Have Not Checked This Item: Some Helpful Ideas

If the child you are observing is not engaged in functional parallel play because she has progressed beyond it, mark the "plays parallel to others with or without objects" item with a +. You will know the child has progressed beyond functional parallel play if you observe her constructing things, pretending in a parallel situation, or playing with a group of children. If, on the other hand, the child has not been observed doing any kind of parallel or group play, you may want to help her learn how.

• Provide a Physical Setup that Fosters Group Activities

Set up your room so that two, three or four children will play together in activities. Put those numbers of chairs at the tables with games or materials for the children to use together during the free choice period. Put your easels side by side so that children can paint in a parallel manner and can begin an interchange of looks and words.

• Invite the Child to Join Group Activity

Your *checklist* observation will tell you which children have not started parallel or group play. Invite these children to join a table, work area or science activity. These children only may manipulate the materials at first, but at least they will be close to another child and can begin by imitation to learn how to play.

☐ PLAYS PARALLEL TO OTHERS CONSTRUCTING OR CREATING SOMETHING

Playing parallel to others constructing or creating something is probably the most popular type of play in an early childhood center. Many activities—especially art activities—place children parallel to one another doing similar constructive projects on their own. With most art activities, children sit next to each other at tables making collages, molding clay or play dough, cutting, and pasting. The children also may sit together in the reading corner looking at books. Two children may pound nails in tiles at the woodworking bench. Three or four youngsters may play at the water table, each filling his own containers. Two or more children may build their own buildings in the block building area.

A child advances from solitary to parallel constructive play when he uses the same type of material with other children in the same location at the same time.

The physical arrangement of the center is most responsible for this type of play. Most centers are organized into activity areas where several children at a time can play with the equipment. This arrangement brings the children together in a parallel manner to work and play on their own with the same materials.

As they mature, the children may want to combine their materials to create something together, but this activity is a long way down the road for most children.

If You Have Not Checked This Item: Some Helpful Ideas

You should be concerned if you have not checked this item for a particular child. If your center is similar to most, not checking this item would mean that the child is not participating in the principal classroom activities. Hopefully, all of your children would spend some of their time working parallel to others in an activity area of their choice on something of their own. Even children who have progressed beyond the parallel play stage enjoy creating their own things next to a friend.

On the other hand, if this is the only "Social Play" item you have checked for a child, you may need to consider the following ideas for involving her in group activities:

- *Try Finger Painting for Two*

Set up a small table where two can sit side by side, and put out finger paints to be shared. Invite one of your reluctant participants and one other child to paint. Do not force the reluctant child. Perhaps you could first involve him in a solitary manner and then ask him if another child could work next to him.

- *Employ Tape Recording for Two*

Hopefully, you have two cassette tape recorders in your program. They are invaluable because they provide an opportunity for two children to play individually with the same materials in a parallel manner. Tape recording is personal and fun. Even the shy child can talk as softly as she likes, as long as she holds the mike up close. She can say anything about herself that she wants, such as her name; the names of her brothers, sisters, or pets; her favorite foods; or where she lives. Then comes the fun of listening to what she has spoken. Two children can record at the same table if they each talk into their own microphones. The children eventually may want to talk into each other's mikes.

☐ PLAYS PARALLEL TO OTHERS IN PRETENDING-TYPE ACTIVITY

"Plays parallel to others in pretending-type activity" is the highest level of the three parallel play items. This level involves dramatic or imaginative play with more than one person but with each person playing his own independent game. The children can be pretending in the block area, in the dramatic play area, at the water table, on the climbing equipment . . . anywhere and everywhere in the classroom and on the playground. Sometimes, it is obvious that the children are parallel playing. Jeff and Joe, for instance, each have a building next to the other and are pretending that one is a hospital and the other is a house. This activity is not cooperative group play because the children are not interchanging anything, neither blocks nor words.

Sometimes, the observer needs to look very closely at the pretend play to determine whether it is parallel or cooperative. Paul and John, for example, actually are playing with the same building, but they are having little to do with one another: John is building a garage for his race car, and Paul is playing with a figure of a person in his house.

Sometimes, several children will be engaged in cooperative dramatic play, and one child will join them as a parallel player who does not interact at all, but who plays his own self-imposed role next to theirs. Parten originally called this "associative play," but recent researchers have found it so difficult to discriminate associative from cooperative play that they call any pretending done in a group, "group play." This categorizing is up to the observer. But, if you have solid evidence that a child truly is doing his own pretending on the periphery of a group, then this parallel play item should be checked.

Observe children carefully on the playground outside, and you may see a great deal of parallel pretend play. Often, children from other classes use the playground at the same time, so the same equipment will be used by children who do not know one another. One child may pretend the slide is a space shuttle launch pad while another child may use the slide as "an amusement park ride." The area under the slide or climber is another favorite site for pretend play. Usually, groups of children will use the area together as a hut or house of some kind. But, sometimes, two children will pretend different uses for the area at the same time.

Pretend play of this parallel nature occurs more often among children who have not yet developed the social skills to interact with a cooperative play group. But, this parallel play is a step in the right direction; it is almost like practicing roles the child will take when she finally joins the group.

Some children from low income families have difficulty joining group dramatic play and thus play in a parallel manner. Some researchers feel that children who have not joined a group in pretend play have not yet developed the social skills necessary for the give and take which cooperative dramatic play requires (Rosen, p. 926).

If certain children have not done any pretend play at all, then they may not have reached the cognitive development level where they are able to see things from another point of view. After all, in order to be a jet pilot, a child must step out of his role as a four-year-old. Again, we see that all development is interrelated. To develop socially, children also must develop cognitively.

Can they learn to see things from another point of view, or must we wait until they are ready? Questions about child development frequently involve the issue of "readiness." We really don't know precisely when each child reaches certain development levels. Even if we did, should we wait around to find out if a child is "ready"? That used to be the style. We would give the child "readiness" tests or "readiness" games until he was "ready to learn," whatever that meant.

Now, we know we should just plunge in, ready or not. The child will learn whatever his developmental level and his own motivation will grant him. Classroom teachers and aides must understand this developmental aspect of children and must accept youngsters' changing development and learning stages. Teachers and aides also must choose materials and plan activities that will promote success among developing children.

Why, then, do we use the *Child Skills Checklist*? Why do we not just plunge in blindly? Because helping a child in the best possible manner requires that we know all we can about the child's level of development and the kinds of things he needs help in. If learning to get along with others is important in his life—and it is—then we need to determine where he stands in regard to this skill, in order to help him proceed from there. Building on skills he already has is one of the most successful approaches we can use.

If You Have Not Checked This Item: Some Helpful Ideas

Some children whom you have not checked already have gone on to group dramatic play and probably will not return to parallel play of this sort. Be sure to mark this item for them with a + instead of leaving the item blank. You should be concerned with children who have not become involved in either parallel play with others or group dramatic play.

What items have you checked for such children? Are they involved at all in solitary, parallel functional, or constructive play? If so, it should not be too difficult to involve them in pretending.

• *Give the Child a Puppet*

With hand puppets, the wearer must take a role other than his own. Let a child first play with hand puppets alone. Then, you can wear one puppet and engage the solitary player in a pretend dialog. Once the child gets the idea, turn your puppet over to another child and say to the first child something like: "The brown bear here, who calls herself Grouchy, doesn't know where bears can find anything to eat in this room. Can your puppet, Pretty Boy, help her?"

• *Bring in Two New Stuffed Animals*

Children enjoy using stuffed animals as pretend people and pretend pets. Invite two children who have not exhibited much pretending to take care of your two stuffed animals for the morning. Then, someone else can have a chance. To get the children started, tell them the animals' names and what the animals like to do. Ask the children if they will help the stuffed animals engage in whatever the animals like to do. Seeing you pretend like this may encourage the children.

☐ PLAYS WITH A GROUP WITH OR WITHOUT OBJECTS

The final three items under "Social Play" involve cooperative group activities, the highest level of social play. This category also has the same three levels: functional, constructive, and dramatic play. Playing in a group with or without objects describes the functional behavior of preschoolers who are first coming together to play: They mill around or try things out rather than participate in a purposeful activity. The activities of toddlers also may take the form of playing in a group with or without objects. This type of play is the least mature of the three types of group play and the least engaged in by three- and four-year-olds during group play.

An example of this functional type of play can be seen in several children coming into the housekeeping area and handling the materials without putting the objects to use. One teacher set up her dramatic play area with doctors' props after her class had visited a clinic. Several children came into the area to play when they first saw the new materials. At first, the children picked up and looked at the various items, playing with the objects in a nonsensical manner. One boy shouted into a stethoscope that was around another child's neck, as if the stethoscope were a telephone. A girl dumped out the contents of the "doctor's bag" onto a table and picked up and examined the contents, object by object. Another girl tried to retrieve the objects from the bag and return them to the bag. No real pretending happened at all in the beginning. The children merely participated in an exploratory sort of play together.

Children come together to play with one another quite early in life. Two- and three-year-olds will search out each other for group play, as mentioned previously. The younger the child, the less structured the play. Functional group play for two-year-olds in the toddler center often revolves around running, climbing over things, and chasing, with lots of squealing and giggling. The two-year-olds may do silly things with objects such as sweeping the doll bed instead of sweeping the floor with the toy broom. Once someone starts this sort of action, everyone has to have a turn. A "follow-the-leader" type of activity is very common at this age. Members of this sort of play group come and go; some members lose interest, and other children join.

Children from low income families tend to engage in more functional group play of this type than in the higher level dramatic play, according to some researchers (Rubin, p. 19). This finding seems to be based principally on the low socioeconomic status of the children and not on their race, according to Catherine Rosen. She found that black middle income children demonstrated as much dramatic play as their white counterparts; whereas, poor children of both races displayed significantly less dramatic play (Rosen, p. 926). Again, this finding may signify that poor children are less mature in social, cognitive, or language development, or that poor children have had less practice in group dramatic play, or that all four of these situations exist.

As a classroom caregiver, you must structure your program so that all children have the opportunity, time, and encouragement to engage in group free play activities.

If You Have Not Checked This Item: Some Helpful Ideas

- *Provide Group Materials*

Children will play with whatever materials are available. If you have puzzles for one, then one child will sit down and play. If you want children to develop social skills, then you need to provide materials for small groups of children. Have four stethoscopes in your dramatic play area to encourage four different children to come together in doctor play. Do the same with four basters or four eggbeaters at the water table. (The children merely may experiment with the materials at first.)

• *Arrange the Classroom for Small Groups*

Young children work best in small rather than large groups. Three, four, or five children together is a comfortable group size. It was noted earlier that two-year-olds cannot play for long with more than one other person. Large groups are just too overwhelming for egocentric children of preschool age. Egocentric individuals simply get lost in large groups.

Move your furniture around to divide large spaces into areas for small groups of children. Break up a large central area with room dividers. Pull bookshelves away from the walls, and use the shelves as dividers for your activity areas. Move your classroom tables away from a large central area, and place each table in a different, smaller area. You can help to manage the size of groups by this type of arrangement. Place four chairs at a table, put four aprons at the water play area, or divide the block area into four building spaces and use masking tape on the floor to suggest the size of the groups that will play there.

☐ PLAYS WITH A GROUP CONSTRUCTING OR CREATING SOMETHING

A more mature group play level for preschoolers involves a group of children coming together to construct or create something. This level of activity requires more cooperative behavior than the previous "Social Play" checklist item. In order to participate in such a creative venture, the players need language, cognitive, social, and creative skills. The children must express themselves verbally, accept assigned tasks, take turns and wait for turns, respect others' rights, and adjust their behavior to the needs of the group.

The children also need physical skills. Large and small motor coordination are necessary to successfully build a hut, paint a cardboard playhouse, or construct a block city.

Just as important are the materials provided. One of Rubin's studies ranked the ten most frequently observed preschool activities, which include

1. Cutting, pasting, and art construction
2. Painting and crayoning
3. Play dough
4. House play, store, doctor, fire fighter
5. Vehicles
6. Sand and water
7. Blocks
8. Science
9. Books
10. Puzzles

(Rubin, p. 21)

Some of these observed activities tended to be nonsocial, while other activities almost always were group-oriented. Children doing painting and crayoning, play dough, sand and water, or puzzle activities usually worked either in a solitary manner or in parallel play with others. These findings seem to tell us that if we want our children to learn social skills, we need to provide more materials which will encourage small group activities.

Rubin found that sex differences affect group play as well. While boys more frequently engage in vehicle and block play (which are both potentially social activities), girls engage in more cutting and pasting, painting and crayoning activities (which are nonsocial). If we want our girls to learn the give and take of group interchange during this important early development period, then we need to provide them with the opportunity to learn about group interaction.

Boys seem to engage more frequently in block play than do girls.

Although free play certainly should allow for children's free choice of activities, you may need to steer individuals toward certain materials and equipment in order to give the children a chance to explore a wide range of activities and to learn skills for getting along in groups.

Most social interactions occur in house play, vehicle play, and, surprisingly, reading activities, Rubin found (Rubin, p. 22). The first two activities involve dramatic group play, but reading is constructive play (the type of activity which teaches skills for getting along in groups). Teachers frequently encourage group interchange before, during, or after the reading of stories. This interchange helps children to take turns, wait their turn, and listen to what others have to say. From such activities can come the creation of group stories on an experience chart or a tape recorder.

Teachers need to be aware of the opportunities in their programs to encourage small group interaction. We tend not to think in these terms. We look to the activities in our classrooms to provide good experiences for children in general, not for children in solitary, parallel, and group play. Yet, if we want to promote the social development of children, we need to provide youngsters with opportunities for learning and practicing social skills.

If You Have Not Checked This Item: Some Helpful Ideas

- *Provide Group Construction Materials*

Put out two or three hand puppets on a table along with a tape recorder and blank tape cassette. Suggest that two or three children record a story that their puppets would like to tell. Show the children how to record if they do not already know how to. The puppets can make up the story as they go along. Expect a lot of laughter on your tape! When one group is done, another can have a turn.

Put two chairs side by side at a small table along with some finger paint, and suggest that two children finger paint on the table surface, making a painting together (or on one large paper if you want to make cleanup easier!). Cleaning up together also can be a valuable team experience for two children.

Outside on the playground, provide two or three buckets of water and paintbrushes for children to "paint" the side of the building or a fence.

- *Have Partners Help*

Whenever possible in your classroom, have one child help another to make something, or to work on a project. For instance, have one child draw around another's hand, foot, or stretched-out body for a self-concept art project.

- *Utilize Cooperative Projects*

Have group scrapbooks for a variety of purposes. All the children with pets can make a scrapbook together, cutting and pasting pictures of animals, birds, and fish from old catalogs. All the children with baby brothers or sisters can make a baby catalog with cut and pasted pictures from maternity advertising catalogs or old magazines featuring families or babies. Make favorite food scrapbooks. Each group of children can make a scrapbook of favorite foods by cutting and pasting pictures of food from magazines. You do not need to purchase real scrapbooks if your budget is low. Any kind of paper can be stapled together. You will need to label the covers with a title and the children's names. Put the scrapbooks in the book corner for everyone to use.

☐ PLAYS WITH A GROUP IN PRETENDING-TYPE ACTIVITY

The ultimate social play experience that most centers provide is dramatic play, the taking of spontaneous roles in imaginary group situations that are made up by the children during free play. As previously noted, Rubin found most of these situations involve house, store, doctor, firefighter, and vehicle play. And as with the solitary and parallel pretending activities, children from low income families do not engage in house, store, doctor, firefighter, and vehicle play as much as middle income group children. A check mark for a child on this item is an indication of his or her social maturity.

A clear sequence of pretend play in young children has emerged over the past twenty years of research. By age two, children can pretend and often play with imaginary objects. The more complex sociodramatic play with several children playing different roles cannot take place until children can articulate verbally, which occurs between two and four years of age. Three- and four-year-old children, probably influenced by the preschool environment, are at the height of their concentration on other children and their use of group dramatic play. Such play gradually becomes more complex with five-year-olds in kindergarten until about age six when the frequency of group dramatic play begins to decline. By age seven, games-with-rules are more prominent, and dramatic play seems to disappear altogether. (Smilansky, pp. 10–11)

Thus, the early childhood classroom needs to take advantage of this recognized sequence of children's activities and to provide the materials, equipment, space, and time to allow and encourage children to engage in group pretend play. Chapter 13, Imagination, discusses the development of a child's imagination and the themes he or she chooses when making up roles and situations in group dramatic play.

In this chapter, we should be concerned with a child's social skills. If she is immature, she may not have developed the "access skills" to enter the group play in the first place. She also must be able to

1. Carry on a conversation
2. Maintain eye contact when speaking
3. Listen to and watch other speakers
4. Adjust own conversation content to be understood
(Smith, pp. 135–36)

In addition, the child must be able to pretend, take a role, take turns, and show respect for others' roles . . . all within a playful framework. These requirements create quite a complex agenda for three-, four-, and five-year-olds. It is no wonder that not all children are successful at social interaction.

Being successful at group dramatic play helps young children to practice and learn the social skills necessary to be successful in life. Some of the skills a child learns through group dramatic play include

1. Adjusting his actions to the requirements of his role and the group
2. Being tolerant of others and their needs
3. Not always expecting to have his own way
4. Making appropriate responses to others
5. Helping others and receiving help from them

In other words, engaging in group pretend play helps to transform a preschool child from an egocentric being who is the center of all attention into a socialized human being who recognizes the existence of others' points of view and who can respond to those points of view appropriately.

If You Have Not Checked This Item: Some Helpful Ideas

▪ *Provide Appropriate Props as Field Trip Follow-ups*

You will be taking your children on field trips to stores, farms, fire stations, hospitals, laundromats, parks, zoos, pet shops, and construction sites. Upon your return, provide a variety of ways for children to represent and talk about this experience. An excellent activity involves providing the children with props to play the roles seen at the field trip site. Many teachers make up a prop box after every field trip. They fill the box with paraphernalia to be used in pretending the different roles, and they label the outside of the box with a picture and words the children soon recognize. Then, the children are free to take such boxes off the shelf and play with the equipment during any free choice period. If children have shown an interest in the field trip, they are more likely to become involved with pretend play afterwards.

A trip to the post office, for instance, could produce a prop box with stamps (cancelled postage stamps or stickers of some sort), a stamp pad and stamper, envelopes, a mail bag (tote bag), a mail carrier's hat, and a picture book about a mail carrier. The book *Be What You Want to Be!* gives dozens of suggestions for making your own props out of discarded materials.

▪ *Change Your Dramatic Play Area from Time to Time*

Everyone is stimulated by change. If you have had housekeeping equipment in your dramatic play period for a number of weeks, try converting the area to something else: perhaps a store or a beauty/barber shop. Talk with the children, and have them help stock the area with empty or discarded items from home.

▪ *Put New Accessory Items in the Block Area*

Group pretend play takes place in areas other than the dramatic play corner. Children can do their follow-up pretending after a field trip in the block corner as well. Mount pictures of the field trip site at eye level on the wall to give children seated on the floor ideas for creating new kinds of buildings. Add appropriate accessories to the shelves within the block area as well. If you have been to a construction site, put out little trucks, figures of people, string (for ropes and wires), plastic tubing, and even stones for the children to choose from. Accessories also can be put at the sand or water tables, but pretending in these areas often involves more solitary or parallel activities rather than group play.

• *Help the Shy Child Get Involved*

You may need to take a role yourself in order to help the shy child get involved in the playing. She may not have the access skills to enter an engaged group. You both can pretend to be visitors going to the store, doctor's office, or house. Let her carry something to give to the other players: pretend money, a ticket, or a box of something to exchange. Once she is involved in the play, you can leave.

REFERENCES CITED

Parten, Mildred B. "Social Participation Among Pre-School Children." *Journal of Abnormal and Social Psychology* 27 (1932): 243–69.

Rosen, Catherine Elkin. "The Effects of Sociodramatic Play on Problem-Solving Behavior among Culturally Disadvantaged Preschool Children." *Child Development* 45(1974): 920–27.

Rubin, Kenneth H. "Play Behaviors of Young Children," *Young Children.* September 1977, 16–24.

Smilansky, Sara. *The Effects of Sociodramatic Play on Disadvantaged Preschool Children.* New York: John Wiley & Sons, 1968.

Smith, Charles A. *Promoting the Social Development of Young Children: Strategies and Activities.* Palo Alto, Calif.: Mayfield Publishing Company, 1982.

OTHER SOURCES

Beaty, Janice J. *Skills for Preschool Teachers.* Columbus, Ohio: Charles E. Merrill Publishing Company, 1984.

Fiarotta, Phyllis, and Noel Fiarotta. *Be What You Want To Be!* New York: Workman, 1977.

Rubin, Kenneth H. "Social and Social-Cognitive Developmental Characteristics of Young Isolate, Normal, and Sociable Children," in Rubin, Kenneth H., and Hildy S. Ross (eds.). *Peer Relationships and Social Skills in Childhood.* New York: Springer-Verlag, 1982.

LEARNING ACTIVITIES

1. Use the *Child Skills Checklist,* "3. Social Play," as a screening tool to observe all of the children in your classroom. Which ones engage mainly in solitary play? in parallel play? in group play? Are any children unoccupied or onlookers?

2. Choose a child whom you have observed engaging in solitary play. Do a running record of the child on three different days to determine the type of solitary play performed. How could you involve the child in the next level of play? Should you? Why or why not?

3. Choose a child whom you have observed engaging mainly in parallel play. What kind of play does the child display? How can you help the child get involved in the next level of play? Use one of the suggested activities, and record the results.

4. Choose a child whom you have not seen doing group pretend play. Use one of the activities from the chapter with the child. Discuss the results.

5. Choose a child whom you have observed and who does not participate in any parallel or group activity. Why do you think the child does not participate in these activities? What particular social skills does the child need to learn? How can you help the child? Try out an activity, and discuss the results.

5

Prosocial Behavior

Prosocial Behavior Checklist

- ☐ Shows concern for someone in distress
- ☐ Shows delight for someone experiencing pleasure
- ☐ Shares something with another
- ☐ Gives something of his/her own to another
- ☐ Takes turns with toys or activities
- ☐ Waits for turn without a fuss
- ☐ Helps another do a task
- ☐ Helps another in need

A second area of young children's social development that is of great concern to early childhood caregivers is the positive aspect of moral development, better known today as "prosocial behavior." It includes behaviors such as empathy, in which children express compassion by consoling or comforting someone in distress or by affirming a person's good fortune; generosity, in which children share or give a possession to someone; turn-taking, in which they share a turn or wait for a turn; and caregiving, in which they help someone to complete a task or help another person in need.

These are some of the characteristics that help people to get along in society, that motivate people to interact with one another, and that help to make us human. Young children are not in the world alone. They are part of a family, a clan of relatives, a neighborhood, a community, a country, and a world of similar beings. To be an integrated member of the "human tribe," the young child needs to learn the tribe's rules of behavior from the beginning.

This learning, you may argue, should happen in the home, and it certainly does, whether or not parents realize they are teaching their children social behavior. Children absorb everything that happens around them: what mom does when the baby cries, what dad does when someone upsets him, and what family members do when they disagree. Every emotional situation presents the young human with forceful patterns of behavior he can model. We know only too tragically that child abusers often come from families of child abusers.

Prosocial behavior can be modeled as well. Both the home and the school should be aware of the powerful lessons taught by behavior modeling, which the child absorbs so readily, especially in emotional situations. The actions of adults in emotional situations can be used to demonstrate the prosocial feelings of caring, sharing, and consoling, too.

Behavior also is taught by methods other than example both in the home and the preschool. Formal—often restrictive—rules for "proper behavior" have been drummed into children from time immemorial. Children are scolded or punished when they behave in an unacceptable manner. They cry, sulk, or slink away, and they may try to behave correctly next time. But, just as often, they stick out a tongue in defiance and grumble, "try and make me!"

111

There is a better, easier way. Many early childhood specialists these days are turning to focus on the so-called prosocial behaviors in a search for ways to raise more humane members of the race. Not only does the learning of prosocial behaviors promise positive results, but it also offers more satisfying responses for both the child and the caregiver. Those who have tried the positive approach claim it is more effective than the negative method and that as children learn prosocial ways to behave, negative behaviors seem to fade away.

Empathy, generosity, sharing, and helping . . . how do you teach these behaviors, anyway? They sound so elusive. Are not some children just "good" naturally?

If children seem to be "good," they probably have maturity and a good "home start." Now, you can add to that maturity and home influence by the way you treat children in the early childhood classroom, and by the way you model behavior yourself, for starters. But first, as with other areas of development, you should know where each of the children already stands concerning his or her development of prosocial behaviors. You will need to observe every child on the eight *Checklist* items and then make plans for the individual support or activities you will provide.

Each of the *Checklist* items in this chapter is an observable behavior that shows if the child possesses a particular prosocial capacity.

☐ SHOWS CONCERN FOR SOMEONE IN DISTRESS

Empathy

Empathy is the capacity to feel as someone else does. A person with empathy is able to understand another person's emotional response to a situation and to respond in the same way, in other words, "to feel for him." Empathy is a step beyond mere sympathy in which one person can respond emotionally to another but from his own perspective. With empathy, you respond from the other person's perspective; you participate in his feelings.

Some psychologists believe empathy is the basis for all prosocial behavior. Until a child has this capacity, she will be unable to behave naturally in a helping, sharing, compassionate manner. Obviously, the child can be forced to perform prosocially whether or not she understands what she is doing. But this forced performance is not empathy. Forced behavior has little to do with the prosocial skills of our concern. Behavior must be natural and spontaneous in order to show that children possess empathy.

Are children born with empathy, or do they learn it? Probably a little of both. Researchers have determined that capacities such as empathy have at least two different aspects which must be considered (Damon, p. 129). Empathy has an affective side which is the emotional response to another's distress or joy, and empathy has a cognitive side which allows the child to see things from another person's perspective.

Until this cognitive development has occurred (as discussed in Chapter 2), the child will have difficulty expressing empathic concern for others because he still will be too egocentric and therefore unable to see things from another person's point of view. Because they lack this empathy, infants and toddlers often mishandle their animal pets. The youngsters have no idea that pulling a puppy's ear or squeezing a kitten might hurt. These actions do not hurt the children, themselves; therefore, why should the pulling or squeezing hurt their pet? This egocentric point of view eventually changes with cognitive maturity and experience, but until a child can view things from another's perspective, he will have difficulty showing empathic compassion for another's distress.

When does this change take place? It happens gradually, of course, as does all development. Yet, some part of the human capacity to respond to distress must be built in, for even infants one day old will become upset and will cry when a nearby baby starts crying. Then, somewhere between one and two years of age, the cognitive change takes place. Children, although they may not act appropriately, begin to show genuine concern for others. Toddlers have been observed giving up their favorite stuffed animal to an older sibling who is crying. They feel comforted by the animal, so why not give it to another in distress. The act of giving demonstrates their developing capacity for empathy.

From two to around six years of age, children begin to react more appropriately to the distress of others around them. This is the age of the children in your class. You will be observing them to determine which ones show concern for another child in distress. Distress may be displayed by someone crying or screaming. It also could be less dramatically disclosed by a child who puts her head down on a table, goes into a corner, or leaves the room after an upsetting incident.

You will note that some children immediately come to the side of the upset child. Others do not. The children that display this empathic concern, of course, may be special friends of the upset child. On the other hand, highly sensitive children who have no particular friendship with the child also will come close. Some youngsters just stand by the side of the distressed child and look at him or her, or look for the teacher. Others actively console the child, touching or speaking to him or her.

If a teacher causes the distress, a similar thing may happen. A child being reprimanded or scolded often will attract a circle of observers. In this case, you will have more difficulty determining empathic behavior because some of the observers are more concerned for themselves and how the teacher feels about them. Others are simply curious. Watch and see who comforts the child after the teacher leaves, before you check this item for them. The children who comfort the child are not necessarily taking the distressed child's side against the teacher. If they stay with the child after the teacher leaves, they more likely have true compassion for the child.

The classroom worker should know that family life and cultural background have a definite influence on empathic response in children. If families stress prosocial behavior, then their children will exhibit it more than children from families who do not teach or demonstrate it.

Some cultures stress consideration of group members more than others. Communal-type cultures, such as the Native American or Asian cultures, often stress concern for group members more than the American culture does. Our culture seems to stress competition among individuals more often than cooperation. The individual is glorified, sometimes at the expense of the group.

On the other hand, even individual animals are shown concern in our culture, which is not always true in many communal cultures where pets sometimes are kicked aside when in the way. Communal cultures tend not to treat the individual person as anything special. The group, itself, is more important. As a child caregiver in the multiethnic, multicultural society that makes up America, you need to be aware of such differences.

Research has shown that community size and the role of women also influence a child's prosocial inclinations. Children from a rural rather than urban setting, from a small rather than a large city, or from a society where women have an important economic function outside the home are more inclined to show concern for others (Damon, p. 132). If the mother works outside the home, then the children must take on responsibilities at an early age. Learning helping and caretaking tasks so early obviously inclines children toward prosocial behavior. Thus, the teacher must know something about the individual child's background in order to make a more accurate assessment of the child's behavior.

If you have not checked this item for many of your children, do not be alarmed. Showing concern for someone in distress is one of the more difficult prosocial behaviors for preschoolers to learn. Distressful situations that happen to others upset onlookers too. Before the onlookers can respond, they often need to overcome their own anxiety. They thus are more apt to step back and let the adult show the concern. You, however, can involve your children in this humane act.

If You Have Not Checked This Item: Some Helpful Ideas

- *Model Empathic Behavior in the Classroom*

You must serve as a model for the children. When something distressful happens to someone, you should show your own concern by going to the person; touching, hugging, or holding the person if this is appropriate; talking to the child; and giving the youngster time and space to feel better again.

A second way to model this behavior is through your actions in distressful situations that happen outside the classroom. If someone is hurt or dies, if a tragic event happens on television, or if something upsetting happens within their families, then you must let the children know you are concerned too.

- *Help the Children to Show Their Own Concern*

Talk to the children both privately and in the group about distressful happenings that have occurred. Encourage the children to ask questions about things they do not understand. Show the youngsters that it is all right to cry and express emotions openly. When a class member is in the hospital, have the class make and send a card.

When children are pretending in dramatic play about people or pets being hurt, listen to see if the youngsters express compassionate feelings even in pretend. You can model a concerned role in pretending too, by expressing your own sympathy when one of the players is pretending to be hurt.

- *Read Books about Showing Concern*

Only One Ant by Leonore Klein, New York: Scholastic Book Services, 1971, tells a series of anecdotes about four children who encounter an injured ant, a spider, a mouse attacked by a hawk, a fish out of water, a bird with a broken wing, and several other distressful events. After each event, the book asks the reader what he or she would do. Then, each of the four children answers the same question, often humorously. This book is an excellent motivation for discussions on questions of empathy.

     Sunflowers for Tina by Anne Norris Baldwin, New York: Scholastic Book Services, 1970, features an inner city girl, Tina, and her brother Eddie who shows concern over her unsuccessful quest for flowers. Tina, in turn, shows her own concern for her unsmiling grandmother by becoming a living sunflower.

     I Have a Sister My Sister is Deaf by Jeanne Whitehouse Peterson, New York: Harper & Row, 1977, is a first person narrative by a young girl about her younger sister, who is deaf. The girl tells all the things her sister can—and cannot—do in a manner showing great concern and sensitivity.

☐ SHOWS DELIGHT FOR SOMEONE EXPERIENCING PLEASURE

Why are we humans always more aware of the bad things than the good? Is it because negative emotions are stronger or more upsetting to us, or because they occur more frequently? Whatever the reason, we seem to give negative emotions more of our attention. Giving negative emotions more attention in the presence of young children can be harmful. We are behavior models for the children, and if the youngsters see us showing more concern over the negative than the positive emotions, then children may get the notion that bad is more important to us than good.

     If we want children to learn a full range of empathic responses, then we, ourselves, need to be aware of and respond to the delightful things that happen to the people around us. How many gratifying things have happened to the children and adults in your classroom recently? Could any of the following be counted:

     A new baby arrived at Sandra's house.
     Richie got new sneakers.
     Jeffrey found the mitten he lost.
     Ken and Donnie finally finished their huge block building.
     The bus driver won a lottery.
     The teacher's assistant passed her CDA.
     Michelle got a new dress.

     How would you have responded to these happenings? As a behavior model, you need to show the children that you care deeply about their successes as well as their troubles. Hug the children, exclaim over them, shake their hands, and laugh and dance around the room if this is appropriate. When children do the same to show their delight in someone else's success, make a point of thanking them for showing someone their pleasure. Celebrate happy occasions. Make your center one that rejoices in the good fortunes of its members.

We do not need to be like some newspapers that feature only bad news. Look for the good things that happen to individuals, and help your children to share in the other person's pleasure by showing him they are happy for him.

Researchers looking at prosocial behavior in preschoolers report that friendly behaviors, in fact, occur more frequently than aggressive behaviors among peers in the group, and that friendly interactions increase at a faster rate than aggressive behavior during the preschool years, especially among the older children (Moore, p. 76).

If You Have Not Checked This Item: Some Helpful Ideas

▪ *Look for Reasons to Rejoice about Individual's Happiness*

Make a list of the good things that have happened to people in your center. Make sure you model the prosocial behavior of rejoicing with the person yourself. Then, invite individual children to do the same.

▪ *Talk about Successes during Circle Time*

Ask children to report on the nice things that have happened to people they know during group time. Start a ritual of going up to one of the children in the circle and shaking his or her hand in congratulations for anything positive that has happened to him or her or in his or her family.

☐ SHARES SOMETHING WITH ANOTHER

Sharing and helping may be the easiest prosocial behaviors for young children to learn because these behaviors involve physical objects as well as feelings. These two prosocial behaviors occur most frequently in the early childhood classroom, which is understandable when you consider the many opportunities children in a group have to learn to share materials with one another. Sharing also is easier to do than some of the other prosocial acts because the child only suffers a temporary loss. The youngster must give up something, but only temporarily.

Again, the child's ability to perform such an action depends upon her cognitive maturity as well as the lessons she has learned from those around her. The younger the child, the more inclined she is to consider the toy she is playing with as her personal possession, whether it is or not. Children still retaining this egocentric view also will try to take the toys they want away from others, and they will be upset if the others do not comply. The fact that these egocentric children want the toy makes it theirs, according to their reasoning.

William Damon's study of the development of a child's sense of justice involved findings about what children considered to be fair in sharing or dividing up candy. The younger children (ages four and five) gave themselves more candy than the older children did. A scale that Damon derived to indicate children's levels of positive justice showed children age four and under justifying their choices simply on the basis of their wishes: that they should get something because they want it.

Children at the second level of the scale (ages four and five) justified their actions on the basis of their size, gender, or whatever characteristic would get them the most. The next level of children (those ages five through seven) preferred to share equally in order to prevent squabbles. Older children must realize that preserving the peace is more important than getting an extra piece of candy. (Damon, p. 136)

In order to prevent squabbles, early childhood teachers need to establish rules governing "property rights" at the outset. When children first enter the classroom, they are confronted with a treasure house of materials to enjoy. The youngsters need to understand that these materials belong to the center, not to specific children. Individuals can use the materials, but the items must be shared, which means letting other children use the items either at the same time (as with paints) or one after another.

Nevertheless, some squabbles over equipment can be expected. The primary way young children learn rules is to test them out. Who gets the favorite toy first? Favorites are often trikes and eggbeaters. Some teachers feel it is best to have several of the favorites in order to avoid problems. Other teachers believe that such problems afford good opportunities for children to learn how to share and take turns.

Researchers find that older children are more likely to share than younger ones. Sharing with peers, in fact, increases dramatically between the ages of four and twelve (Damon, p. 128). If a toy belongs to the center, young children are more likely to share the item than if it belongs to them personally. Most teachers ask children to keep toys from home in their cubbies. The youngsters can show the toys to the class at circle time, but afterwards, the toys must be put away until time to go home.

Because sharing is such an important prosocial skill in the preschool center, everyone must spend time helping individuals to learn the skill. You may want to start by observing the prosocial behavior of every child in your class to see which children already know how to share and which ones may need help in learning this skill. Some children will share toys, food, turns when asked by another child, but many still need the teacher to make the request.

If You Have Not Checked This Item: Some Helpful Ideas

- *Model Sharing Yourself*

Sharing is one of children's behaviors that is definitely influenced by adult modeling behavior. Adults often ask children to share with their peers, but how often do adults ask a child to share with them? Try it. Set up a situation where a child who has had difficulty in sharing must share a seat, a piece of equipment, or an activity with you. For example, invite him to paint at your table. Then, set out one jar of paint that the two of you must share. Verbalize as you work on your painting. Let the child know he is doing well in sharing the paints.

- *Use Group Toys*

Encourage a small group of two, three, or four children to construct a building using one set of Lego building blocks. Have several children work on a large puzzle together.

Using a "group" toy together teaches children how to share.

- *Set Up a Food-Sharing Experience*

Bring in one apple, one orange, or one melon for each small group at your snack tables. Discuss with the children how they can share the piece of fruit. Let them help you divide it equally.

☐ GIVES SOMETHING OF HIS/HER OWN TO ANOTHER

Generosity

A great deal of research has been done on this aspect of prosocial behavior, perhaps because researchers easily can measure whether or not children are willing to give a possession to someone else. Most studies show that as children increase in age, their generosity also increases. The reason behind this finding, however, is not so clear.

We assume that as children become cognitively more mature, they will be less concerned with themselves as the center of everything, and they will be more aware of others and others' needs. We also expect that as children grow older, they will have more experiences with social customs through the teachings of their family, friends, school, and church. In other words, the children will have learned how society expects them to behave.

But, other things affect young children's giving. Length of ownership is one. Children seem more willing to give up a possession they have had awhile than something they just have obtained (Smith, p. 210). Perhaps the novelty eventually wears off.

The item they are giving also makes a difference. It may be a toy, an item of food, a piece of candy, or money. Whether the children have more of the same item also makes a difference. Reasons for the giving have a bearing too. Is the item given out of friendship, because someone asks, because someone has a need, or because an adult suggests that it might be a nice thing to do? Older children are more apt to respond to adult suggestions or pressure.

Children are more likely to share a favorite toy rather than to give it up totally. Formal occasions for giving such as birthdays or religious holidays teach children about giving. The child's egocentric nature often shows itself when he or she wants to give mom a toy truck or doll for her birthday.

Teaching generosity, however, is tricky in our society. People send children mixed messages. Adults tell children it is a good idea to give to people in need, but then, the youngsters see those same adults turn away charity solicitors at the front door. Children hear adults refuse to lend a lawn mower or power tool to a neighbor who has a need. "Let him buy his own," the adults say, "Let him work as hard as we did to buy this one."

We have a very material-possession-oriented culture. Children learn this from television and adult responses to television messages. And children witness how strongly we adults feel about our cars, stereos, and microwave ovens.

Not all cultures value personal material possessions so highly. People of many Pacific islands, for instance, teach their children from the start that giving is more important than possessing. These people practice what they preach by simply giving a possession to a neighbor or relative who admires or needs it. The people feel that they are enhanced when the person accepts something from them.

Nevertheless, as preschool teachers we need to be aware of how this prosocial behavior works with the children in our classroom, regardless of our society's confusion over the issue. Use the *Child Skills Checklist* to determine which children will give a possession to someone else. Are these the same children you have checked on the other prosocial behaviors? What other characteristics do the children share? Have the youngsters been given a great deal of responsibility in their families? Prosocial behavior such as generosity often is more evident in such children. Are they children who seem more mature in all areas of development? We know that generosity increases with age and maturity.

If You Have Not Checked This Item: Some Helpful Ideas

- *Be a Model of Generosity*

Let children see you give something of yours to someone in need: an item of clothing, a book, food, or money. How do you feel about this? In our society, we often are reluctant as adults to begin this kind of giving ourselves. We have been conditioned to acquire material possessions and to guard against losing them. Will the giving get out of hand? Will people take advantage of us? How genuine is your own generosity?

- *Articulate Generosity*

When situations arise where giving is appropriate, talk to your children about it. Maybe they could donate some money or services to help someone in need.

- *Read Books about Giving*

Louie by Ezra Jack Keats. New York: Scholastic Book Services, 1975, tells about the little nonverbal boy Louie who says his first words at a puppet show put on by neighborhood children when he becomes entranced by the doll puppet Gussie. Louie grabs Gussie at the end of the show, but the children convince him to give her up because she has to go to her own home. Later, Louie's mother tells him someone has left him a note which tells him to follow a long green string. At the end of the string, Louie finds Gussie waiting for him. The children evidently had a change of heart when they saw someone who needed the puppet more than they did. Ask the children in your classroom how they feel about this story. Would they have done the same thing?

Tico and the Golden Wings by Leo Lionni. New York: Pantheon Books, 1964, tells a folktale-like story of a little bird in India that is born without wings and lives without them until a wishingbird grants his wish and gives him a pair of golden wings. But, Tico learns that he can never be happy until he gives away all of the golden feathers one by one to people in need.

Our country's books reflect our values. Very few of today's children's books present stories about generosity and giving like the two books mentioned previously. Many, many more books focus on themes of individual children striving and trying to accomplish things on their own.

☐ TAKES TURNS WITH TOYS OR ACTIVITIES

☐ WAITS FOR TURN WITHOUT A FUSS

These two items reflect a different aspect of generosity: alternating the use of toys, equipment, or activities with other children, and taking turns with patience. Opportunities for learning and practicing these prosocial behaviors occur much more frequently in the early childhood classroom than occasions for giving. In order to maintain a smoothly running program, you must help children learn at the outset how to take turns and wait their turns in the group situation.

Those children with brothers and sisters at home may have learned this behavior already; although, sometimes, the children may have learned inappropriate behavior such as the biggest or strongest gets the first turn. Research also has shown that authoritarian parents do not necessarily help children to learn this prosocial behavior. When parents strictly control their children's actions, the children have less motivation and fewer opportunities to develop moral reasoning and turn-taking on their own (Eisenberg, p. 854).

In order to grow from an egocentric being, whose only concern is satisfying his own wants, to someone who understands the wants of others, the young child must learn to see things from another person's perspective, as previously mentioned. To do this, the child needs the freedom to be able to function on his own in an open environment. His parents can support this development best by helping him to understand the views of others and by encouraging him to participate in decision making about his own behavior. Following the dictates of authoritarian parents gives him little opportunity to develop these skills.

For the young child, warm, supportive mothering also makes a difference in the development of prosocial behaviors. As children move into elementary school, the best support they can have at home is a nonauthoritarian mother who allows and encourages her children to act on their own.

Children can regulate their own numbers during free play if the environment is arranged so that they understand its use.

But, in the preschool, the children must learn to take turns and wait for turns. You can help the children most by setting up the environment so that it speaks to these needs. Arrange activity areas for three, four, or five children at the most, and put signs or symbols for these numbers in every area. Then, children can regulate their own numbers during free play. Let the children take tags to hang on hooks or pegboards, tickets to put in pockets mounted on the wall, or their pictures covered with clear contact paper to hang in the area where they want to work.

Many centers start the day with a circle time. During this time, the teacher lets the class know what activities are available, and the children choose activities by taking tags. If a child finishes playing in her chosen area before free choice time is over, then another child can pick up the tag and take his own turn. This is how children learn about taking turns and waiting their turn.

But, the teacher must let the children learn on their own. Directing individuals into particular areas is the same as the authoritarian parent telling his or her children what to do. If we want children to develop prosocial behaviors, the youngsters must be allowed to experiment with turn-taking alone.

Giving children this freedom takes forbearance on the part of the preschool staff. It is so much easier for adults to make choices for children. After all, children take so long to make up their minds, and allowing many children this freedom creates confusion. But, we must remember the purpose of the free choice period in the first place: to allow children to learn how to make their own decisions based on their own interests and needs, and how to deal with the consequences of their choices. Through freedom of choice, children also learn that another child may have the same choice as theirs, and that they may have to wait before their choice is available.

Children also learn by using timing tools such as a kitchen timer or three-minute hourglass when several children want turns using favorite toys or equipment. One child can hold the timer while another uses the toy for three minutes. When it is the next child's turn, the child after her gets to hold the timer. Some children enjoy controlling the timer as much as playing with the toy!

If You Have Not Checked This Item: Some Helpful Ideas

- *Have Children Practice Turn-Taking in Dramatic Play*

Set up a particular play area such as beauty shop or barber shop, and put out two or three chairs for the customers. Then, the children will have to wait their turn just as in real life. Or set up a bakery shop or other facility where people must take tickets to be waited on. Have tickets available for the children to take. Perhaps one child could be the ticket taker. Set up a traffic light in the classroom for the children to use in their big truck play. The light can be a cardboard milk carton with holes cut out and covered with clear food wrapping paper colored red, yellow, and green. Not only will children learn safety rules, but they also will realize that cars and people must wait their turns before using the road at a street crossing.

- *Bring in a Special Plaything or Activity to Teach Turn-Taking*

Introduce a new toy at circle time, and have the children help set up the rules for playing with it, such as the number of people who can use the toy at once and for how long. The children may want to use the kitchen timer you have provided to keep track of the time. One child surely will want to keep the time. The teacher also can help children sign up for turns on a chart if this method seems better. Timers also work well with other favorite center toys such as trikes and tape recorders.

- *Read Books about Taking Turns*

Everybody Takes Turn by Dorothy Corey. Chicago: Albert Whitman & Company, 1980, is a book of similar pictures on two pages showing first one child, then another taking turns. A simple line of text tells whose turn it is.

☐ HELPS ANOTHER DO A TASK

Along with sharing, helping another do a task is by far the most common prosocial behavior exhibited in the preschool classroom, possibly because this behavior is much less of a cognitive act. Children simply assist someone in doing a task. They may be asked or they may volunteer to help when they see that a peer or the teacher needs assistance with something. The children do not need to understand or intellectualize about what is happening. They do not need to take another person's perspective. They just need to lend a hand, so to speak. Most children already have learned this activity at home, and they soon realize that the early childhood classroom also expects children to help out.

Research shows that this behavior may occur three times more than any other prosocial act. Even so, helping others to do a task is not all that frequent in proportion to other behaviors. Seeking help occurs about six times more frequently than giving help among three-year-olds (Moore, p. 77). But, as children grow and develop through the early childhood years, helping behavior increases. Whereas slightly more than half of the youngest children assessed in one study (three-year-olds) gave some form of help, 100 per cent of children nine and ten years old provided assistance (Smith, p. 216).

The youngest preschoolers, nevertheless, may have some problems with helping. The youngsters may not know when to help or how much help to give. Sometimes, children overdo their help, becoming bossy and not knowing when to stop. Other times, children do not help enough and simply stand around watching before the task is finished. The best way for them to learn the cues for appropriateness in such social behavior is to plunge in and to try various responses. Other children are not shy about telling peers what those peers are doing wrong.

You, on the other hand, need to set up activities that require children to give assistance. Setting tables for snack and lunch, getting out cots or mats for naptime, getting out paints and mixing them, filling the water table, feeding the pets, and helping with cleanup are a few activities that will involve children in helping. These tasks are multiple learning situations for cognitive concepts as well as for learning when and how to help.

Children may have favorite chores as well as chores they try to avoid. Making up a "helpers" chart gives every child a chance at doing every chore. Let the children help design the chart. It can contain pictures as well as titles for every job. Children can hang their name tags on the chart daily during circle time or once a week. New jobs can be added from time to time as needed. Use your creativity to invent the jobs. A few jobs you may want to include are

Mail carrier: delivers notes to office
Zoo keeper: takes care of pets
Aquarium attendant: feeds fish
Door attendant: opens and closes door
Chef: helps prepare snack
Waiter/Waitress: sets tables
Gardener: waters plants

You cannot expect young children to do all the work in the classroom. Picking up blocks in the block corner is a case in point. One or two children easily can empty the shelves in building a complicated construction. Putting all the blocks back in proper order during cleanup time may be an overwhelming chore for two. A teacher should get down on the floor with the children and lend her assistance, just as the children help her from time to time.

If children are not helping at all, you need to engage them in chores. Chores do not need to be drudgery. Children enjoy doing grown-up things. Youngsters have no idea that pickup is any less interesting than getting toys out, unless adults make pickup seem "less glamorous." In fact, you should make cleanup in your room a fun thing to do.

If You Have Not Checked This Item: Some Helpful Ideas

- *Invite a Helper to Your Class on a Weekly Basis*

Anyone engaged in an occupation is a helper. Perhaps a different parent could visit the classroom on a weekly basis to talk to the children about how he or she helps.

One class created a new job on its helpers chart each week after the "helper" had visited. Sometimes, the children had to stretch their imaginations. After a telephone lineman visited the children, they finally decided to add the job "telephone attendant" in which one child every day would be allowed to answer the classroom phone.

- *Use Games for Pickup and Cleanup*

Block shelves fill up much easier when they are hungry monsters waiting to be fed by the children or when the children do pickup to music, trying to finish before the record is over. Long blocks can be bulldozers pushing the blocks or toys over to the shelves. Have your children help you think up other pretend games at cleanup time.

• *Read a Helper Story*

Herman the Helper by Robert Kraus, New York: Windmill Books, 1974, tells the colorful underwater story of Herman the little octopus who helps his mother, father, brothers and sisters, friends, enemies, and finally himself.

☐ HELPS ANOTHER IN NEED

This particular behavior is perhaps the most difficult prosocial skill for young children to attain. Helping another in need is an extension of the first item, "shows concern for someone in distress." Whereas showing concern involved "compassion," a psychological support, helping another in need involves "caretaking" or "giving nurturance," a physical act of giving help. The help may consist of giving affection (hugging, touching), positive attention (getting help, giving help), reassurance (verbalizing support), or protection (standing by, protecting physically).

For young children, giving these things is difficult because the youngsters must first overcome their own anxiety caused by the stressful situation. Then, they must have an understanding of how to act. In emergency situations, even adults often are confused and have difficulty knowing what to do.

Even very young children have been observed taking action when another child or person is in distress, but the instances are rare compared to other prosocial acts. Toddlers have been seen giving their bottles or cuddly toys to siblings who cry in distress. Giving something to the victim of distress seems to be the main response of young children. They more often seek help than give it, however. In addition, those who seek help in the preschool more often approach adults than peers, although older preschoolers begin to turn to their companions for help.

Crying or uttering distressful sounds is supposed to trigger an empathic response in others, according to psychologists. Scientists look to the animal world and note the intricacies of response in many species. Have we humans lost much of this seemingly instinctive concern? We read in the news or see on television the instances of adults ignoring victims who call for help. Much of this inattention seems to be a defensive reaction on the part of people who not only do not want to get involved in the trouble, but also feel they might be victimized themselves.

Can helping be taught to children? Studies show that children can learn helping behaviors in pretend or symbolic situations, but when a real circumstance occurs, the youngsters still may not respond. Children with nurturant caregivers do give more help and do express more sympathy. So, it seems that modeling behavior does promote prosocial helping. (Yarrow, p. 254)

What kinds of situations that call for help might occur in the classroom? Injury is one situation. Children or adults may fall and hurt themselves, cut themselves, or burn themselves. Losing something is another happening that requires help. Children may lose mittens, money, or a toy. Accidental damage also necessitates assistance. Children may spill paint on themselves, fall in the mud, or spill milk or other food. They may drop and break a dish, a record, or a toy.

How can children help? Depending upon the situation, they could go for help if an adult is not in the immediate vicinity. They could comfort the victim by talking or touching. They could help pick up spilled things, look for lost things, or give information to help the adult solve the problem.

Children are more likely to give help to others when with someone. Teachers should take advantage of this by involving the children in helping situations whenever possible, rather than doing all the helping themselves. When children are involved on their own, teachers should step back and allow the youngsters to do what they can.

If You Have Not Checked This Item: Some Helpful Ideas

• Discuss Helping with the Children

When helping behavior by others occurs, spend time in small and large groups talking to the children about it. Sometimes, television events seen by children are good discussion items.

• Read Books about Helping

The previously mentioned book, *Only One Ant* (p. 115), is good for motivating a discussion about helping. If the children like the story, read it more than once, and see how many solutions they can propose for the various helping situations.

Swimmy by Leo Lionni. New York: Knopf/Pantheon, 1963, is a children's favorite. The book tells about the little black fish Swimmy who helps a school of little fish to swim unafraid like the biggest fish in the sea.

The Mysterious Giant of Barletta by Tomie de Paola, New York: Harcourt Brace Jovanovich, Publishers, 1984, is an Italian folktale about a giant statue in a little town that comes to life and saves the town from an army. Children will enjoy hearing some of the Italian words used and will love the pictures of the huge "colosso" (the mysterious giant). Although the text is long for preschoolers, teachers can "read" the pictures.

Now One Foot, Now the Other by Tomie de Paola, New York: G.P. Putnam's Sons, 1981, is a touching story of Bobby and his Grandfather Bob, who has a stroke. Bobby never gives up hope that his grandfather will recover—even after his parents do—and finally finds a way to help his grandfather walk and talk again, just as his grandfather had helped him when he was little.

• When You Model Helping Behavior, Talk about It

You will help children all year long. Talk about what you are doing with the children, and help them find ways to assist you.

- *Encourage Children to Help One Another*

If a child needs a shoe tied or a coat zipped, ask another child to help.

REFERENCES CITED

Damon, William. *Social and Personality Development.* New York: W.W. Norton & Company, 1983.

Eisenberg, Nancy, et al. "Prosocial Development: A Longitudinal Study," *Developmental Psychology* 19, no. 6 (1983): 846–55.

Moore, Shirley G. "Prosocial Behavior in the Early Years: Parent and Peer Influences," in Bernard Spodek (ed.), *Handbook of Research in Early Childhood Education.* New York: The Free Press, 1982.

Smith, Charles A. *Promoting Social Development of Young Children: Strategies and Activities.* Palo Alto, Calif.: Mayfield Publishing, 1982.

Yarrow, Marian Radke, et al. "Learning Concern for Others," *Developmental Psychology* 8, no. 2 (1973): 240–60.

OTHER SOURCES

Lickona, Thomas. *Raising Good Children.* New York: Bantam Books, 1983.

Webb, Roger A. (ed.) *Social Development in Childhood: Day Care Programs and Research.* Baltimore: The Johns Hopkins University Press, 1977.

LEARNING ACTIVITIES

1. Use the *Child Skills Checklist,* "4. Prosocial Behavior," as a screening tool to observe all of the children in your classroom. Which ones demonstrate the most prosocial behavior? Do they also have friends in the class? Which children show few of the prosocial skills? How do these children get along with the other children in general?

2. Choose a child who exhibits few of the prosocial skills. Do a running record of the child on three different days to determine how he or she works and plays with the others. Do an activity with the child to help him or her share, take turns, or help. Record the results.

3. Choose a child who is a good helper, and try to involve him or her in getting another child to participate in helping. Discuss the results.

4. Try two of the ideas under "If You Have Not Checked This Item . . ." with a child who shows few prosocial skills. Discuss the results.

5. Read one of the children's books from this chapter with a group of children, or do an activity with a group to promote prosocial skills. Discuss the results.

6 Large Motor Development

Large Motor Development Checklist

- [ ] Walks down steps alternating feet
- [ ] Runs with control over speed and direction
- [ ] Jumps over obstacle, landing on two feet
- [ ] Hops forward on one foot
- [ ] Pedals and steers tricycle
- [ ] Climbs up and down climbing equipment with ease
- [ ] Throws object overhand to target
- [ ] Catches thrown object with hands

P hysical development for young children involves two important areas of motor coordination: movements controlled by the large or gross muscles and motions controlled by the small or fine muscles. This chapter will focus on large motor development, involving movements of the whole body.

Because motor development is an obvious and visible aspect of children's growth, we sometimes take it for granted. Of course, children will grow bigger, stronger, and able to perform more complicated motor tasks as they age. But, do all children really develop these abilities? What about the awkward child who seems to trip over his own feet? What about the child who never can keep up with the others? Is the "accident-prone" child overly eager or underdeveloped? How can we tell, and can we do anything to help such children?

Early childhood caregivers must know that yes, children do develop physically in a predictable sequence of skills that can be observed; that there are individual differences in this growth as well as developmental lags in some children; and that yes, we can do something to help.

First, we need to become familiar with the entire sequence of normal large motor development. We need to know its origins, patterns, and range for individuals. Then, we need to apply this knowledge to the children in order to determine whether they are developing predictably within the normal range, or whether they may need special help. Finally, we should assemble a repertory of activities to help the child who is lagging behind in this development.

MOTOR DEVELOPMENT IN INFANCY

The infant uses motor skills as tools to explore himself and then the world around him. At first, his movements are reflexive or involuntary. He sucks when his mouth touches something. He jumps at a loud noise.

Soon after birth, however, three types of rudimentary movement abilities appear. The nonlocomotor or stability skills involve developing control of the head, neck, trunk, and, eventually, the ability to sit and stand. Manipulative skills involve reaching for, grasping, and releasing. And locomotor skills involve creeping, crawling, and, eventually, walking. (Gallahue, pp. 5–6)

Muscular maturation follows both a predictable sequence and a direction. Large muscle coordination develops before small muscle synchronization. In

129

other words, the infant or young child develops arm movement control before finger control. Development is also *cephalo-caudal* in direction; that is, it begins at the head and progresses to the feet. Control of the head and upper trunk occurs in the infant before control of the legs and feet. Development also occurs in another direction: from close to the trunk out to the extremities, which is called *proximo-distal.* (Allen & Goetz, p. 130)

Many of the infant's first movements are random. He lies on his back in a bassinet or crib and kicks with his legs or waves his arms. Should he happen to strike a mobile or rattle with either arms or legs, he usually will try to repeat the movement to cause the same interesting sound and touch effect. In repeating the movement over and over, he begins to gain control over his muscles, so that the movement eventually will become voluntary and controlled.

His rate of development occurs in a predictable sequence and is related closely to the maturation of his central nervous system, the integrating agent. Even though an infant's motor skills cannot develop until the neuromuscular system is ready, a rich environment filled with stimulating sights, sounds, and people motivates the child to initiate and to continue to practice movements.

Are we saying, then, that the environment and the infant's experience with it can improve his motor development? Yes, when the required maturation level has been reached. If there had not been a mobile in the baby's bassinet, he would not have struck it with his arm and then would not have continued to practice this movement. Even if his neuromuscular system was not mature enough for him to control this movement, then the mobile's presence still might keep him trying until the proper maturity had developed.

Fraiberg's work with blind infants shows the importance of such environmental factors in the development of motor skills. The blind babies developed trunk control and sitting stability within the same time range as sighted children. The blind babies even could support themselves on hands and knees. But, they never learned to creep. They had no visual stimuli (like sighted babies had) to motivate them to move across the floor. Their caregivers had to find other means to stimulate them to attempt locomotion. (Schickedanz, p. 146)

This is one of several studies that has proved the importance of sensory stimuli, especially sight, sound, and touch, in the development of large motor skills. We also know that caring adults must interact with infants from the beginning; adults must encourage, support, and praise children for the accomplishment of motor skills, as adults do for all aspects of children's development.

Because this encouragement, support, and praise tends to happen almost automatically in most families, we seem to think infants and young children develop these skills on their own with little support from adults or the environment. A look at infants and children in institutions where little or no human or material support was offered, in fact, proves otherwise. Hunt and several other American psychologists visited orphanages in Iran that had an infant-caregiver ratio of 40-to-3, where many of the two-year-olds could not sit up, and where most of those children in their fourth year could not walk alone yet! (Pines, p. 59) The quality of early child care does indeed make a difference.

The range for mastery of a particular skill varies from one month to four-to-six months in young children. Developmental delays may result when early reflexive movements somehow fail to become integrated into higher level voluntary movements. (Allen and Goetz, p. 131) Birth defects, handicapping conditions, certain illnesses or injuries, or neglect may cause this lack of integration. Children whose early movement patterns have not become integrated into voluntary responses either do not learn the higher level skills or learn to compensate in some atypical manner.

Large motor skills, then, play an important part in the infant's learning first about himself by moving his body parts, and then about his world as he responds physically to the people and materials around him. His environment plays an important role, as well, in stimulating this development. He gains more and more independence through the movements he is able to master, and when he finally walks, the world is his to explore.

The eight items under Large Motor Development on the *Child Skills Checklist* are neither a complete list of large motor skills nor a sequence of skills, although one skill may precede the other. Instead, these eight items represent a sample of important motor behaviors that children should have acquired by age five.

It is important to screen all the children in your class at the outset using this or a similar list of skills in order to identify children needing special help. Knowing that large motor development precedes small motor growth, you must help all of your children to be prepared in this first area in order to be successful in the small motor tasks expected of them in the reading and writing soon to come.

☐ WALKS DOWN STEPS ALTERNATING FEET

One-Year-Olds

Walking is the skill that separates the infant from the toddler. It occurs around the end of the first year or the beginning of the second year. The child finally is able to move around in an upright position unaided by people or furniture. This movement gives him a freedom he scarcely can comprehend. Now, he can investigate in a twinkling all those intriguing items in the room that seemed so far away. And he is able to see things from a different perspective altogether: upright.

Try it yourself. Get down on your hands and knees, and look around you. What do you see? Baseboards, table and chair legs, people's shoes. (No wonder shoes are so important to young children!) See something of interest across the room? Try crawling over to it. By the time you arrive, you may have lost much of your interest in the object you sought. Think what walking upright must mean to the child. Suddenly he has a freedom he never knew existed. He can go anywhere that is not blocked off on his own. His eye level reaches a wholly new order of things that, in turn, stimulates increased practice of his new skill.

Beginning walkers are not independent all at once. They still move cautiously and appreciate a helping hand. They do not have the stamina of older children. But, they are on their way. They walk with such a wide stance that some child care workers call them "waddlers," and older more balanced walkers "toddlers." The children's wide stance helps them balance and offsets their top-heavy trunk. As their legs grow longer and their balance improves, they will not have to waddle to move forward without falling. They use their arms to balance themselves, as well, and they do not swing their arms as mature walkers do.

Two-Year-Olds

Two-year-olds, on the other hand, do not need to pay so much attention to balance and can concentrate more on toddling along. They still monitor their walking to some extent and may stop for obstacles, but a quick stop seldom brings them down on their seats like when they were age one. Beginning two-year-olds should be able to walk upstairs alone placing both feet on a step, and they love to do it. By age two-and-a-half, they desperately strive for independence in their locomotion (remember the "terrible two's"?), but they still need supervision because of their disregard for safety. Older two-year-olds may be able to alternate feet going upstairs, but they still walk down two feet on a step.

Three-Year-Olds

Three-year-olds walk in adult fashion. Their trunk is no longer top-heavy, and they have mastered walking to the extent that they no longer need to watch their feet or balance with their arms. They swing their arms as they walk, just like adults. They still may fall occasionally on uneven ground, but they are not so far from the ground that falling hurts too much. Now, they can walk upstairs alternating feet unaided, although most three-year-olds put two feet on a step coming down. The balance of some children this age is good enough to allow them to walk a straight line, one foot in front of the other.

Although growth occurs in a predictable chronological sequence, it seems to happen in spurts. It seems almost as if the body has to stop and assimilate all the development that has occurred before going forward again. This "assimilation stop" often happens at the half-year age. Children who walked and ran smoothly at age three may seem to have a "relapse" at age three-and-a-half. They suddenly act uncertain with their large motor skills and even may seek the hand of an adult as they walk along, especially going up or down stairs. They may have good days when everything about their bodies seems to work well, and bad days when they stumble and fall. (Caplan, p. 177)

Four-Year-Olds

Four-year-olds have control of and take great pleasure in using their bodies. Children age four can walk confidently in many ways: forward, backward, sideways, tiptoeing, or striding along. They are able to walk a circular line for the first time without losing their balance. Most can walk both up and down stairs alternat-

Three- and four-year-olds get practice stepping up and down on stools and platforms as well as on stairs.

ing their feet. Although their skipping is not at all perfected (most can do it only with one foot), some start to roller skate.

Four is an age of great exuberance and expansiveness. If you do not provide enough walking, running, and climbing activities in your center, four-year-olds may make their own. They definitely need an opportunity to practice their large motor skills both inside and outside.

Five-Year-olds

Five-year-olds are at the adult stage in walking. This is another period of great growth when children spurt up as much as two or three inches in a year. Much of this growth occurs in the legs, which lengthen more quickly than the other body parts. Boys may be a bit taller and heavier than girls, but they are about a year behind the girls in physiological development. (Caplan, p. 237)

Children this age can walk a straight line for about ten feet without stepping off it. Most can skip with alternating feet now. Even the less active five-year-olds now can walk down stairs alternating feet. They can keep time to music with their feet and may enjoy dancing. Five-year-olds are less expansive and more controlled than four-year-olds in all of their actions, but children age five still love to use their large motor abilities in play.

If You Have Not Checked This Item: Some Helpful Ideas

- *Practice Walking*

Studies show that children between the ages of two and six demonstrate observable improvement in basic motor patterns after repeated performance with adult encouragement. Instruction in the movement does not seem to help, but practice does. (Flinchum, p. 28)

Play follow-the-leader in the classroom and outside with yourself as the leader who sets the pace. Do all kinds of walking motions, and be sure everyone has a chance to copy you before you change to the next movement. March, shuffle, stride, giant-step, tiptoe, bunny hop, and skate.

Set up a walking-hopping-sliding trail in your classroom or large motor room with contact footprints stuck to the floor in various patterns of movement that involve both one foot and two.

- *Practice Step Climbing*

If your room is at ground level in a building with a second story, make it a practice to take children up and down the stairs every day. If you have no stairs, go for a field trip to a building that does have stairs, or get a rocking-boat-steps piece of large motor equipment for the children to practice on. Some playground equipment also has stairs, but ladders are not the same.

- *Walk to Music or Other Rhythms*

Play different records or pieces of music with different rhythms, and have your children try to walk around the room keeping time. Have them walk to the rhythm of hand claps or drum beats. Speed up and slow down the claps or beats; make syncopated sounds.

- *Walk to Chants or Poems*

Read some of the animal verses from Clare Cherry's *Creative Movement for the Developing Child*, Belmont, Calif.: Fearon Publishers, 1971, and have the children imitate the way the particular animals walk.

Bring in animal pictures and discuss how the animals walk. Let the children make up simple verses about rabbits hopping or deer moving silently through the trees. Let the children demonstrate.

Read the book *Just Suppose* by May Garelick, New York: Scholastic Book Services, 1969, and have the children pretend to move like the animals described.

- *Play Charades*

Have two or three children demonstrate how an animal walks, and let the others guess what animal it is.

☐ RUNS WITH CONTROL OVER SPEED AND DIRECTION

Running may be the large motor skill you think of when you consider young children. They seem to be perpetual motion machines. You suspect running is the principal method of movement for some children. But, others run somewhat awkwardly, and they spend much less time running than the rest of your children.

What should you expect of the two-, three-, four-, and five-year-olds in your program? As with walking, you will need to know the whole range of development for this skill before you can decide where each of your children stands and how you best can help.

Two-Year-Olds

Running involves moving forward with some rapidity by placing one foot in front of the other, in which there is a brief period of no contact with the running surface. Although one-year-olds move quite rapidly in a hurried sort of walk (which some people may call a run), they maintain contact with the surface at all times. The true, unsupported run does not occur usually until sometime between the second and third year (Gallahue, p. 25).

A two-year-old's running is not as smooth as it will be at age three. A two-year-old still has short legs and a top-heavy trunk. He runs rather stiffly and has trouble with turning corners and with coming to a quick halt. This difficulty does not stop him from using this newfound skill, however. Two-year-olds in the classroom seem like a lively bunch of young puppies scampering here and there, squealing, and giggling. Because they cannot control their stops easily, two-year-olds are forever bumping into things or each other and falling. They quickly pick themselves up and are off again without a backward glance.

Teachers should provide time and space in the classroom not only for allowing two-year-olds to practice running, but also for giving these human dynamos a chance to let off steam. Otherwise, you may have great difficulty controlling these children for any length of time.

Three-Year-Olds

Running is much smoother for three-year-olds. Their body proportions have grown and changed from a top-heavy appearance. Their legs are now longer and more coordinated in their movements. They have more control over starting and stopping than two-year-olds, but they still have not mastered this skill completely. Since their large motor skills are so much more automatic, they can abandon themselves to the pure enjoyment of running.

Then, at about age three-and-a-half, many children go through an awkward stage where some of the smoothness of their large motor movements seems to disappear. Teachers need to be aware of these "disequilibrium" times in order to support the child during his "bad days," knowing he will return to his smoothness of motion sometime soon. (See p. 132.)

Such children should not be confused with the truly awkward child.

Cratty's studies have found most so-called "awkward" children are boys who seem to show a development delay in motor coordination. These boys exhibit an exaggerated awkward behavior. Some of this behavior may be the result of "learned helplessness" obtained possibly from parents who overreact to their children's every little problem. (Cratty, p. 36) On the other hand, the physical awkwardness of these boys may be more in the eye of the beholder, especially if a teacher compares them with the best-coordinated boys in the class.

A wide range of individual differences exists regarding physical development, as in every other aspect of development. Some children simply will never be highly coordinated. Others may grow up to be professional athletes. The sensitive teacher needs to work with each child, encouraging and supporting him to accomplish all he is capable of. Pressure and ridicule simply have no place in the early childhood classroom. The teacher needs to find interesting motor activities in which the awkward child can succeed, and to avoid those activities that pit one child against another in competition.

Can awkward children be helped? Whether they can be assisted seems to depend upon their age and the severity of their problem (Cratty, p. 37). Providing a wide range of interesting motor activities that are fun to participate in seems to be the best answer. Three-year-olds are at an ideal age to begin such a program. And because some so-called awkward children are simply beginners at the activity or half-year children having a "relapse" (See p. 132.), it is useless to label them as abnormal. Children are children; they are all different in looks, likes, and abilities. Each of them needs your special affection and support as he or she progresses through the sometimes rocky road of physical development.

You need to be aware of these ages and stages as they apply to your children, nevertheless. Take time to visit this year's class next year; you may see some surprises. The awkward boy then may be the best runner around. The sedentary girl who would never join in then may be the leader of the physical activities. A year makes such a difference in the development of young children.

Four-Year-Olds

Expansive four-year-olds are good runners. Their movements are strong, efficient, and speedy. They can start and stop without difficulty, and they like to zoom around corners. They seem to know what their bodies can do and to enjoy putting their bodies through the paces. Give them space and time to run.

Some four-year-olds are labeled "hyperactive" because they never seem to stop. Be careful of such labels. Only a doctor can diagnose this condition of hyperkinesis. Some children are just more active than others, often wearing out parents and teachers in the process. Sometimes during their children's age of four period, with its characteristic exuberance and surplus energy, parents worry most about hyperactivity. Surely, these parents reason, a way exists to slow down such children. Maybe the doctor will put these children on drugs.

Using drugs to combat so-called hyperactivity is a very serious decision to make for such young children in our overmedicated, drug-dependent society. Really active children probably always have been that way, but as four-year-olds, their activity seems exaggerated. You may want more than one medical opinion before deciding what to do. True hyperactivity is sometimes difficult to distinguish from the normal surplus energy of an active four-year-old.

Five-Year-Olds

As mentioned previously, five-year-olds seem to spurt up in height, mostly in their legs. They are more mature runners than four-year-olds, and many of them love to join in games that test their abilities. Their speed and control has increased, and they seldom fall when running across uneven surfaces, like four-year-olds some-times do. Their running games, like the rest of their actions, usually are not as noisy and out-of-bounds as the running games of four-year-olds.

If You Have Not Checked This Item: Some Helpful Ideas

- *Use Simple Running Games*

Preschool running games should not be competitive. The awkward child may give up trying if he or she is always last. Instead, simple circle games should be used to strengthen running skills. Old classics like "Duck, Duck, Goose" are still favorites of three- and four-year-olds as they walk around the outside of the circle and tap someone who then chases them around to the empty space. No one wins or loses. Games-with-rules often are too complicated for preschoolers, who learn to make the right responses and enjoy the running in simple games like "Duck, Duck, Goose."

- *Employ Directed Running*

You can make up all kinds of inside and outside running activities. For instance, one child at a time can run to the tree and back until all have had a turn. Make the activity more complicated by having the children follow a second direction: Run to the tree; run around it once, and then, run back.

- *Have the Children Run to Music*

Get the children running to music in the large motor area. Have them run fast or slow, loudly or quietly, according to the music.

- *Involve the Children in Running to Chants*

Young children need to run. If you do not have the inside space, or if the weather outside is bad, then have them run and hop in place to a simple chant you have made up, like

> *I'm a kangaroo-roo-roo*
> *See me run-run-run*
> *Have some fun-fun-fun*
> *In the sun-sun-sun*
> *Watch me hop-hop-hop*

Never stop-stop-stop
Then I run-run-run
In the sun-sun-sun

- *Try Imaginative Running*

Let the children pretend to be cowboys riding their horses or jet planes going down the runway. Have them pretend to be animals that run, such as deer or dogs. Put up pictures of animals that run, and have the children imitate them.

☐ JUMPS OVER OBSTACLE, LANDING ON TWO FEET

Jumping is a skill that involves taking off with one or two feet and landing on both feet. Jumping is sometimes confused with leaping, which involves taking off on one foot and landing on the other, or hopping, which is done all on the same foot. The *Checklist* item mentions "landing on two feet," so that observers will not confuse jumping with leaping or hopping. The obstacle you are looking for can be anything—a mark on the floor, a block, a toy, a stick, a low barrier, a book, a rug, or a box—any item the child perceives as something to be jumped over.

Jumping as a large motor skill, however, can be done with the child springing up and landing in the same spot, jumping forward and landing on both feet, jumping from the floor or ground over an obstacle, or jumping from a height such as a step or a chair and landing on the floor.

Two-Year-Olds

Real jumping is not performed by children much before age two. They have to develop some proficiency in walking and running before they can attempt jumping. Their first try around age one-and-a-half may be a sort of hesitation on the bottom step of the stairs and then a bouncing step off with one foot. By age two, the children actually may make their first real jump off the bottom step with two feet.

Also, sometime between ages two and two-and-a-half, many children make their first jumps off the ground with two feet. This takes strength in their lower extremities, which occurs last in children due to the cephalo-caudal direction of development.

Three-Year-Olds

Some children become quite proficient jumpers by age three, but many do not, and we should not expect them to. They must have developed the strength first and then must be encouraged to practice the skill. (Most parents do not encourage their children to jump off steps or from furniture!)

Three-year-olds, though, are becoming more long-legged and coordinated. If they are not too heavy, most probably will be able to do some jumping with practice. In jumping over an obstacle, most children start by leading with one foot. Springing up with both feet simultaneously is more difficult, but possible for some.

Four-Year-Olds

Four-year-olds are much more proficient jumpers, and by age four-and-a-half, most can accomplish any type of jumping: up, down, forward, or over. They may not be able to do a sequence of different actions, though, such as hopping, skipping, and jumping, although they perform some or all of these activities separately. One study showed only forty-two percent of preschool children jump well by age three; whereas, seventy-two percent jump well by age four-and-a-half (Zaichkowsky, p. 39).

Four-year-olds can jump higher up in the air and farther down from higher elevations. The second step from the bottom of the stairs is now their big challenge, one you may want to redirect because of its potential for injury.

Five-Year-Olds

Five-year-olds, of course, are long, high, far jumpers, if they have had practice. Maturity is important, as previously noted, but just as necessary is practice of the skill along with encouragement and praise from adult caregivers. If children have been ridiculed because of their awkwardness or lack of physical accomplishment in the past, then you may have to spend much of your time helping them improve their self-image.

They may not want to try because they have performed so poorly in the past. This may have been due to undeveloped muscular strength and/or coordination, lack of practice, or a half-year "relapse" stage. Now, they need to try again to prove to themselves they really do have physical skills. Have them jump over a line on the floor. If they succeed, draw two parallel lines (or use masking tape). As they become successful, let them separate the tape to wider and wider positions. They can do this on their own in a corner of the room if they do not want an audience in the beginning. Most five-year-olds soon will feel secure enough to jump anywhere.

At this age, jump roping first appears. Girls may try to make this activity their exclusive sport, but teachers can be the rope turners so that every class member who wants to participate can have a turn. Again, do not force the awkward child. Before you introduce a jump rope to five-year-olds, be sure to check out the jumping skills of all the children individually so that no one will be embarrassed in front of peers if he or she tries to jump rope and fails. This failure sometimes happens, and it may prevent a child, especially a boy, from ever putting himself in such an embarrassing situation again, which means he may not participate in group sports in school.

Competition has no place in the early childhood large motor program, as mentioned previously, and neither do total group activities that play up the weaknesses or inabilities of individual children. Total group games such as jump rope seem like such innocent fun, but they are not enjoyable for the awkward child. It is better to let three children at a time play with a small jump rope than to insist that all children try to play with a big jump rope, if one of those children will be embarrassed by his or her lack of ability. Knowing how to handle different children results from observing and recording the large motor abilities of your children before introducing new activities.

If You Have Not Checked This Item: Some Helpful Ideas

- *Work with Individual Children Who Show Poor Skills*

If children are age four and five and still cannot jump, then you should try an activity such as jumping over lines, mentioned under "Five-Year-Olds." If children are age three or younger, you do not need to be so concerned, since jumping may not be well developed yet.

- *Use Chair Jumping*

Have a "chair jumping day" when individuals or small groups get to jump from one of the small chairs in the room, and you measure their jumps. Keep a record of each child's jumps on a chart or notebook so individuals can see how well they do each week. Do not measure the results against the others in the class; otherwise, the activity becomes a competition. Let each child try three jumps, for instance, and have a different child be the measurer for each jumper.

You might want to measure with sticks you have color-coded to certain lengths, a yard stick, or a piece of string you mark off and later measure against a ruler. Whether or not you record in inches, centimeters, or merely red sticks will be up to you and the cognitive development level of your children. You do not need to be absolutely exact with the youngest ones. They will be delighted to find they jumped for two red sticks and a blue stick the first time, and for three red sticks the second time.

It is probably good to have a special chair that you cover with contact paper to keep the seat from being scratched. Let the children know that this is the only "jumping chair," and put it away when not in use.

- *Try Concept Jumping*

When children are learning the concepts "up," "down," "over," "forward," and "in place," you might try having the youngsters act out the motions by jumping. Ask the others to guess what kind of jump a child made, or let one child call out a concept and another child try to demonstrate it by jumping.

- *Utilize Jumping Animals*

Put pictures of jumping (leaping, or hopping) animals on the walls at child eye level, and have the children try to imitate the animals. Use photos of the kangaroo, kangaroo rat, frog, toad, rabbit, deer, and Mexican jumping bean, for example.

Have a "Mexican Jumping Bean Day" at your preschool when the children can squat down on the floor completely covered over with cloth squares they have colored (such as old sheets and rice sacks). Play Mexican music, and have the children listen for a "ting" you will make on a triangle or a click on a castanet. At that sound, have your human "beans" pop up in a jump and quickly settle back down until the next signal. Or, you can call out the names of the children one by one for them to jump. This activity works especially well if the children have seen and know what real jumping beans do.

☐ HOPS FORWARD ON ONE FOOT

Hopping is the large motor "bounding" skill in which the child takes off and lands on the same foot. Jumping uses both feet together, while leaping uses alternating feet to take off and land. A child can hop in place or hop forward for one or more steps. This *checklist* item asks you to identify the children in your class who can hop forward (obviously on one foot because they are hopping).

Children need balancing skills before they can hop. They also need the leg length and strength to do jumping first. This means that not many children truly will be hopping before three years of age, and maybe not until age three-and-a-half. In fact, hopping is not well developed in most children before age four.

There are large individual differences in this skill like in other areas of development, but the largest difference can be seen in the genders. Four- and five-year-old girls almost always hop more and better than boys. At first, we may reason that, of course, girls are a bit more physically mature than boys of this same age. Still, someone else may argue that boys generally have a greater proportion of body muscle tissue throughout life than girls.

The truth seems to lie instead in the differences in opportunities and encouragement for hopping between girls and boys. Hopping is a girl's skill in our society. Games such as hopscotch and jump rope, which appear among five- and six-year-olds, are examples. These games are played principally by girls, not boys. Challenge a boy to play hopscotch, and he soon finds that girls his age are much more skilled hoppers, just as the girls are better jump rope jumpers.

There is no reason why a boy could not become skilled at hopping if he practiced. But, until some new hopping challenge appears that appeals to boys, this improvement probably will not occur. Check the children in your class. How do the boys compare with the girls? Ask the children about the hopping games they play at home. Children who play few or no hopping games probably will have great difficulty doing any hopping, whether they are boys or girls.

If You Have Not Checked This Item: Some Helpful Ideas

- *Create a Hopping Trail*

Make a hopping-tiptoeing-walking trail in your classroom or large motor room with cut out contact footprints that show hopping steps on one foot, then walking steps with both feet, then hopping steps on the other foot, tiptoeing, and jumping.

- *Hop to Music*

Find a bouncy but slow record, and let the children try to hop and jump to it. Most four-year-olds will not be able to do more than four or five hops at a time, but the children can change to jumping.

• *Hop to Drum Beats*

Let the children make different movements to different drum beats you play. A one-thump beat can mean to walk, a two-thump beat can signify to hop, and a quick-time beat can indicate to run. See if the children can follow your rhythm. Do not change your beat too quickly since most children are really beginners when it comes to moving to rhythm.

☐ PEDALS AND STEERS TRICYCLE

Using a wheeled vehicle takes both strength and coordination of legs and feet, and with a tricycle, a child must have arm strength and coordination as well. Preschool children must have practice with a tricycle. Many children learn on such equipment at home, but others do not because their parents cannot afford or there is no room for trikes. Your program should find a way to provide all children with such challenging opportunities to put their developing motor skills to use.

Two-year-olds have not reached the stage where their legs are long enough or coordinated enough to pedal. These youngsters may sit on a riding toy and push themselves along, but pedalling usually comes later. By age three, though, most children can learn to pedal a tricycle and even to steer it enough to avoid obstacles.

By age four, they should be riding it smoothly without bumping into things, and with practice, they will soon be able to manipulate U-turns easily. Somewhere between ages five and six, many children are even ready to ride a small bike (Caplan, pp. 232, 266).

If You Have Not Checked This Item: Some Helpful Ideas

• *Provide More Than One Trike*

A tricycle is often the most popular piece of equipment in your center. If you have only one, it will be the focus of many squabbles over turn-taking. It is better to have more than one trike and thus to avoid at least some of the conflicts. Set up a turn-taking system ahead of time. If you use your trikes outside, talk with the children before they go out, and have the youngsters choose what they want to do first on the playground. You can write down their names. Then, all will be aware of who gets to use the trikes first. Use a kitchen timer if there is a waiting list of riders.

Usually, the presence of trikes alone will motivate children to ride. If your observations show you that particular children avoid riding, set up an individual riding opportunity for "new riders" so that they can practice on their own. You might be able to have this "new riders session" in a hall in your building, as long as you supervise.

- *Make a Trike Path*

If your playground is mainly grass, it will be difficult to use trikes unless you have a hard surface path. Sometimes, you can arrange to have a construction company donate to the center the blacktop material left over from a job.

Some Chicago area preschools found an ingenious way to make a trike path: They persuaded several companies to donate old conveyor belts (the kind used to move boxes from trucks into stores). When placed on the grass, the belts were just the right size for trike paths!

☐ CLIMBS UP AND DOWN CLIMBING EQUIPMENT WITH EASE

Climbing, like trike riding, involves use of the arms as well as the legs. Climbing is, in fact, an outgrowth of creeping. Most children begin climbing as soon as they can creep over to an item of furniture and pull themselves up. If they are allowed, they will creep up the stairs. They will try to creep down, too, and soon will find out that a backward descent is the only kind that works!

Climbing induces use of arms as well as legs.

Most two-year-olds are avid climbers. Once they walk upright and are able to see the world from a new perspective, they want to see more. Climbing is their method to see or reach farther. Parents of two-year-olds soon put away all breakables. Some late two-year-olds even will try climbing to the top of a jungle gym, although they cannot climb down.

Many three- and four-year-olds enjoy climbing on all sorts of play equipment and available objects, including jungle gyms, ladders, ladder climbers, dome climbers, slides, rope climbers, trees, rocks, poles, and drain pipes. By the time they are in your program, children this age should be able to climb down as well as up with ease. Remember, though, some children may be going through one of the disequilibrium periods previously mentioned.

Although it takes some bravery in addition to muscle strength and coordination to be a successful climber, many of your children will be able to develop this skill if they have the opportunity. You should consider providing climbing equipment and climbing possibilities both inside and outside your classroom.

Safety factors, of course, should be considered. Since falling is the main concern with climbing, be sure that floor or ground surfaces are cushioned. Padding can be used inside. Sand or wood chips are preferable to grass or hard surfaces outside.

Not all children will attempt to climb. Do not force the reluctant ones. You can encourage, and help children if they try to climb, but if they refuse, they should not be forced to try. Not all children will want to accomplish climbing skills, which is perfectly acceptable. Children have as much right to their own personal choices and interests as adults. Were you a climber when you were age four?

If You Have Not Checked This Item: Some Helpful Ideas

- *Provide a New Piece of Climbing Equipment*

A packing crate (with splintery edges sanded down) is often a tempting piece of climbing equipment that is used either inside or outside. Ladder steps can be fastened to the outside of the crate, if necessary, or children may use a step stool to climb the crate. Cargo netting is also an excellent piece of climbing equipment. Fasten it to a wall inside that has padding underneath or to a horizontal bar outside. A small stepladder also may prove to be useful for climbing in your classroom.

- *Build a Loft*

Lofts not only give preschool children extra space for various new activities, but lofts also provide a new perspective on the activities below. Some lofts use ladders to reach them; others use steps or stairs. Some have several means of entrance. Even nonclimbers often learn to manage all the methods of access because being up in the loft is such fun.

- *Have a Multiple-Access Slide*

A multiple-access slide is perhaps the most valuable piece of large motor equipment you can purchase. With this climbing-sliding device, children have a reason for climbing: to get to the platform at the top of the slide. A multiple-access slide usually has steps, bars, or ladders to help the children climb up, and the youngsters soon know how to use these access tools. A multiple-access slide is an excellent piece of equipment for inside if you have room.

• *Make an Obstacle Course*

Use planks, sawhorses, barrels, ladders, and boxes to create an obstacle course. Rearrange them frequently. Children can climb up, over, and under the objects.

☐ THROWS OBJECT OVERHAND TO TARGET

Throwing and catching are two important upper body large motor skills. Throwing appears first. Although there are several ways to throw, such as overhand, underhand, and sidearm, we are primarily concerned with overhand throwing in early childhood programs.

Throwing appears early in life. Two-year-olds frequently try to throw things such as food or clothing, sometimes in frustration. The throwing action of two-year-olds, however, is more of a jerky, sidearm movement. If they should try to throw a ball, they usually stand facing the target, using both forearms together to sort of push the ball forward. The ball generally dribbles away, almost accidentally.

Photographic studies made of children throwing reveal four distinct patterns in the development of throwing, including

1. Two- and three-year-olds throw mainly with their forearms using little or no footwork or body rotation.
2. Three-and-a-half-year-olds throw with more body rotation and arm range.
3. Five- and six-year-olds start to throw with a forward step on the same side as their throwing arm.
4. Six-and-a-half-year-olds throw maturely, stepping forward with the opposite foot. (Zaichkowsky, p. 40)

The children in your classroom should be able to develop throwing skills to some degree. Three-year-olds can throw without losing their balance. Four-year-olds can begin to use more mature motions. Throwing takes practice, not so much instruction as opportunity. Children have to work out how to throw by themselves as their muscles and coordination mature. Give the youngsters many throwing opportunities in your classroom, and they will do the rest.

What can they throw? Let them try inflated beach balls, yarn balls, sponge balls, Nerf balls, beanbags, clothespins, and even small pillows. Large balls are better than small ones for beginners. Soft or light balls are easier to control than hard balls at first.

Where can the children throw? They can throw to you, to another child, to themselves (play catch), at a target, into a box, into a bottle, or at the wall. They can throw in the classroom or outside. But they need to throw. Neither boys nor girls will develop this skill to a mature degree without practice.

Definite evidence shows that practice counts with this large motor skill. Earlier, our society considered boys to be better throwers than girls. "To throw like a girl," was a derogatory comment often made about boys who threw poorly. It described the immature throwing stance of stepping forward on the same foot as the throwing arm and throwing from the elbow. This phrase does not have to be true.

Now, we know that even grown men in cultures where throwing is not emphasized use the same immature throwing form. On the other hand, many modern girls in our own society do not "throw like a girl." Through early childhood programs like yours as well as early elementary physical education training, girls have had the same experience as boys. Girls' throwing maturity is evident if you watch them perform in any of the Cinderella softball leagues.

Still, you must realize that throwing skills are only at the beginning of their development in the early childhood years. Mature throwing probably will not develop much before age six. You can give it a good start, though, if you offer varied and interesting throwing opportunities to your children.

If You Have Not Checked This Item: Some Helpful Ideas

* *Use Beanbags*

Beanbags are easy to grip, light to throw, and fun to use. Make your own by filling bright cloth squares with beans or rice. Have children throw the beanbags into a box or at a target.

* *Read a Book*

The Mysterious Tadpole by Steven Kellogg, New York: The Dial Press, 1977, tells the story of a little boy whose uncle in Scotland sends him a tadpole for his birthday. The tadpole eventually grows into a Loch Ness Monster, and the boy must find it a place to swim as well as supply it with its favorite food, cheeseburgers.

Children love the story, and you easily can convert it into a beanbag game: Make the monster's green head (an oval) on the outside of a cardboard carton; cut out a large hole for the monster's mouth; and make beanbag "cheese-burgers" out of three cutout circles. To make the beanbags, use two brown circles from supermarket bags or brown cloth and one slightly larger orange circle from orange construction paper or cloth. Sew or staple the circles together, putting the orange one between the two brown ones, and fill the paper or cloth with rice. So you never have heard of paper beanbags? They work. For busy child caregivers who do not sew, paper beanbags are as good as cloth ones.

Even the most reluctant thrower in your class will want to try to feed the "mysterious tadpole" with beanbag cheeseburgers. Have the children stand behind a line not too far from the box at first. Let them throw either overhand or underhand, whichever is easier.

What other books have an animal character the children love and something appropriate that could be thrown?

What about *Harry the Dirty Dog* by Gene Zion? (New York: Harper & Row, 1956). Someone could make a sketch of Harry, mount it on a cardboard backing that would stand up, and place it in an empty plastic wash basin. The children could have fun throwing dry sponges at Harry.

☐ CATCHES THROWN OBJECT WITH HANDS

This last *checklist* item is the most difficult of the large motor skills listed for preschool children to accomplish. In addition to having upper body maturity, children also must possess eye-hand coordination in order to be successful in catching thrown objects with their hands.

Three- and three-and-a-half-year-olds are still at the stage of trying to catch mainly by holding their arms straight out in front of their bodies. They usually only are successful if the ball is large and thrown directly into their arms with little force. Even five-year-olds only catch a chest-high ball sixty to eighty percent of the time. (Cratty, p. 126).

In addition to the necessary practice, this particular skill also requires nervous system maturity. The child is being asked to respond to moving objects of varying speeds. His response time is much slower than that of an older child or adult. Even when he seems to be ready for the ball to arrive in his hands, he may not be able to bring them together in time.

Girls, it seems, are more successful than boys in ball catching, perhaps because they have more mature eye-hand coordination. All children need as much practice in catching as in throwing. You, however, need to be aware that they may not succeed as well in catching because they are not ready developmentally.

If You Have Not Checked This Item: Some Helpful Ideas

• *Throw Large, Soft Objects for Catching*

It is better to start developing catching skills with objects other than balls. You might start by throwing a small, soft pillow to each of the children in a small group and letting them throw it back to you. When you begin to use balls, start with an inflated beach ball. It is large enough and light enough for children to catch with their arms at first and then with their hands. Stand close enough to the children to be able to aim the beach ball accurately. Throwing underhand may make it easier for you to get the beach ball into each child's hands. As individuals' skills improve, you can use sponge balls, yarn balls, and bouncing balls.

TABLE 5. Large motor skills

Age	Walking	Running	Jumping	Pedalling	Climbing	Throwing
Eight months–one year	Walks in a wide stance like a waddle				Climbs onto furniture and up stairs as an outgrowth of creeping	
One–two years	Walks in a toddle and uses arms for balance (Arms are not swung.)	Moves rapidly in a hurried walk, in contact with surface	Uses bouncing step off bottom step of stairs with one foot		Tries climbing up anything climbable	Throws items such as food in a jerky sidearm movement
Two–three years	Walks upstairs two feet on a step	Runs stiffly, has difficulty turning corners and stopping quickly	Jumps off bottom step with both feet	Sits on riding toy and pushes with feet	Tries climbing to top of equipment, although cannot climb down	Throws ball by facing target and using both forearms to push, uses little or no footwork or body rotation
Three–four years	Walks with arms swinging; walks upstairs alternating feet; walks downstairs two feet on step	Runs more smoothly, has more control over starting and stopping	Springs up off floor with both feet in some cases, jumps over object leading with one foot	Pedals and steers tricycle	Climbs up and down ladders, jungle gyms, slides, and trees	Throws overhand with one arm; uses body rotation; does not lose balance
Four–five years	Walks up and down stairs alternating feet; walks circular line; skips with one foot	Displays strong, speedy running; turns corners, starts and stops easily	Jumps up, down, and forward	Rides trike rapidly and smoothly	Climbs up and down ladders, jungle gyms, slides, and trees	Uses more mature overhand motions and control but throws from elbow
Five–six years	Walks as an adult, skips alternating feet	Shows mature running, falls seldom, displays increased speed and control	Jumps long, high, and far; jumps rope	Rides small bicycle	Displays mature climbing in adult manner	Steps forward on throwing arm side as throws

REFERENCES CITED

Allen, K. Eileen, and **Elizabeth M. Goetz.** *Early Childhood Education: Special Problems, Special Solutions.* Rockville, Md.: An Aspen Publication, 1982.

Caplan, Theresa and **Frank.** *The Early Childhood Years; The 2 to 6 Year Old.* New York: The Putnam Publishing Group, 1983.

Cratty, Bryant J. "Motor Development in Early Childhood: Critical Issues for Researchers in the 1980s" in *Handbook of Research in Early Childhood Education* by Bernard Spodek (ed.), New York: The Free Press, 1982.

Flinchum, Betty M. *Motor Development In Early Childhood: A Guide for Movement Education with Ages 2 to 6.* St. Louis: The C. V. Mosby Company, 1975.

Gallahue, David L. *Developmental Movement Experiences for Children.* New York: John Wiley & Sons, 1982.

Pines, Maya. "A Head Start in the Nursery," *Psychology Today.* September 1979.

Schickedanz, Judith A., et al. *Toward Understanding Children.* Boston: Little, Brown, and Company, 1982.

Zaichkowsky, Leonard D., et al. *Growth and Development: The Child and Physical Activity.* St. Louis: The C. V. Mosby Company, 1980.

OTHER SOURCES

Ames, Louise Bates, and **Frances I. Ilg.** *Your Five Year Old: Sunny and Serene.* New York: Dell Publishing Company, 1979.

————. *Your Four Year Old: Wild and Wonderful.* Dell Publishing Company, 1976.

————. *Your Three Year Old: Friend or Enemy.* New York: Dell Publishing Company, 1976.

Beaty, Janice J. *Skills for Preschool Teachers.* Columbus, Ohio: Charles E. Merrill Publishing Company, 1984.

Torbert, Marianne. *Follow Me, a Handbook of Movement Activities for Children.* Englewood Cliffs, N.J.: Prentice-Hall, 1980.

LEARNING ACTIVITIES

1. Use the *Child Skills Checklist*, "5. Large Motor Development," as a screening tool to observe all of the children in your classroom. Which ones are the most physically accomplished? Which need the most help? What are their ages?

2. Choose a child who seems to need a great deal of help in large motor development. Do a running record on three different days to determine what the child can do physically. Do an activity with the child to promote a skill he or she needs help with. Record the results.

3. How do the girls and boys of the same age in your program compare with one another in each of the Large Motor Development Checklist items? How do you explain any differences or similarities? Can you make any conclusions about gender differences based on your observations?

4. Choose a child who needs help in throwing. Practice throwing with him or her using one or more of the ideas from the text. Discuss the results.

5. Have a staff member involve children in a new large motor game while you observe and record. Discuss your results as compared with an original screening of large motor abilities. What conclusions can you draw?

7 Small Motor Development

Small Motor Development Checklist

- ☐ Shows hand preference (which is _____)
- ☐ Turns with hand easily (knobs, lids, eggbeaters)
- ☐ Pours liquid into glass without spilling
- ☐ Unfastens and fastens zippers, buttons, Velcro tabs
- ☐ Picks up and inserts objects with ease
- ☐ Uses drawing/writing tools with control
- ☐ Uses scissors with control
- ☐ Pounds in nails with control

S mall motor development involves the fine muscles that control the extremities. In the case of young children, we especially are concerned with control, coordination, and dexterity in using the hands and fingers. Although this development occurs simultaneously in children along with large motor development, the muscles near the trunk (proximo) mature before the muscles of the extremities (distal), which control the wrists and hands.

Thus, it is important for the young child to practice use of the large muscles before he or she becomes involved in small motor activities to any extent. Delays in developing large motor coordination very well may have a negative effect on the development of small motor skills. But, once small motor involvement is possible for the child, preschool caregivers should encourage him to engage in all types of manipulative activities so that he can learn and then practice the skills needed to use his hands and fingers with control and dexterity.

REFLEXES

Surely infants and toddlers use their hands and fingers without much previous experience, you may counter. Why, then, do three-, four-, and five-year-olds have a different situation? The difference is important. It involves voluntary versus involuntary movements. Infants move their arms, hands, and fingers through reflexes, not voluntary movements. These involuntary movements are assimilated by the nervous system as it matures in order for the child to be able to control his movements in a voluntary manner. As these initial reflexes disappear, the child must purposefully learn to replace them by using and controlling his hands and fingers in a voluntary manner.

A very large number of reflexes are present in the infant. They include the Moro, or startle, reflex in which the infant throws out its arms with a jerk and lets out a cry; the rooting reflex in which the infant turns its head and opens its mouth when touched on the side of the cheek; the sucking reflex in which the infant sucks if its lips or mouth are touched; the walking reflex in which the infant makes stepping movements when held in an upright position on a surface, and the swimming reflex in which the infant makes swimming movements when held in the water with its head supported. Many more reflexes exist. (Zaichkowsky, p. 37)

The reflex most connected with small motor hand skills is the grasping reflex, or palmar grasp, in which the baby clamps its fingers around anything put in its palm. This grasp is so strong in the beginning it will support the infant's weight and can be used to lift the baby entirely off a surface. It is difficult, in fact, for the infant to let go. You may have to pry its fingers apart.

Involuntary responses such as the grasping reflex have their origin in the lower brain stem and spinal cord, and they eventually come under the control of the higher brain centers of the nervous system as the child matures. This higher part of the brain inhibits these initial reflexes after they have finished their task of aiding the survival of the helpless newborn, and the higher brain center allows voluntary movements to replace them.

The initial reflexes fade away within their own recognized timetable, depending on individual differences, of course. Rooting and sucking usually disappear after three months; walking and swimming usually vanish after five months, and Moro—the last to go—usually leaves after nine months. When such reflexes persist after their allotted time, it may be an indication of brain impairment. (Zaichkowsky, p. 37)

The grasping reflex lasts until about age nine months. Thus, infants cannot start to control hand and finger actions voluntarily before this time. Infants may reach for things—but not very accurately—before age six months; then, letting go is the infants' main problem. They can grasp an object easily but find it extremely difficult to let go. Even year-old children may struggle to release an object voluntarily, and some do not gain control of "letting go" before a year-and-a-half of age.

READINESS

We understand that like the large motor skills, voluntary small motor skills just do not happen; they must be learned naturally and then practiced by young children. But, is there a certain time period when particular skills can be learned best? Again, we face the problem of "readiness." When is the child's neuromuscular system mature enough for him to control his movements and perform certain actions? Should we wait until he is ready? Not necessarily. As with large motor skills, we should encourage children to use their small muscles as soon as possible. Because each child's development is different, this time period may differ for each.

All of us carry a biological time clock that we have inherited within us. For some of us, small motor development occurs in "textbook fashion," just as the charts for average physical growth indicate. For others, this development happens just a bit behind or ahead of the charts. This staggered individual development will exist in all of the children in your program. Each child has his or her own built-in biological clock. But, you do not know what time it is for the child except in general terms, and neither does the child. Since everyone's development occurs in a particular sequence, the best we can do is to assess the child's development and then provide him or her with appropriate activities, materials, and encouragement.

Is there a "critical moment" when small motor skills must be learned or it will be too late? Not really, except in broad, general terms. The best time to learn a small motor skill seems to be when the skill is changing most rapidly (Zaichkowsky, p. 36), but because this time is not easy to determine, it is best to offer many types of activities for all of your different children and to help the children get involved with those activities that offer both success and challenge.

In order to know where your children stand in their small motor development at the outset, you may want to screen them using the eight Small Motor Development Checklist items. These items are observable behaviors that demonstrate handedness as well as acknowledged small motor skills of young children in the areas of rotation, manipulation, and dexterity.

☐ SHOWS HAND PREFERENCE (WHICH IS _____)

Many but not all of your children will have developed a hand preference by age three. You may want to take note of this preference, but you should not be concerned about it. A great deal of interest and controversy—as well as incomplete understanding—surrounds the development of handedness, or *lateral dominance* as it is called. Lateral dominance also includes the development of a foot preference and eye preference. These preferences may or may not be the same as the hand preference.

Infants tend to use both hands in the beginning. This is due to reflexive rather than voluntary movements. As the neuromuscular system matures enough for voluntary movements to occur, the infant may begin to show a preference for one hand. In the beginning, this preference may not be very strong, and because involuntary movements do not disappear all at once, the infant may use both hands for many months.

This slight preference but use of both hands seems to be the case at age one. By age two, the child may begin to prefer using one hand over the other. By age two-and-a-half, about fifty-eight percent of American children have established a dominant hand, and by age three, about seventy percent have established dominance. Then, this percentage does not increase much until age eight-and-a-half. By age eleven, ninety-four percent of children have established a preferred hand, and the remaining children are ambidextrous, having mixed dominance. (Zaichkowsky, p. 75)

Not all of the world is the same. Hand preference development in Japanese children is similar to that of American children until about age two-and-a-half. But, between then and age four-and-a-half, its development is much slower. Only fifty percent of Japanese children establish hand dominance by age four-and-a-half. (Zaichkowsky, p. 75)

This is an important finding because we know that children develop in the same sequence and within the same timetable around the world. Differences, therefore, must be due to cultural influences . . . in other words, the child's environment. In America, we particularly are concerned with handedness, and many parents go out of their way to help their child develop right-handedness. They put emphasis on the right hand by handing things to his right hand or having him use his right hand to eat, hold, or throw. They give him praise and positive feedback when he is successful.

Such practice accompanied by feedback and positive reinforcement is, of course, the best way to develop any motor skill. Evidently, the Japanese are not so concerned with hand dominance at an early age and have allowed their children to develop it individually. In the end, parental influence seems to make little difference because ninety percent of the human race eventually uses the right hand for small motor activities. More boys, by the way, are left-handed or ambidextrous than girls.

Foot dominance is somehow different. Even infants often show a clear-cut preference for one foot over the other. By age five, ninety-four percent of children have developed foot dominance.

Our concern over handedness always has centered around children's ability in learning to read and write. Will lefties have more trouble? Will children with mixed dominance have learning problems? Should you try to change a child's hand preference from left to right? The answers are not all that clear. A great deal of controversy exists regarding the relationship between perceptual-motor development and learning disabilities. There is still so much we do not know about human development.

The best advice at the moment, it seems, advocates helping a young child develop a hand preference, whichever it may be. It will be more useful for her to be right-handed in this predominantly right-handed world if she has no strong preference. But, if she favors her left hand, then help her to develop skill in using it. Whatever you do, act with support and encouragement, not pressure.

Children need to succeed. A strong hand preference will help them perform small motor tasks with dexterity. Find out the hand preference for each of your children, and help them to develop it with practice and positive feedback.

If You Have Not Checked This Item: Some Helpful Ideas

- *Do Not Make a Fuss*

You may want to know if the child has established handedness and with which hand, but keep your efforts at a low key. Encourage the child to use whichever hand he prefers so that he will become more skillful in using it.

☐ TURNS WITH HAND EASILY (KNOBS, LIDS, EGGBEATERS)

Twisting or turning movements done with the wrist, hand, and fingers by rotating the wrist and/or forearm take several different forms. The child may enclose a doorknob with her hand and try to twist and then pull the knob to open the door. Depending upon the size and stiffness of the knob and door, she may or may not succeed at first. Or, she may not be tall enough to make her small motor skills work effectively. Turning a key in a lock involves this same type of motion.

Another form of small motor rotating involves vertical turning at the wrist or rotating the forearm while the fingers are gripping an implement, a cranking type of movement. Eggbeaters, food mills, and can openers use this motion. Still another type of small motor rotating uses the fingers to twist a nut onto a bolt, turn a screw into a hole, or twist a lid onto or off of a jar or bottle.

Children at an early age can accomplish this motor skill. Two-and-a-half- and three-year-olds, for instance, can turn a doorknob if they can reach it. They love to screw and unscrew lids or tops on jars and bottles. Have your parents collect empty plastic bottles and containers of all sizes along with their screw top lids, and keep the items in a box in the manipulative area of the classroom for the children to practice on.

Small motor control is especially far from perfect with the younger children; things have a way of slipping out of their fingers from time to time. Thus, it is important to use only unbreakable containers such as plastic—never glass—in the classroom.

This same hand-rotating skill also is used by three-year-olds and older children as they try to put together a puzzle. Whereas two-year-olds often will try to jam a puzzle piece into place and will give up if it does not fit, older children will rotate the piece to try to match the shape of the hole.

Watch and see how your children put puzzles together. Obviously, perceptual awareness is also at work in this instance, but children first need the small motor rotating skill in order to use their shape recognition ability. Puzzles of differing complexities should be an item on your shelves of manipulative materials. These puzzles offer excellent practice for finger dexterity and eye-hand coordination, as well as the cognitive concepts of matching, shapes, and part-to-whole relationships.

Three-year-olds can turn an eggbeater, and they love to do it. Be sure to have more than one eggbeater at your water table, since the eggbeater is usually a favorite implement and the focus of many squabbles if only one is available. Children like to try turning food mills and can openers as well, but sometimes, youngsters do not have the strength to succeed in turning these items if the things to be ground or opened are too difficult to handle.

At age three-and-a-half, many children show a temporary lack of coordination in small motor skills, just as they do with the large muscles. If you are aware of this "relapse," you should not be overly concerned when some of your most coordinated children seem suddenly awkward. (See p. 132.)

If You Have Not Checked This Item: Some Helpful Ideas

• *Have a Collection of Food Utensils for Play*

Visit a hardware store that has a large assortment of food preparation utensils, and stock up on all kinds of grinding, squeezing, and cranking types of implements. Better still, visit a flea market, and buy the same things and more secondhand. Some of the old-fashioned hand tools of great grandma's kitchen will make a big hit in your classroom. Keep the items in your housekeeping area, near the water table or on your manipulative shelves, and watch what your children do with them.

- *Make a Nuts-and-Bolts Board*

Fasten bolts of differing sizes to a sanded-down board, and give the children a box of nuts to screw onto the bolts. The children will need to use their size-sorting as well as small motor skills.

- *Get Sample Doorknobs*

Ask a building supply company for sample doorknobs, door locks, bolts, or other similar items when it no longer uses the particular model on display.

- *Collect Old Locks and Keys*

Have a box of old locks and keys for children to experiment with. The youngsters will need persistence as well as motor skills to match up and make the locks and keys work.

- *Try an Orange Squeezer*

Bring in an orange squeezer that works by hand, and let your children take turns twisting half an orange on it to make juice.

☐ POURS LIQUID INTO GLASS WITHOUT SPILLING

Two-year-olds are able to hold a glass of milk, at first with two hands and then with one. Most parents really are not concerned that their children do more than this holding. Pouring tends to be an adult activity that mothers do for their children. Many nursery school teachers and day-care personnel feel the same way. Why should children learn to pour? Won't they just make a mess if they spill? Isn't it much quicker and more efficient if the adults in the classroom do the pouring?

Children must not learn to pour simply to develop a helping activity but to practice and acquire small motor coordination as well. Pouring is an excellent real activity that children can participate in and that is both helpful to others and, more importantly, helpful for their own small muscle development.

Long ago, Maria Montessori, the renowned Italian early childhood educator, recognized the value of pouring by including all sorts of pouring activities in her "daily living exercises," which taught children small motor skills such as eye-hand coordination. Today, Montessori children still learn by pouring rice before they finally pour liquids successfully from small pitchers.

The size of the pitcher is the key to successful pouring. Put a small pitcher on each of your children's snack or lunch tables, and let the youngsters help themselves to juice or milk. If they should spill, they can help clean up with a soft sponge . . . another good small motor exercise.

Allowing children to pour may not be as efficient as having an adult pour the drinks, but you need to think about the purpose of your program. Is it to take care of a group of children, or is it to help young children develop their own skills and learn to take care of themselves? Young children take a great deal of pride in being able to do adult-type tasks. Performing these tasks not only makes them feel grown up but also gives them a real sense of self-worth and accomplishment.

There will be accidents. Spills are part of the price children pay for the complicated task of growing up. Remember the problem of releasing the grip, in which children actually have to learn how to let go because some traces of the palmar grasp reflex may still remain? And if they do not have their minds on what they are doing, they may release their grips without meaning to. Again, make a spill a learning experience, not an embarrassment. The children will enjoy squeezing out the cleanup sponge.

Three-year-olds may need to use both hands for pouring. If the pitcher is small enough, four- and five-year-olds often can handle it with one hand.

If You Have Not Checked This Item: Some Helpful Ideas

• *Have Pouring Implements in Your Water Table*

Have several sizes and types of plastic pitchers in your water table. Some can be large with lids on the top; some can be small and open at the top. All should have handles. Children can do much of their initial pouring practice here without worrying about spilling.

• *Use Pouring Implements on Your Food Table*

Have small plastic or ceramic pitchers that the children can use to serve themselves. You can fill these small-sized containers as they empty. Again, the flea market is a good source for interesting pouring implements such as vinegar cruets and small metal pitchers.

☐ UNFASTENS AND FASTENS ZIPPERS, BUTTONS, VELCRO TABS

Unfastening and fastening zippers, buttons, and Velcro tabs are self-help skills we want children to accomplish in order not only to take care of themselves, but also to help them develop small motor dexterity. Young children want to do things for themselves. Often, they have trouble accomplishing unfastening and fastening tasks because their motor coordination has not developed sufficiently. But, just as often, their difficulty has to do with lack of practice because the adults around them do everything for them.

It is interesting to note that economically disadvantaged children frequently develop small motor dexterity before children from middle income families do. Economically disadvantaged children have more practice. In fact, preschoolers in many large, one-parent families are expected to help dress themselves when the working mother has her hands full getting herself ready for work every morning, the baby ready for the sitter, and breakfast prepared for everybody before she has to leave.

If mother and father do all the buttoning and fastening of clothing for their preschooler, the child misses an excellent opportunity for learning how to do it on his own. He may even resist when the preschool teacher encourages him to try, wanting the teacher to perform the same function as his mother.

Three-year-olds are able to unbutton first—always an easier task—but many also can button large buttons on clothing if given the chance to practice. Most three-year-olds also can fasten regular snaps but may have trouble with the heavy-duty, jeans-type snap. Even four-year-olds seldom have the finger strength necessary to make these heavy-duty snaps work.

Four-year-olds should be able to button and unbutton clothing with little difficulty. They can unzip zippers, but they often need help getting started with jacket zippers that come apart completely.

Four-year-olds can undo zippers with ease but sometimes need help in getting started with zipping up jackets.

Many shoes and articles of clothing now are fastened with Velcro-type fasteners. This seems to be the easiest fastener for children to handle. A Velcro fastener is pulled apart by gripping the end between the thumb and forefinger and pulling; it is fastened merely by pushing one Velcro-covered tab against the Velcro backing. Preschoolers have the strength and coordination to do this type of unfastening and fastening with ease.

Velcro tabs are the easiest type of shoe fasteners for preschoolers to handle.

If You Have Not Checked This Item: Some Helpful Ideas

▪ *Use Buttoning/Zipping Boards*

Make or purchase several boards that will help your children acquire and practice these skills. If you make your own boards, have only one skill practiced on each board: buttoning on one, zipping on another, and snaps on yet another. Have these boards available in the manipulative area of your classroom.

- *Talk with Parents*

Talk with parents about the importance of their child's development of small motor coordination. Let them know the kinds of activities their children will be doing in your class. Suggest some of the activities the children could be doing at home, such as self-help skills like dressing themselves—including buttoning, zipping, and snapping clothing—or helping to dress younger members of the family.

☐ PICKS UP AND INSERTS OBJECTS WITH EASE

Manipulative Materials

Picking up and inserting objects is the small motor skill most frequently promoted in the early childhood classroom. This skill involves manipulation of items by gripping them between the thumb and fingers and inserting or placing them somewhere else. Using puzzles, pegboards, and stacking toys; lacing; sewing; weaving; stringing beads; and sorting small items call for this skill. Playing with Lego bricks, Tinkertoys educational toys, geoboards, formboards, Bristleboards, and many plastic table games also requires the presence of picking up and inserting skills.

All classrooms should have a permanent space for manipulative activity of this sort, with shelves at the children's level equipped with many materials for easy selection and return. There should be a table in the area next to the shelves as well as floor space for playing with the larger toys.

The selection of materials should cover a wide range of children's abilities, as well. Wooden puzzles, for example, should include simple, single pictures with pieces showing an entire part of the picture for beginners, as well as more complicated pictures with many pieces for older or experienced children.

Teachers should plan to check all of the manipulative materials at least once a week to be sure all the parts and pieces are there. If some pieces are missing, either replace the pieces or remove the material. It does not help beginners to try to make puzzles or play games with pieces missing; many beginners soon give up in this case.

It is not necessary to put out all of the manipulative materials that the program owns at once. Add a few new ones to the area every month, and remove some of the old ones. Save some of the more complicated table toys for challenging the experienced children later in the year. If you have a limited supply of materials, consider trading with other programs.

Children's Skills

You should know which children visit the manipulative area during your free play period. Use the Small Motor Development Checklist as a screening device to help you find out. Are children avoiding the area because they are not comfortable with small motor skills? Do boys mainly avoid the manipulative materials?

Once you know which individuals avoid manipulation tasks, you will be able to sit down at a table with a single child and challenge him or her to make a puzzle with you, stack blocks, or sort shapes into a formboard. If you are keeping file card records of each child, you can add this information to his or her card. You or your co-workers may need to spend time every day with children who need extra practice with small motor skills. You may need to encourage these children to complete some of the small motor activities on their own.

Gender Differences

Our society seems to encourage girls to engage in small motor activities more than boys. Even the women's movement has not changed the way many parents raise their children. Boys still are encouraged to run outside and climb trees or play ball. Girls are given manipulative-type toys for their play. As a result, many girls are more dextrous with their fingers, while boys are more skillful in large motor activities such as running and throwing.

In the end, all children need to be skillful and at ease with both large and small motor activities. Once involved with formal education, both genders will need to handle writing tools and reading activities. Girls who are more skillful with finger dexterity and eye-hand coordination have an edge over boys in writing and reading at present. Is this skill imbalance perhaps the reason more boys than girls have problems in learning to read?

If You Have Not Checked This Item; Some Helpful Ideas

- *Use Bead-Stringing*

Put out all kinds of materials for both boys and girls to use in making necklaces. Have macaroni and all sorts of pasta shapes available; the children can color them first by painting. Bring in little sea shells with holes drilled in them (hobby shops may do this) as well as acorns and horse chestnuts in the fall, plastic or wooden beads, and any other small items you can find. Save tops from plastic bottles and tops of magic markers; punch holes in them, and use them for stringing necklaces and bracelets.

- *Make a Geoboard*

Make a one-foot-square wooden board of some thickness, and pound in headless nails over the surface of the board in rows one inch apart. Allow the nails to protrude above the surface of the board about an inch. Let the children string colored rubber bands over the tops of the nails, making all kinds of designs. Older children can try to copy design cards you have made, as well. Make foot-square cardboard cards with dots for the nails in the exact arrangement as the geoboard. On each card, draw in outlines of items such as a red square, a blue triangle, or a yellow rectangle, and let the children try to copy each shape with similar rubber bands on the geoboard. Designs must be simple for three- and four-year-olds, since their cognitive copying powers are still at an early level. Kindergarten children will have an easier time copying geoboard designs. If this play becomes a favorite activity, then you will need more than one geoboard.

- *Make Pegboards*

Ask a building supply company for scraps of pegboard it normally would throw away. You can cut the scraps to child-size shapes and sand down the edges. The pegboard does not have to be square. Triangular pegboards are just as useful and appealing. Get boxes of colored golf tees for pegs, and let the children use the tees in the same way rubber bands are used on the geoboards. You may want to make simple designs on paper or cardboard for the children to copy on their pegboards, as well. Graph paper is helpful if you do not want to spend time measuring spaces.

- *Have Parents Help*

Have a parent "Board-Making Bee" to help stock your classroom as well as to make enough extra boards to take home for their children to play with. You almost always can attract parents to come to your program to help like this if they know they will be making educational games they also can take home. Besides helping their children both at home and at school, the parents, themselves, can be learning the importance of small motor activities for their children. Too often, adults tend to look upon all children's activities as play, as an unimportant entertainment. Parents need to be aware that play is essential to their children's physical, mental, and social development as human beings. Such parent group activities may change parents' outlook.

☐ USES DRAWING/WRITING TOOLS WITH CONTROL

Preschool programs for two-, three-, and four-year-olds should not be concerned with "teaching" children how to draw pictures or write words. Some of your older children may—and probably will—progress to this stage of development and may be able to do some pictorial drawing and word writing naturally, but these skills do not need to be your goal for all children. Instead, you should provide children with opportunities to use writing and drawing implements of all kinds in order to encourage development of their small motor finger strength and dexterity, and their eye-hand coordination.

The first time preschoolers use crayons, pencils, or magic markers, they usually hold the writing tools in the so-called "power grip," with all of the fingers clamped fist-like around the implement. This grip does not give the children much control over the marks they will make, since the entire hand, wrist, and arm is involved in the movements rather than the fingers. As their motor skills develop and they have the chance to practice, children eventually switch to the "precision grip," holding the implement between the thumb and fingers.

Watch and see which of the children use this mature grip and which still seem to prefer the fist clench. Ask their parents what writing or coloring tools the children have at home. Some children, because they have no materials, may not have had practice like others. You may want to send home a few crayons and paper for those children who need more drawing and writing practice.

Are your children using these tools with their preferred hand? Check and see. Children often pick up an implement with either hand and start to use it whether or not the hand works well. You might have children try switching hands if you already have identified their handedness and if they are crayoning with the non-dominant hand.

The stubby fingers of preschoolers sometimes have more success gripping a thick tool, although some youngsters prefer regular pencils and crayons. Magic markers are already thick and easy for the preschoolers to use. Easel paintbrushes are thick enough but usually too long for children to control readily. You may need to cut off a few inches and sand the brushes down. Day-care supply houses finally have gotten the message and are coming out with properly proportioned paintbrushes for preschoolers.

Art and writing skills for preschoolers will be discussed more fully in Chapter 11, Written Language, and Chapter 12, Art Skills.

If You Have Not Checked This Item: Some Helpful Ideas

- *Use Coloring Books*

Coloring books are quite controversial with preschool program people. Some are concerned that these stilted, stereotyped pictures will substitute in the classroom for creative art. It seems we have missed the point. Coloring books have little to do with art, but a great deal to do with small motor skills. Coloring books should be kept on the shelves with manipulative materials. Children love to fill in the outline pictures with various colors. At first, children merely scribble over the pictures with one color. As they gain control of the crayons, the youngsters work more carefully using different colors. Finally, the children are able to stay within the lines, a very satisfying accomplishment for the child struggling to control the use of his fingers.

Using coloring books, in fact, is an excellent pre-writing activity for young children if the books contain simple pictures with large spaces. You can use the books a different way by having children try to trace over the outlines of the pictures with a crayon or magic marker.

- *Have a Writing Table*

Place a small table in your library corner. Have primary pencils, regular pencils, magic markers, ball-point pens, crayons, and notebook or tablet paper available to scribble on. Let the children pretend they are writing.

☐ USES SCISSORS WITH CONTROL

Learning to cut with scissors takes a great deal of coordination and practice. Children who have had practice with this activity at home may be way ahead of those who have not, regardless of age. Sometimes, the scissors, themselves, make it difficult for youngsters to learn how to cut. The blunt scissors found in many preschools are often dull and difficult to manipulate, even for adults. Try the scissors yourself, and loosen and sharpen them before giving them to the children. Really good scissors cost money, but they are a worthwhile investment when you consider what fine practice they give children in developing strength in their hands and coordination in their fingers.

For children who have not learned to cut, you can provide help in several ways. Show them how to hold the scissors with their favored hand. As with crayons, children sometimes pick up scissors with either hand and will not have much success if they are trying to use the non-dominant hand. Have a child cut in two a narrow strip of paper stretched taut between your two hands. Once she can do this cutting without difficulty, get another child to hold the paper, and let each take a turn holding and cutting. Give them a task of cutting all the yellow strips into small pieces.

On another day, show the child how to hold the strip of paper in her own hand and cut with the other hand. Handedness especially may be confusing for her with this activity. She needs to keep the scissors in her dominant hand. Let her practice on different kinds of paper, including construction paper, typing paper, and pages from magazines. Finally, draw a line on a sheet of paper, and let the child practice cutting along the line. Be sure to have at least one pair of left-handed scissors.

Most four-year-olds can cut along a straight line without difficulty, but many have trouble turning corners and following a curved line. The children need all kinds of practice in cutting. Whenever you are preparing art materials for the children to use, especially cutouts which need to be pasted, try to involve the children in helping to do the cutting.

If You Have Not Checked This Item: Some Helpful Ideas

- *Use Wrapping Paper Ribbons*

Let children practice cutting wrapping paper ribbons into confetti. Ribbons have more body than ordinary paper and so cut easier. Save the confetti for a celebration.

- *Read a Book to Promote Cutting*

Let's Make Rabbits by Leo Lionni, New York: Pantheon Books, 1982, is a simple story about a talking pencil and a pair of scissors who get together and decide to make rabbits. The pencil draws a rabbit, and the scissors cuts out a collage rabbit, and the two rabbits immediately become best friends. The teacher can trace out the circular pieces which make up the rabbit and help the children to cut out their own collage rabbits.

The Trip by Ezra Jack Keats, New York: Scholastic Book Services, 1978, tells the story of the inner city boy, Louie, who moves to a new neighborhood where he does not know anybody, so he creates his own world in a shoe box peep show. Directions for making the peep show appear on the last page. Although making the peep show is too complicated for most young children to do on their own, teachers can prepare some of the materials and can ask children to help with the cutting and pasting.

☐ POUNDS IN NAILS WITH CONTROL

Holding a nail and pounding it with a hammer held in the opposite hand is the most complicated small motor skill discussed thus far. Many children will not be able to do it well until they are older and more coordinated. Even adults often have difficulty with this skill. Try it yourself, and find out.

Handedness makes a difference and so does arm and wrist strength. The small toy hammers found in play sets should not be used. They are not heavy or strong enough to have much effect other than frustrating the pounder. A small adult hammer is better.

Both boys and girls should be encouraged to pound. It is an excellent activity to develop small motor strength and coordination. If you do not have a carpenter's bench in your room, you can set up a woodworking area by hanging tools on the wall from a pegboard and using several tree stumps as pounding surfaces. Often, building supply companies will provide you with various wood scraps.

To get children interested in this or any activity area in your classroom, simply go into the area yourself, and begin pounding something. Pounding always attracts attention, and soon, children will want to do the same thing the teacher is doing. Again, you should check to make sure they are holding the hammer in their favored hand. You easily can control the safety factor by limiting the number of hammers or tree trunks available for pounding.

If You Have Not Checked This Item: Some Helpful Ideas

- *Use Soft Materials*

Do not start your pounding activities with wood. Children need to acquire the pounding skill before they will be able to drive a nail through wood. Start with a softer material such as fiberboard, ceiling tiles, or Styrofoam™. Children also love to pound nails through the holes in Tinkertoys educational toys.

- *Use Large-Headed Nails*

The children should use large-headed nails at first. Most tacks are too short for the pounder to hold, but roofing nails or upholstering tacks are large enough and long enough to work well.

REFERENCES CITED

Zaichkowsky, Leonard D., et al. *Growth and Development: The Child and Physical Activity.* St. Louis: The C.V. Mosby Company, 1980.

OTHER SOURCES

Beaty, Janice J. *Skills for Preschool Teachers.* Columbus, Ohio: Charles E. Merrill Publishing Company, 1984.

Caplan, Theresa, and Frank Caplan. *The Early Childhood Years: The 2 to 6 Year Old.* New York: The Putnam Publishing Group, 1983.

Dunn, M. L. *Pre-Scissors Skills.* Tucson, Ariz.: Communication Skill Builders, Inc., 1979.

Schickedanz, Judith, et al. *Toward Understanding Children*, Boston: Little, Brown, and Company, 1982.

Thompson, David. *Easy Woodstuff for Kids*, Mt. Rainier, Md.: Gryphon House, 1981.

LEARNING ACTIVITIES

1. Use the *Child Skills Checklist*, "6. Small Motor Development," as a screening tool to observe all of the children in your classroom. Pay special attention to which hand each child seems to favor. Also, note which children spend time in small motor activities and which ones do not.

2. Compare the children in your classroom on their *Checklist* results in both large and small motor development. Do you see any relationships?

3. Choose a child who seems to need a great deal of help with small motor skills. Do a running record of him or her on three different days, concentrating on small motor skills. Do a learning activity with the child based on the results.

4. How do the girls and boys of the same age compare with one another in small motor skills? What conclusions can you make based on your observations?

5. Put out a new small motor activity for the children to use. Observe and record the results of their play. What conclusions can you draw?

 Cognitive Development:
Classification & Seriation

Cognitive Development: Classification & Seriation Checklist

- [ ] Recognizes basic geometric shapes
- [ ] Recognizes colors
- [ ] Recognizes differences in size
- [ ] Sorts objects by appearance
- [ ] Discriminates things that are alike from those that are different
- [ ] Puts parts together to make a whole
- [ ] Arranges events in sequence from first to last
- [ ] Arranges objects in series according to a certain rule

CREATING KNOWLEDGE

Cognitive development of preschool children is concerned with how they develop their thinking abilities. We are only at the beginning of our understanding of how this development takes place. The work of researchers like Swiss psychologist Jean Piaget in his investigation of how knowledge is created (See Table 6.) and psycholinguist Noam Chomsky in his exploration of how language is acquired has given us new insights into how children think as well as how their thinking evolves.

The use of the computer and the work on "artificial intelligence" to program the computer to work like the human brain have added even more understanding of the brain's workings and of its unimagined complexity. The technological advances in time-lapse photography, videotaping, and other laboratory observation methods for infants and children have given us entirely different perspectives on child development. Still, we are only at the gates, the mere frontiers of understanding intellectual ability and how it develops.

What we do know about intellectual ability is something quite startling to those unfamiliar with recent findings: Children create their own knowledge. Using the physical and mental tools they are born with, children interact with their environment to make sense of it, and in so doing, they construct their own mental images of their world. The brain seems to be pre-programmed to take in information about objects and their relationship to one another. What do things look, feel, taste, sound, and smell like? What can they do? How are they like one another? How are they different? What happens if you touch, push, or throw them?

USING PLAY

Another startling finding, for those new to the field, involves the principal way children create this knowledge: They do it by playing with things, people, and ideas. Most people think of play as something recreational, something we do for enjoyment, and something rather inconsequential. For adults, this definition of play

171

TABLE 6. Piaget's stages of cognitive development

Sensorimotor Stage
(Birth to age 2)

Child thinks in visual patterns ("schemata").

Child uses senses to explore objects (i.e., looks, listens, smells, tastes, and manipulates).

Child learns to recall physical features of an object.

Child associates objects with actions and events but does not use objects to symbolize actions and events (e.g. rolls a ball but does not use ball as a pretend car).

Child develops "object permanence" (i.e. comes to realize an object is still there even when out of sight).

Preoperational Stage
(Age 2 to 7)

Child acquires symbolic thought (i.e. uses mental images and words to represent actions and events not present).

Child uses objects to symbolize actions and events (e.g. pretends a block is a car).

Child learns to anticipate effect of one action on another (e.g. realizes pouring milk from pitcher to glass will make level of milk decrease in pitcher as it rises in glass).

Child is deceived by appearances (e.g. believes a tall, thin container holding a cup of water contains more than a short, wide container holding a cup of water).

Child is concerned with final products (i.e. focuses on the way things look at a particular moment, "figurative knowledge," and not on changes of things or how things got that way, "operational knowledge"), and he cannot seem to reverse his thinking.

Concrete-Operational Stage
(Age 7 to 11)

Child's thoughts can deal with changes of things and how they got that way.

Child is able to reverse his thinking (i.e. has ability to see in his mind how things looked before and after a change took place).

Child has gone beyond how things look at a particular moment and begins to understand how things relate to one another (e.g., knows that the number two can be larger than one, yet, at the same time, smaller than three).

Formal-Operational Stage
(Age 11 +)

Child begins to think about thinking.

Child thinks in abstract terms without needing concrete objects.

Child can hypothesize about things.

NOTE: Information from Forman, pp. 69–93 included

may be true, but for infants and young children, play is a way of trying out and finding out. Children fool around with toys, their clothing, their hands and feet, sounds, words, and other people. Youngsters use their senses of taste, touch, sound, sight, and smell in a playful manner with anything and everything they can get their hands (or feet) on, in order to find out what an object is, what it feels like, what it sounds like, and what they can do with it. The fact of the matter is that child's play is practice in learning to think.

From the time he is born, the human infant pursues such information with a single-minded determination. At first, everything goes into the mouth. Then, the infant bangs objects against the side of the crib to see what sound they make, to feel their impact, to see what they will do, and to find out what will happen. The toddler has an extra advantage. He has expanded his field of exploration by learning to walk. Suddenly, the world's objects are his to touch, pick up, shake, throw, taste, and take apart. He uses his senses to "play" with his world in order to find out what it is like. And as soon as he can talk, he plays with words and word sounds as well.

All of the information extracted through this playful exploration of the environment is filed away in predetermined patterns in the brain, to be used to direct or adjust the child's behavior as he continues to respond to the stimuli around him. We now know that this knowledge is organized by the brain in predictable patterns from a very early age. Some of these patterns even may be inherited. Recent highly sophisticated research with two- and three-year-olds has convinced psychologists that children may be born with the ability to make distinctions between animate and inanimate things, and to understand cause and effect (Pines, p. 48).

Yet, if the child does not have the opportunity to explore his environment—if his environment is uninteresting or sterile, or if his caregivers are harsh, controlling, or neglectful—he may not develop his intellect to the same extent as children without these handicaps. Witness the apathetic children in the Iranian orphanages who hardly could walk at age four. (See p. 130.) Yet, when Dr. Hunt trained their caregivers to use vocal play with newly arrived infants, an overwhelming change took place in them. Not only did these youngsters learn to walk and talk on schedule, but even their appearance and their facial features also changed for the better. (Pines, p. 63)

ASSESSING DEVELOPMENT

How have the children in your classroom fared in the construction of their own knowledge? They need to have built up mental representations of objects, ways to differentiate things by appearance, ways to tell what kinds of things are alike, and ways to decide how things fit together to form a whole or a part of a sequence or series. These are the types of patterns or concepts the brain forms in organizing the data it takes in.

You will need to assess each of your children by observing his or her ability to accomplish the eight *Checklist* items at the head of this chapter. The first six of these items refer to classification skills the child needs to know, and the last two items involve skills for arranging things in a series. You must plan activities or playful exploration periods for children to use in order to continue developing their intelligence.

☐ RECOGNIZES BASIC GEOMETRIC SHAPES

The development of thinking begins with the infant seeing, hearing, and feeling things in his environment: his mother's face, the nurse's face, and his bottle or mother's breast. His brain takes in these important visual perceptions and stores them in particular schemes or patterns that are mental representations for the objects and events he experiences. His brain seems to be pre-programmed to pay attention to certain things in his environment and to ignore the rest.

Research has shown, for instance, that an infant looks longer at the human face than at anything else around him (Schickedanz, p. 152). The infant seems, in fact, to prefer visual stimuli that have a contour configuration. He is beginning his construction of knowledge.

The first aspect of this knowledge is called "figurative knowing" because it deals with shapes and configurations as well as the patterns of movements, tastes, smells, and so on (Saunders, p. 117). The infant will have to recognize these objects and shapes again and again. He will need to respond to his caregivers, his bottle, his rattle, and other environmental objects in an appropriate manner. Perceptual recognition, then, is the earliest form of the infant's store of knowledge.

But, as the young child learns new things (as he acquires new mental constructions), an interesting phenomenon occurs. He seems to store his new knowledge in previously constructed categories, which become very general in nature. For instance, not long after he learns that his own specific four-legged pet is a "doggie," he categorizes all four-legged creatures—even cats and teddy bears—as "doggies." In other words, his brain overgeneralizes. As it matures, it eventually will have to learn more discriminating features and to develop new categories for a variety of different animals. This refinement seems to take place especially between ages two and four.

This first *Checklist* item on shape is concerned with this refinement in perceptual recognition. In order to think, the child needs to know and discriminate among basic shapes of things. We start with geometric shapes because the concept of shape is one of the first concepts to emerge in the child's cognitive development. He needs to distinguish between a circle, a square, a rectangle, and a triangle, not in order to do geometry, but to be able to categorize mentally and to distinguish among the objects in his environment.

Adults are often surprised to learn that young children overgeneralize about shapes, too. At first, children view all enclosed figures as being the same. In other words, youngsters think that a circle and a square are the same. They have difficulty distinguishing one shape as different from another. They need to learn the special features of the shape that distinguish it from a similar shape. Surely, they can look at a circle and a square and see the difference, you may think. But, the point is they cannot in the beginning. The brain evidently processes this visual input all in one category. Children have to create new categories by learning the difference between shapes.

This learning takes place not just by a teacher telling the child, "This is a square," "This is a circle," but more effectively by the child playing or exploring with all of his senses about what makes a particular shape a circle or a square. Seeing pictures of the various shapes is helpful, but it is too abstract as the only method for young children to learn. Youngsters need hands-on activities with three-dimensional materials as well.

Your program should provide the children with many such experiences. Since the children learn these classification skills through the senses, you should give the youngsters all kinds of sensory play opportunities. Play with dough, for instance, allows children to make dough balls, which the youngsters flatten into circles with their hands or roll flat with a rolling pin and cut into circular cookies. Sensory learning involves taste, touch, smell, and sight in this instance. Clay and play dough provide similar sensory experiences.

Blockbuilding is an excellent medium for creating squares, rectangles, and triangles. In the beginning, you will need to provide a vocabulary of new terms for the shapes the children are making. Can the children build a triangle, one of the most difficult shapes? Their triangles probably will be rather rounded in the beginning because corners are hard for the children to deal with. The brain seems to use the circular shape as the model in its overgeneralizations. Put masking tape on the floor in the shapes of squares, rectangles, and triangles, and let children try to build these shapes with their blocks.

The diagonal line appears last in children's learning. For this reason, triangles and diamonds are very difficult for children to copy. See Chapter 9 on space and Chapter 12, Art Skills, for further discussion on shapes.

If You Have Not Checked This Item: Some Helpful Ideas

- *Start with One Shape at a Time*

Children need to focus their attention on one concept before expanding it to include other aspects. The circle is good to begin with because children are used to the roundness or ovalness of the human face. They need to experience examples of all kinds of circles. Let the youngsters see how many circles they can discover in the classroom. Did they find the wheels on toy vehicles, the casters on the doll bed or office chair, or the mark on the table made by a wet glass?

How long should you concentrate on this shape before including a second shape in their explorations? It depends on your children and their interest. Be sure every child has a chance to have enough sensory involvement with circles so that he or she can internalize it. This internalization may take several weeks, depending on the age and experience of your children. Bring in a collection of things that contains some circular shapes, and let each child try to sort out the circles. Include items such as bottle tops, coasters, jar lids, and rings. Then, have the children try sorting blindfolded. If some children are frightened by having a blindfold tied over their eyes, let them shut or hold a hand over their eyes.

▪ *Have the Children Make Their Own Circles*

Use circle-making activities that involve molding clay, shaping dough, finger painting, cutting out circles, cutting out jack-o-lantern tops, stamping circular shapes on paper, and tracing around circular objects.

When the children finally have a strong sense of circleness, introduce the square as the next shape.

▪ *Read Books That Have Stories or Pictures of Shapes*

Wheels Go Round by Yvonne Hooker, New York: Grosset & Dunlap, 1981, is an interesting cardboard book containing large colorful pictures of vehicles and their wheels. From steamrollers to go-carts, vehicles with wheels that are cut out appear on every other page in the book, each wheel increasingly smaller. On the page opposite each vehicle is a four-sentence rhyming description of the vehicle. Children will enjoy feeling the roundness of the cutout wheels and may want to trace the wheels on paper.

Round in a Circle by Yvonne Hooker, Grosset & Dunlap, 1982, follows a similar cardboard book format with square, circle, and triangle shapes cut out of every other page from things like an artist's easel, a television, a balloon, and a teepee.

Tatum's Favorite Shape by Dorothy Thole, New York: Scholastic Book Services, 1977, is the story of little Tatum who has trouble in school keeping straight the different shapes until his mother plays a shape-finding game with him at home.

☐ RECOGNIZES COLORS

Another way the brain can classify things is by color. Research shows that infants as young as four to six months of age begin discriminating colors (Richardson, p. 123). Children develop color perception shortly after shape recognition, although they seem to talk about colors first. This "color talk" reflects the fact that the people around the children make more reference to color than shape. The children, in fact, may be able to name many colors just as they name numbers, without truly knowing what the names mean. Just because a child tells you he knows red does not mean that he really does know the color. Ask the child the color of his shirt or her dress. Ask the youngster to find red in the classroom.

Color, like shape, is a type of visual perception the child's brain uses to help classify and sort out the world. Although the child sees colors from the beginning, he now needs to put names to the different ones.

Again, concentrating on a single color at first and then adding others works best. Basic colors such as red, yellow, green, and blue, plus black and white, are usually easier for children to recognize at first. But, you must take advantage of seasonal colors as well. Orange certainly should be a part of your classroom during the Halloween season.

Allow children to "play" with sorting colors the same way as with sorting blocks. Give them things like poker chips or golf tees, and let the children see if they can find all the reds. Some children will be able to sort out all the items by color, but everyone does not have to perform this way at first. Allow the children to play with paints. You may want to put out only one color of paint plus white paint at the easel at first. Let the children experiment with the look and texture of all the shades of "redness" as the youngsters mix red and white paint. Give the children plenty of time to experience one color before you focus on another.

As your group begins its investigation of other colors, you can add those one by one to the easel. Have color lotto cards, colored plastic blocks, and many other table games featuring colors. Be sure to bring in many different items of the color you are exploring. If you have bilingual children, be sure everyone learns color names in both languages.

Handicapped children can learn color concepts along with all of the other youngsters. Set up your activities so that children with physical and mental disabilities can participate. If you keep concept games in the manipulative area, be sure the shelves are low enough for everyone to reach.

If You Have Not Checked This Item: Some Helpful Ideas

- *Let the Children Mix Colors*

Let children have the fun of mixing colors. Put out squeeze bottles of food coloring, spoons for stirring, and plastic cups or muffin tins full of water. You may want to use only one or two colors at first, or you may want to let children discover how mixing blue and yellow together makes green, since this is such a dramatic change. At another time, use cups of predissolved colors, medicine droppers, and muffin tins full of clear water.

There are many different ways for children to play with colors. The youngsters can finger paint with the color you are focusing on. When they add a new color to their repertory, add the same one to the finger paint table.

- *Have the Children Cut or Tear Colored Paper*

Colored construction paper can be used in many ways. When they have learned two or three colors, let the children cut up pieces of construction paper that are these colors and use the pieces for a sorting activity or for making collages. Do not confuse children by combining shape and color activities when the youngsters first are learning color concepts.

- *Play Concept Games*

Children love to play any game that focuses on them. A game that asks them to identify the color of their clothing makes an excellent transition between activities: "The boy with the blue and white sneakers may go to lunch; the girl with the red and white top may go next; all the children with brown pants may go."

- *Read Color Books*

Many picture books feature colors. One of the most simple, yet dramatic picture books, is Leo Lionni's classic *Little Blue and Little Yellow*, New York: Astor-Honor, 1959, in which a little blue circle and a little yellow circle want to play together but are not allowed to by their blue family and yellow family. When the two circles finally do come together, a dramatic change takes place: They, of course, become green. Cornell University Early Childhood Specialist Sue McCord has added a most effective method for demonstrating this blue-yellow combination: She reads the story at naptime with the room darkened and two flashlights covered with blue and yellow cellophane playing on the ceiling as the children watch from their cots. The yellow circle and blue circle on the ceiling turn just as green as paint when they finally come together.

Another classic is Margaret Wise Brown's *The Color Kittens*, recently reissued by Golden Books, New York: Golden Press, 1977. The book tells about Brush and Hush, two kitten painters who have all of the colors in the world except green and spend the story trying to find green.

Other favorite books featuring colors include the following:

Freeman, Don. *A Rainbow of My Own*. New York: Puffin Books, 1978.
Hoban, Tana. *Is It Red? Is It Yellow? Is It Blue?* New York: Greenwillow, 1978.
Kellogg, Steven. *The Mystery of the Flying Orange Pumpkin*. New York: The Dial Press, 1980.
Kellogg, Steven. *The Mystery of the Magic Green Ball*. New York: The Dial Press, 1978.
Kellogg, Steven. *The Mystery of the Missing Red Mitten*. New York: The Dial Press, 1974.
Robinson, Deborah. *Anthony's Hat*. New York: Scholastic, 1976.
Stinson, Kathy. *Red is Best*. Toronto, Canada: Annick Press, 1983.
Zolotow, Charlotte. *Mr. Rabbit and the Lovely Present*. New York: Scholastic, 1962.

- *Create Book Activities*

Besides reading these books to the children, think of other fun activities that can extend the book experience while helping the children learn colors. *Anthony's Hat*, for example, can be played as a game. The book features the little boy Anthony who gets a beautiful black hat for his birthday, but when he wears it outside to show his friends, a number of different items drop on it and turn it different colors, unbeknownst to Anthony. One child in your classroom can sit in a chair with a hat on and his eyes covered while another child drops a colored cloth or item of clothing over the hat. The first child then can guess what color his or her hat is now.

If you purchase paperback books, you can cut up a duplicate copy of *Anthony's Hat*, mount the pictures on cardboard with a sandpaper backing, and let the children use the pictures to retell the story. You also can let the children play with the pictures on a flannelboard.

☐ RECOGNIZES DIFFERENCES IN SIZE

As the young child constructs his own knowledge by interacting with the objects and people in his environment, his brain seems to pay special attention to the relationships between things. Size is one of those relationships. The child must understand the property of size, like the properties of shape and color, in order to make sense of his world.

There are various orders of size, usually thought of in terms of opposites: big-little, large-small, tall-short, long-short, wide-narrow, thick-thin, and deep-shallow. Direct comparison of objects based on one of these aspects seems to be the best way for young children to learn size.

Natural Curiosity

The children already should be making sensory explorations of objects in the classroom. Are they? We know that infants are born investigators. They not only are predisposed to explore their surroundings with their senses, but they also almost are driven by some inner urge to try out, get hold of, and get into everything that is within reach. We call this "natural curiosity" when its results are positive. But, we say other, less pleasant things about it when infants, toddlers, and preschoolers get into things that they should not be investigating.

Yet, all investigations by children are part of the same natural urge to find out. We should cultivate this drive in children, for it is their principal motivation for learning. Some parents encourage their children to pursue this drive; some do not. You can see this parental influence—or lack of it—in the behavior of your preschoolers. Some children seem to have retained their natural curiosity; others have not, maybe because their original investigations were stopped by their parents.

Rather than stop such investigations, some parents realize it is better to "child proof" the house by putting dangerous and breakable items away, covering electrical outlets, and blocking off stairs and cupboards. Then, the child can explore without creating negative consequences for anyone.

If children, instead, have been scolded constantly, punished physically, or restrained from exploring their environment, many eventually give up. You may have to talk with their parents about how children learn, and to work with the children in trying to reactivate their natural curiosity.

Bring in some new, interesting, but unknown item, and watch to see which of your children try to find out about it. For instance, seal an onion in a box covered with colored wrapping paper and punctured with several holes. Put it on a display table in your classroom with a sign reading: "Guess what's inside!" Then, observe and record which children are curious enough to try to find out.

They will have to ask what the sign says. You can tell them, but do not give them any other hints. Does anyone shake the box, smell it, or poke in or try to see through the holes? Does anyone ask another child or another classroom worker what is in the box?

Let the children tell their guesses to the tape recorder, individually, and ask them to give their names and to say why they each think they are correct.

Later at circle time, you can play the tape, discuss it, and then open the box to see if anyone guessed its contents correctly.

This activity can help you in two ways: first, you can determine who are the curious children and which ones never seem to notice or do not have the courage to make a guess; second, it should motivate your children to do sensory exploration. It may even remotivate those who seem to have lost their natural curiosity.

Repeat this activity every few days for several weeks, and see if it makes a difference in your children's sensory exploring abilities, guessing abilities, and interest in new things. In addition, you should take the lead in modeling the behavior you want your children to exhibit. When you come to something new, explore it yourself with your senses, and make your own educated guesses. Shapes, colors, and now sizes are some of the properties you and your children should be focusing on.

Comparisons

Comparing one object with another is one of the best ways to investigate the properties of something new or different. This is, in fact, how the brain works. It takes in and evaluates data about the new object on the basis of what the brain has processed previously about a similar object.

When you first are using comparisons with your children and are focusing on the concept of size, be sure to use objects that are alike in all of their properties except size. This is not the time to use different colored or different shaped items. Instead, try using two similar objects, one that is large and one that is small at first.

Opposites

Making a direct comparison of two objects that are similar in every aspect except size is one of the best methods to use for teaching children the concept of size. Use things such as two apples (a big and little one), two cups, two blocks, two books, and two dolls. Be sure to talk in positive terms ("This one is big. This one is little"), rather than in negative terms ("This one is not big"), which only may confuse the child. Also be sure the children are making comparisons of the two objects, themselves, and not of the objects' position in space. Some children look at two similar objects and say that the closest one is biggest because it looks bigger to them than a more distant object.

Use the size opposites "big" and "small" in all sorts of comparisons in your classroom before you move on to other aspects of size such as "tall" and "short." Children's brains seem to overgeneralize with many of the size opposites, equating "big" with "tall." That overgeneralization may explain why, in Piaget's classic experiment, they believe that a tall, thin container of liquid has more in it than a short, wide container, although both contain the same amount. In other words, "tall" means "big" or "more" to most young children.

Use the words for size opposites whenever you can in the classroom: "Look, Alice has built a tall building, and Bonnie has made a short one." "Who can find a thick pencil? Who can find a thin one?"

If You Have Not Checked This Item: Some Helpful Ideas

- *Play Size Transition Games*

When you are waiting with the children for lunch to be served, for the bus to come, or for something special to happen, it is a good idea to have a repertory of brief transition games, fingerplays, or stories available. This time provides an excellent opportunity for concept games such as: "The girl wearing the skirt with wide stripes may stand up." "The boy wearing the T-shirt with narrow stripes may stand up." Or, play a guessing game with your fingers. Hold your hands behind your back, and ask your children to guess which hand has a big finger held up and which has a little finger, held up. Then, show them. Can one of your children then be the leader of this game?

- *Read a Size Book*

Some children's books feature size. A favorite one is Steven Kellogg's *Much Bigger than Martin*, New York: The Dial Press, 1976, in which Martin's little brother fantasizes about what it would be like to be much bigger than his brother. The illustrations are hilarious.

Fast-Slow High-Low, a Book of Opposites, by Peter Spier, Garden City, N.Y.: Doubleday & Company, 1972, is a wordless picture book with one set of opposites on each double page. The book is illustrated by many pairs of similar but opposite objects or people. The many examples may be confusing to children who are just at the beginning of their understanding of differences, but it is a good book for most kindergarten children. You may want to pick out only certain pages to use at a time: big-small, long-short, deep-shallow, tall-short, or wide-narrow.

☐ SORTS OBJECTS BY APPEARANCE

Once they have begun to notice the similar properties of objects, children can begin to group or classify the objects, an ability that is necessary in cognitive development in order for the brain to sort out and process the wealth of incoming data obtained through the sensory activities of the child. Sorting objects and materials gives children practice in this skill and involves identifying the similarities of objects as well as understanding relationships (i.e., which items belong together because of their similarities).

Piaget and other researchers have noted that children progress through a sequence of sorting skills, and each skill is more complex than the previous one as the youngsters' cognitive abilities develop.

The earliest sorting skill to appear is simple classification, which many two- and most three-year-olds can do. Children doing simple classification can sort or group objects that actually belong together in the real world. For example, they can group together all of the toy animals that live on the farm in one set and all of the toy animals that live in the zoo in another set if the youngsters have had previous experiences with such animals. This activity is not quite true classification because it is based on associations between the animals and their homes rather than likenesses or differences of the animals.

Another type of simple classification in which young children place things that "belong together" into a group involves putting all of the toy trucks, cars, and motorcycles together in a group because "you can drive them," or putting the proper hats on all of the dolls, or putting all of the blocks together because they make a house.

Less verbal children seem to do as well in simple classification tasks as verbal children (Richardson, p. 181). These simple classification tasks do involve real classification skills. In order to perform them, children need to understand the rule for sorting and to follow it with consistency. In addition, the youngsters must discriminate likenesses and differences based on function or some other rule in order to place objects in the correct group. The main difference between this kind of sorting and real classification is that simple classification is based on something other than appearances only, and the groups formed are not true classes.

A more mature type of classification that many three-year-olds and most four- and five-year-olds can do involves classifying objects into separate sets based on a common characteristic like color, for instance. You can ask the children to place all the red blocks in one set and all the blue blocks in another.

The problem most young children have in doing this kind of sorting involves consistency. They have difficulty keeping in mind the rule upon which the sorting is based. Often, they will start sorting objects on the basis of color but will switch in the middle of the task to some other property, like shape, and even will switch again before they are finished.

Children need to practice with all kinds of sorting games, activities, and collections, and the youngsters love this practice. Give a child a box of mixed buttons and let the individual sort it out in any way he or she chooses. Talk with the child afterwards, and ask how he or she decided on which buttons to put in each pile. Look around your classroom for other objects to sort, things such as dressup clothing, blocks, and eating utensils.

By age five, children with experience can sort objects into intersecting sets based on more than one characteristic, using color as well as size, for example.

If You Have Not Checked This Item: Some Helpful Ideas

- *Use Block Sorting*

Have children help sort out a certain type of the unit blocks during cleanup before putting them back on the shelves. This activity will give you an indication of which children can and cannot sort objects based on appearances. Make this activity a game, though, and not a task.

Block pickup gives children an opportunity to practice sorting skills.

- *Play with Lotto Cards*

Make or purchase simple lotto cards that the children can match. You can mount different colored construction paper onto cardboard, cover it with clear contact paper, and cut it into playing card size. Have at least four cards for each color. Mix the cards up, and let the children try to sort them out.

Get several duplicate catalogs from companies such as car dealers, and cut up the catalogs, mounting four similar car pictures on each set of four cards.

- *Make Collection-Sorting Games*

Take a shoe box, three empty margarine containers that have a hole cut in the top of them, and a collection of three kinds of seeds. You can use beans, three sizes of paper clips, or any other collection you can think of instead of the seeds. Let the child dump the collection into the top of the shoe box and sort it piece by piece into the margarine cups. This activity provides good small motor practice as well.

☐ DISCRIMINATES THINGS THAT ARE ALIKE FROM THOSE THAT ARE DIFFERENT

The classification skill previously discussed under "sorting" asked whether children could group objects by appearance, especially on the basis of things that looked alike. This next *Checklist* item looks to see if children can discriminate things on the basis of being alike or being different. That is, can the children tell which items are alike and which are different by looking, feeling, and by smelling?

We know that infants build up mental constructs of the objects and people in their environment. Recent technology has helped us determine the kinds of things infants like to look at. Time and again, infants seem to prefer things that are familiar but slightly different. As they grow older, for instance, children look longer at pictures of faces that are a bit more complex than those they are used to. (Schickedanz, p. 151)

Thus, we know that the brain is stimulated by a moderate level of novelty and that even at a very young age, children can recognize differences in visual stimuli. We also know that the infants who do well on such tests of development are babies who have had the freedom to move around the floor of their homes and not just the bottom of their playpens. These well-developed infants also have had a variety of toys to play with and responsive mothers. (Schickedanz, p. 152)

Preschoolers and kindergartners also should be able to distinguish likenesses and differences in objects around them on the basis of the objects' look, feel, sound, smell, and taste. Montessori programs and others include materials such as "smell cylinders" that children must try out in order to match the pairs that smell the same. Fabric sorting games and texture boards also are used to promote sensory discrimination. Many young children even learn to distinguish musical sounds that are the same and those that are different.

In order to develop or refine their skills of discrimination, young children need a great deal of sensory practice and the freedom to explore and play with the objects in their environment. This need is one of the reasons why a "free play" or "free choice" period is so important in the classroom. Besides providing such time for children, you also need to provide the appropriate sensory materials for learning to discriminate likenesses and differences.

Have collections of materials that can be matched such as small cars, miniature people, plastic table blocks, and lotto cards of birds or animals. Observe to see which of your children can distinguish likenesses and differences easily and which need more help.

If You Have Not Checked This Item: Some Helpful Ideas

- *Use Color Discrimination Activities*

Activities that involve discriminating colors are different from those in which children learn to recognize one color at a time. On one of the tabletops in your manipulative area, put strips of masking tape in parallel rows six inches apart. Color each strip a different color. Let children place items from a set of things (such as cars, people, animals, and buttons) on the strip with the matching color.

▪ Encourage Shape Discrimination

You can provide the same kind of motivation for children to sort out shapes from a collection. One way to provide this inducement is to cut out contact paper shapes of the unit blocks, just as you do for shelf symbols, only this time stick the shapes to pieces of cardboard that you place here and there on the floor of your block corner when the children have finished building and are ready to pick up. Then, let the youngsters stack up the right blocks on top of the proper cutout block symbol. When all the blocks have been categorized this way, the children can slide the cardboards over to the shelves and put back the blocks on the proper shelves without any trouble.

▪ Read a "Find-the-Animal" Book

Several books hide pictures of animals or other objects within the illustrations and challenge children to try to find the pictures.

But Where is the Green Parrot? by Thomas and Wanda Zacharias, New York: Delacorte Press, 1968, is a beautifully done book containing a large brightly colored train, house, toy chest, garden, and circus against a white background, with a text that describes the various colored items on each page but challenges the children to find the green parrot hidden somewhere on the pages.

Find the Cat by Elaine Livermore, Boston: Houghton Mifflin, 1973, is an interesting, simple story about a dog searching inside a house for the cat that has made off with its bone. This book is more of a challenge for young children than the previous book, since the illustrations are more complicated black line drawings against a yellow background. This book calls for sharp eyes to discriminate the shape of the cat on each page.

☐ PUTS PARTS TOGETHER TO MAKE A WHOLE

Thus far, we have observed children to find out if they can recognize shapes, colors, and sizes, sort objects on the basis of similar appearance, and discriminate things that are alike from those that are different. These classification skills indicate children's cognitive development, for the brain constructs knowledge about its world through classification. Observation tells us where the children stand in their development and what kinds of experiences we should be providing them in order to further this development.

This next *Checklist* item asks us to observe whether children are able to use their recognition of the various properties of objects by putting them together to make a whole. All through their lives, children's brains will be called upon to organize pieces of knowledge in this fashion. In the beginning, youngsters learn to organize information about concrete objects. Later, they will need to organize abstract information and ideas in order to make inferences and draw conclusions.

Some people are better at seeing "the whole picture" than others, just as some children can sort, match, and categorize concrete objects better than others. You will want to find out which children in your classroom can see the whole picture and which need help and practice in putting together parts to form a whole.

Many young children see parts as separate entities in themselves and do not see the relationship of parts to a whole. Three- and four-year-olds are just at the beginning of this organizational aspect of their knowledge. The most common uses of part-whole relationships in your classroom may be the manipulative activities of making puzzles or putting together take-apart toys, and the art activities of making models in clay or play dough or creating representational pictures (for your more advanced children). When children are creating their own wholes, they often omit important parts. As cognitive development occurs, children refine their abilities to create wholes, and they see their omissions.

A common kind of part-whole relationship activity that preschool children often engage in is making puzzles.

Putting parts together to make a whole is yet another aspect of "figurative knowing." (See p. 174.) The child's brain has stored perceptual information about the things the youngster has dealt with and now must mentally reproduce a previous state of affairs: what something looked like previously when it was whole. In order to be successful in making a simple puzzle, for instance, children need to represent the whole puzzle in their minds as they move the pieces.

While perceptual information is concerned with actions as they occur in the present, the mechanism for reproducing past or future images in a child's mind involves cognition. As we know, cognition develops in children in a sequential manner as they interact with their world and mature in their thinking. Children's brains assimilate information from the interactions the youngsters have been experiencing, and the brains organize this information into a system of concepts, relationships, and rules that in turn reproduce the mental images necessary for children to form wholes out of parts (Cowan, p. 42).

This balance between biological maturity and physical experience works the same in a child's cognitive development as it does in his or her physical development of being able to throw a ball, for instance. In the beginning, the child is awkward and not entirely successful. With practice and maturity, a child is able to perform more smoothly. With no practice at all, the individual may have difficulty even though he or she is mature enough to perform. Your program should provide this practice.

If You Have Not Checked This Item: Some Helpful Ideas

- *Make Flannelboard Pictures*

Have children practice assembling pictures of familiar objects and people on a flannelboard. You can make your own flannelboard quite simply by covering a piece of cardboard with flannel or felt. For the pictures, color and cut out large figures from a coloring book. Mount them on cardboard, back them with sandpaper, cover them with clear contact paper for protection, and cut them into their separate parts: arms, legs, head, and body for people; wheels and body for cars; legs, head, tail, and body for animals. Keep each picture in a marked manila envelope. Trace the whole picture on the outside of the envelope so that children will know what the picture looks like.

You not only may want to use one large flannelboard with a group, but also consider making small, individual flannelboards to be kept on the shelves of your manipulative area along with the envelopes containing the picture parts for your children to assemble.

- *Have Toys that Can Be Taken Apart*

It is much easier for young children to take something apart than to put it back together. They need encouragement and practice on this second part of the skill as well. A number of commercial toys can be manipulated in this way. If you do not find any in your regular stores, try a hobby shop.

☐ ARRANGES EVENTS IN SEQUENCE FROM FIRST TO LAST

In observing children to determine their cognitive development, we have been concentrating thus far on the classification aspects of what is known as "logico-mathematical knowledge." Children display three aspects of this knowledge

1. **Classification abilities:** The ability to understand particular characteristics or properties of objects, and the ability to group things into classes with common properties.
2. **Seriation abilities:** the ability to understand "more than" or "less than," and the ability to arrange things systematically in a sequence or a series based on a particular rule or order.
3. **Number abilities:** the ability to understand the meaning and use of numbers, and the ability to apply numbers in counting and ordering.

(Saunders, p. 120)

The last two *Checklist* items in Chapter 8 involve seriation abilities in children, while the first two items in Chapter 9 deal with number abilities. All three of these aspects are part of a child's "operative knowing," that is, the system of knowledge he has constructed about his world through the organization of his perceptual experiences.

In order to arrange events in a sequence, the child first has to recognize their properties and relationships. How are they alike? How are they different? What is the common thread that creates their relationship to one another? Then, the child must understand order, that something comes first, something happens next, and something occurs last. His practice in sorting things by appearance should help him to note both properties and relationships among events as well.

But, just as the young child often changes the rule he is using as he sorts a number of things, he also displays inconsistency in arranging events in a sequence. It is as if his immature mind cannot hold for long the rule upon which the sequencing is based.

Cards with action pictures frequently are used in sequence games. The cards show sequences of an action from beginning to end, with one part of the sequence on each card. For example, one set of cards may have pictures of a pencil sitting on a desk, rolling off the desk, falling through the air, hitting the floor, and lying on the floor. Three- and four-year-olds often arrange only the first and last cards correctly. Another card set may show a baseball being thrown, going straight through the air, being hit by a bat, looping through the air, and being caught by a person with a baseball glove.

Such sequence cards really are not appropriate for preschoolers, since games with rules are beyond many of them at their developmental level, and since many of the cards depict events that are unclear and difficult even for adults to arrange. Some preschoolers will be able to arrange three easily understood sequence cards in proper order. Kindergartners, with their increased maturity, are more successful. When asked to tell about a series of events in the order they occur, many children can do it correctly if the events are familiar. But, if the sequence is too long and complicated, the best most preschoolers can do is to identify the correct beginning and ending.

Ask your children to relate their favorite stories that you are familiar with. Do the youngsters get the plot sequence in the right order? Ask them to tell you what they would do in a fast food restaurant in order to get something to eat. Did they include all the essential steps?

If You Have Not Checked This Item: Some Helpful Ideas

- *Use an Instant Print Camera*

Children learn best from their own actions. Take a series of three photos of a child performing an action: for instance, bringing in a birthday cake, blowing out the candles, and eating the cake; or building a house, completing the house, and knocking it down. Cover the photos with clear contact paper for protection, and put the sets in envelopes for the children to play with. If the youngsters understand number sequence, you can number the pictures on the back for the children to check on their accuracy.

- *Use an Illustrated Recipe Chart in Cooking*

Use a large chart with each step in the cooking process numbered and illustrated in sequence. Discuss each step with the children as they do it. Ask them which step comes next, and then what.

You may discover that some of the preschoolers' problems with sequencing can be explained by their incomplete understanding of a particular process. For instance, children who had completed all of the steps in the recipe chart for making a birthday cake and were ready to put it in the oven were asked, "What should we do next?" Some said, "eat it;" others thought that candles should be put on, but nobody understood that the next step was to bake it!

- *Make Your Own Sequence Cards*

Coloring books often show simple drawings of people or animals in a sequence. You can cut out the drawings and mount them on cardboard for use in your table games area. Comic books, of course, show pictures in a sequence. If you find any that are simple enough or appropriate for preschoolers, you also can cut and mount these comics in sets. Furthermore, you can buy duplicate paperback storybooks, and you can cut out and mount sets of three sequence cards from the favorite stories.

- *Make a Pictorial Daily Schedule*

Draw or paste pictures to illustrate the time blocks of your daily schedule in the order they occur. Display this pictorial schedule prominently, and discuss it with the children whenever the need arises, using questions such as: "What do we do first today?" "What comes next?"

☐ ARRANGES OBJECTS IN SERIES ACCORDING TO A CERTAIN RULE

The final item involving seriation asks us to observe children to see if they can arrange objects in a series based on a certain rule, from the biggest to the smallest, from the tallest to the shortest, from the hardest to the softest, or from the loudest to the quietest, for example.

Young children usually are able to form a series if they are provided with cues. Montessori size cylinders, for instance, are supposed to be arranged in a board with graded holes of the proper size. Children fit the cylinders from large to small in the increasingly smaller holes with this self-correcting activity. The youngsters match the size of the cylinders with the size of the holes and find out by trying which cylinders do or do not fit. Once they have learned the concept, many children are able to line up the cylinders in the proper order without cues from the board.

Stacking blocks, boxes, and rings works on the same principle of arranging items in a series from the largest to the smallest. Even toddlers soon learn that the largest item will not fit into a smaller one and that if one item is left over, they need to start over again to find their mistake. The point is that children play these learning games on their own, and the youngsters learn the concept through their play.

It is true, though, that three- and four-year-olds have difficulty forming a consistent series from a large number of items when no cues exist, just as they have trouble in sorting out large collections or arranging many action cards into the proper sequence. Although children are able to compare two items on the basis of size, as soon as several other graded items are added, the youngsters have difficulty arranging the items in the proper order.

Most preschoolers understand the concept of bigger and smaller, but when this concept is applied to a series, the complexity of the many comparisons seems to confuse the youngsters. How can an object that is bigger than one item at the same time be smaller than the item that precedes it?

You may find that you have not checked this particular *Checklist* item for any but the most mature children. This finding is to be expected with three- and four-year-olds. Five-year-olds are more successful. You may decide to add a number of new series games and activities to your manipulative or science/math areas in order to promote this skill. Be sure the new materials provide enough cues for your children to be successful. Most of all, be sure the new activities are fun to do.

If You Have Not Checked This Item: Some Helpful Ideas

- *Arrange Children*

Have groups of three children at a time arrange themselves from tallest to shortest. Mix up the children so that the shortest child in one group may not be the shortest in another group.

▪ *Read Books That Feature Series*

The traditional classic stories of *Goldilocks and the Three Bears, The Three Little Pigs,* and *The Three Billy Goats Gruff* all feature a graduated series of characters, from the biggest to the smallest, along with their graduated series of furniture, cereal bowls, houses, and even noises. Children love these stories and will want to say aloud the repetitious dialog or sounds as you read or tell the stories. The youngsters may want to act out the stories as well.

You can cut out the pictures of the three characters from extra paperback copies of each of these books. You can mount the characters on sandpaper and use them with your flannelboard activities. Can your children arrange the characters in proper order from biggest to smallest? What about from littlest to biggest?

REFERENCES CITED

Cowan, Philip A. *Piaget with Feeling: Cognitive, Social and Emotional Dimensions.* New York: Holt, Rinehart and Winston, 1978.

Pines, Maya. "Can A Rock Walk?" *Psychology Today.* November 1983.

Pines, Maya. "Head Start in the Nursery," *Psychology Today,* September 1979.

Richardson, Lloyd I., et al. *A Mathematics Activity Curriculum for Early Childhood and Special Education.* New York: Macmillan Publishing Co., 1980.

Saunders, Ruth, and Ann M. Bingham-Newman. *Piagetian Perspective for Preschools: A Thinking Book for Teachers.* Englewood Cliffs, N.J.: Prentice-Hall, 1984.

Schickedanz, Judith A., et al. *Toward Understanding Children.* Boston: Little, Brown, and Company, 1982.

OTHER SOURCES

Beaty, Janice J. *Skills for Preschool Teachers,* Columbus, Ohio: Charles E. Merrill Publishing Company, 1984.

Forman, George E., and David S. Kuschner. *The Child's Construction of Knowledge: Piaget for Teaching Children.* Washington, D.C.: National Association for the Education of Young Children, 1983.

Osborn, Janie Dyson, and D. Keith Osborn. *Cognition in Early Childhood.* Athens, Georgia: Education Associates, 1983.

LEARNING ACTIVITIES

1. Use the *Child Skills Checklist*, "7. Cognitive Development," as a screening tool to observe all of the children in your classroom. Which of your children did you check for most of the items? How did these children do on other areas of the *Checklist,* for example, in Small Motor Development?

2. Choose a child whom you found did not have many checks under Cognitive Development. Observe the child on three different days, making a running record to help you get a more detailed picture of his or her cognitive skills. Plan an activity to help this child, and record the results when you use it.

3. What are the ages of the children who had the most checks on the *Checklist?* What are the ages of those with the least checks? What are the children's backgrounds? Can you make any inferences about cognitive development based on this information?

4. Choose a child who needs practice in discriminating likeness and difference, set up activities for the child to practice this skill, or play some appropriate games with him or her. Record the results.

5. Read one of the children's books from this chapter with a child you have identified as needing help in a particular cognitive development area. Discuss the results.

 Cognitive Development:
Number, Time,
Space, Memory

Cognitive Development: Number, Time, Space, Memory Checklist

- ☐ Counts by rote to ten
- ☐ Counts objects to ten
- ☐ Knows the daily schedule in sequence
- ☐ Knows what happened yesterday
- ☐ Can build a block enclosure
- ☐ Can locate an object behind or beside something
- ☐ Recalls words to song, chant
- ☐ Can recollect and act on a series of directions

T his second chapter on children's cognitive development continues the discussion begun in Chapter 8 but deals with several different aspects: children's learning to understand the concepts of number, time, and space, as well as the development of memory. Two *Checklist* items are devoted to each of these aspects. Observers will need to watch and listen to children as the youngsters work and play naturally in the classroom, displaying evidence of their cognitive development.

As with all *Checklist* items, those under Cognitive Development are not a test of children's abilities, but a listing of behaviors that children possibly can accomplish. Cognitive development observers should not set up the particular activities listed in this chapter and then record as children try to perform the tasks; instead, the observers should keep an overview of children in the classroom and check these activities as behaviors are performed naturally. If there is no opportunity to see the behaviors performed, then the observer needs to record "*N*" rather than leaving the item blank.

☐ COUNTS BY ROTE TO TEN

Learning the concept of number is important for young humans to accomplish. They will be dealing most of their lives with numbers involving size, distance, amounts, time, temperature, costs, money, and measurement. As each child's mind quests to create its own knowledge, the children will be going through a predetermined sequence of development, internalizing the information gained from their sensory interactions with their world, as noted earlier.

Even two-year-olds display a rudimentary knowledge of numbers when they hold up two fingers to show you their age and count aloud "one, two." This counting is more of a parrot-type response and does not indicate a true understanding of "two years." Some two-year-olds and most three- and four-year-olds are able to count by rote to ten, and sometimes even higher. Again, this rote counting does not mean that the children understand the concept of number in the beginning.

Often, in fact, children do not get the sequence correct in their counting, or they even may leave out a number or two. These mix-ups are understandable

Preschool children can count off the days of the month, but a true understanding of time comes later.

since the children are performing a memory task. The youngsters' counting is really chanting, as in a nursery rhyme. You will find that if you ask them, the children really do not know the meaning of each word. In fact, their chanting of numbers seems more like one long word instead of ten separate ones: "onetwothreefourfivesixseveneightnineten."

This type of counting is partly a factor of language experience; the children are at the very beginning of this experience. In order to understand the meaning of each number word, the child must form a mental image of it. You cannot expect this mental image formation of two-year-olds. By age three, some children will have formed mental images of certain numbers because the youngsters have had sensory experience with the use of numbers in the environment. It is therefore important for parents and other adults to use numbers frequently in the children's everyday living and to involve children in the use of numbers with activities such as measuring, weighing, counting out items, counting out money, and playing games involving counting moves.

With infants and toddlers, chanting numbers, and singing and chanting number rhymes such as "one-two, buckle my shoe," are an important prelude to understanding number concepts and should be encouraged. But, before children can be expected to know the meaning of each number, they first must accomplish several of the skills mentioned in Chapter 8, which are dependent both on maturity and practice.

The children will need to be able to place objects in a series and to understand that an object is bigger or smaller than another object. The youngsters will need to be asking questions such as "how many?" And, of course, the children will need to know the names of the numbers. Some of these skills just are surfacing in the preschool classroom, but many children will not fully grasp the concepts of seriation and number much before the age of seven or second grade (Cowan, p. 181).

For children who can count to ten rapidly but seem to have no understanding of numbers or of counting real things, try having them count to seven or to nine. The children will have to slow down and think about what they are doing. They may not be able to stop at a number other than ten at first. Play games with individuals or small groups asking each to count to a number other than ten that you will call out. Make the games exciting. Children who have not learned to count will soon be picking it up in order to play the game.

If You Have Not Checked This Item: Some Helpful Ideas

- *Play Number Chanting Games*

Say or sing chants, such as "one little, two little, three little Indians," using fingers or even children who jump up, sit down, or perform some other action.

- *Chant Backwards*

Use number chants in all sorts of ways. Children love to count down 10–9–8–7–6–5–4–3–2–1–0 before the missile or space shuttle blasts off. Have them make models in their woodworking area or with clay, or ask them to bring in toy spaceships.

- *Read Counting Books*

1,2,3 *to the Zoo* by Eric Carle, New York: Philomel Books, 1968, is a wordless picture book with a number symbol on each double spread page and a large colorful illustration of animals in a train car on the way to the zoo. Although the numbers show one-to-one correspondence with the animals, the book is principally a counting book because it has no words.

Moja Means One: Swahili Counting Book by Muriel and Tom Feelings, New York: The Dial Press, 1971, gives the numbers one-through-ten in regular number symbols but with the number name in the Swahili language on each double page. One sentence of text describes the African scene or custom portrayed. Children enjoy learning new names for things.

Ten, Nine, Eight by Molly Bang, New York: Greenwillow Books, 1983, is a simple counting book that shows a little black girl and her father as they count down the objects in her bedroom before she goes to sleep.

☐ COUNTS OBJECTS TO TEN

Three-, four- and five-year-olds can master simple one-to-one correspondence, which is what we are asking them to do when they count objects. Counting objects to ten is the children's next step in the sequence of learning number concepts. At first, the youngsters try to rush through their counting chant without actually including all of the objects. The children are more concerned with saying all of the numbers than with making sure each number represents an object. When the youngsters understand the task, they will learn to do it accurately.

Start with fewer items than ten in the beginning, just as you did with number chanting. Then, the children will learn to stop before they get to ten. Also, have the children touch each item as they count. If they skip one, have them try again. Or, have them hand you an item as they count it.

Learning to do sorting, as discussed in Chapter 8, is good preparation for counting things. Putting a cup with a saucer or a hat on a doll helps the children understand one-to-one correspondence. Now, they must apply their learning to numbers. They learn by their sensory actions that the number "one" represents the first object, that "two" represents the second, and so on. This learning is the first step. But, counting in a progression still is not the same as understanding one-to-one correspondence.

The children may be able to count a row of ten children and still may not be able to choose four of them. Once they are able to count up to ten objects in a progression, the youngsters will need practice in picking out a particular number of items, such as three dolls, five blocks, or seven dominoes. Phrase your questions or directions to give the children practice with both activities. "How many red markers are there?" asks them to count in a progression. "Bring me eight napkins" takes them one step further in their development of number concepts.

Recording Numbers

To support your children's number activities, you must record their counting. You should not use number symbols at first; instead, use several familiar pictures or shapes to represent the amount. For example, keep an attendance chart with all of the children's names, and mark a symbol for each child present. Then, the children can count the symbols. Put signs in each activity area with a particular number of stick figures to represent the number of children allowed in the area at once, or have a certain number of hooks on the wall and name tags to hang on them in each area. Check from time to time with the children in the area; have them count how many youngsters are there, and have them check whether this amount is the proper number.

Use charts and bar graphs at appropriate times to record numbers. Hang a calendar chart near the guinea pig's cage, and record the number of carrots he eats every day by pasting or drawing carrot symbols. Record how much each child's seeds grow every week by posting a chart with the child's name and having him or her measure with a ruler or stick marked with a green dot for every inch. Let the child count and record the proper number of green dots after his or her name each week, or use a bar graph that can be colored in up to the height the plant has reached.

Later in the year when the children have shown that they understand one-to-one correspondence, you may want to use real number symbols along with the picture symbols. Numbers alone are too abstract for most children this age.

If You Have Not Checked This Item: Some Helpful Ideas

- *Have the Children Count One Another*

Any activity is more meaningful to a young child if it involves him and his peers directly. Have children help you take attendance in the morning by going around and counting how many children are present. Have the counters touch each child. Give the counters help with numbers above ten.

- *Have Many Counting Materials*

Fill your manipulative or science/math area with counting materials or games. Use egg cartons; let the children fill the sections with items and count how many things are there. Use buttons, seeds, dominoes, spools, paper clips, and macaroni as items for filling the cartons.

- *Read Number Books*

One Bright Monday Morning by Arline and Joseph Baum, New York: Knopf Pantheon, 1962, is a cumulative counting book of the objects seen by children on the way to school each day of the week.

One Snail and Me by Emilie Warren McLeod, Boston: Little, Brown, and Company, 1961, is a hilarious cumulative counting book with each page showing another odd menagerie of animals that a little girl has with her in the bathtub. Humorous illustrations and rollicking rhymes help children to count groups of animals from one to ten.

Bunches and Bunches of Bunnies by Louise Mathews, New York: Scholastic, 1978, shows several sets of rabbits on one page, the total number on the next page, and a rhyming text that multiplies the sets to get the total number. Although the multiplication is certainly inappropriate for young children, they can ignore it (or learn from it if they can) and still can have fun counting the groups of bunnies in comical antics.

- *Have Children Set the Table*

Let the children set the table for meals and snacks. The children will need a set number of forks, plates, cups, and napkins for each table. This real task excellently teaches one-to-one correspondence.

☐ KNOWS THE DAILY SCHEDULE IN SEQUENCE

Understanding Time

Time is the next cognitive concept we need to look for in young children. Three-, four-, and five-year-olds are only at the beginning of their temporal understanding. We need to provide them with simple activities involving time, but we cannot expect the youngsters to develop a mature understanding of so abstract a concept during the preschool years and kindergarten.

Time comprehension has a number of different aspects: 1) the ability to understand what comes "before" and what comes "after," 2) the ability to describe past events, 3) the ability to anticipate and plan for future events, 4) the ability to describe the order or sequence of things, 5) the ability to understand the passage of time and how it is measured (with clocks and calendars), and 6) the ability to understand units of time (such as seconds, minutes, hours, days, weeks, months, years, and centuries).

The child's ability to arrange things in a sequence or series based on a particular rule or order was discussed in Chapter 8 under seriation abilities. This knowledge that events may occur in a particular order with something happening first, something next, and something last generally precedes a child's understanding of time intervals.

Because young children are still egocentric, looking at everything exclusively from their own point of view, they do not perceive time as adults do. To young children, time occurs because they are there. For example, "snack time" and "nap time" do not happen unless they participate. They learn to understand the movement of the hands on the clock only very superficially; the youngsters usually only know that two hands pointing straight up means lunch time. Calendars, likewise, have little meaning for the children, although youngsters can memorize the names of the days of the week.

One of the problems is that time is a very abstract concept. It is not something you can see. Even adults realize that the passage of time seems uneven in different circumstances. If we are occupied, it goes quickly; if we are bored, it drags. For young children, the present moment is most important. Their comprehension of past and future is limited to periods of time not too distant from the present.

Time is one of the basic organizing dimensions of the child's experience (Cowan, p. 126), and as such, time needs to be considered an important part of the child's cognitive development. Although the young child will not develop a mature perception of time while in your classroom, you need to be aware of each child's present development in this area in order to provide activities and support for its continued growth.

Using the Daily Schedule

Since the child learns best from things and events that involve him directly, using the daily schedule to help him understand the concept of time is a good place to begin. First of all, you must have a daily schedule that is clear and consistent. The activity periods can be of various lengths as long as they follow one another in the same order daily. A brief transition activity between each period helps children to understand that the next period is about to begin.

A full-day program might consist of the following:

A.M.	P.M.
Arrival	Nap time
Morning circle	Free choice
Free choice	Snack
Snack	Afternoon circle
Outdoor play	Departure
Toilet	
Story	
Lunch	

If you follow this same schedule consistently day after day, children not only feel secure about what will happen, but they also come to an understanding about the sequence of things. The ability to represent mentally and to remember the order of events are essential ingredients in the young child's development of the concept of time. Even if your morning free choice period varies in length from day to day, the children will still know that it comes after morning circle and is followed by snack time.

The morning circle time is essential in bringing about awareness of this sequence, in helping children to make choices and to plan for future activities, and in giving them an awareness of time in general. The *Checklist* observer should attend the morning circle in order to hear which children give appropriate answers to the teachers' questions about the activities to follow and which do not seem to understand time intervals.

Although many teachers do calendar activities at this time as well, they need to be aware of children's superficial understanding of calendars and clocks. We really cannot expect children to understand these abstract concepts much before age seven.

But, four-year-olds are aware of established sequences and become upset if things are not done in the regular order. If one of your periods is to be omitted, this should be made clear at circle time. On the other hand, the length of the activity periods can vary without anyone seeming to notice. Teachers who have had to shorten their day by several hours report that the children hardly notice the difference as long as the activities follow one another in regular sequence.

Giving children advance notice that a period is coming to a close is another method for helping them to understand the passage of time. "Five more minutes before cleanup time," may not have the same meaning for young children as it does for adults, since children still do not completely understand "minutes." But, youngsters do know that this signal means the free choice period is almost over and that they must soon help to clean up.

Having some kind of transition between each activity period also helps a child to order the day mentally. When everyone finally has arrived and it is time for morning circle, you could give a transition signal by playing a chord or song on the piano, or by singing a transition song such as

Good morning to you,
Good morning to you,
Good morning everybody,
Good morning to you.

Come sit in our group,
Come sit in our group,
Good morning everybody,
Come sit in our group.

(Tune: "Happy Birthday")

When circle time is finished, you could play a concept game as a transition to send the children to their activities: "All the children with red on may go to their activity area." Free choice period usually ends with cleanup. When children are finished with that, they go to the snack table in most centers. The transition to outdoor play could be a song that will send the children to get their outdoor clothes on

We're waiting to go out,
We're waiting to go out,
Jill and Joe and Rodney too,
Get ready to go out.

We're waiting to go out,
We're waiting to go out,
All the girls at table one,
Get ready to go out.

(Tune: "The Farmer in the Dell")

When they come in from outdoor play, the youngsters already should know that they should go to the bathroom and wash their hands once their coats are hung up. From the bathroom, they generally will go over to the library corner where one of the teachers will be waiting with a book to read. The transition activity to lunch could involve something from the story you have just read

Harry, the dirty dog, is looking for a hungry boy or girl to go to the lunch table. Everyone, close your eyes, and wait for Harry to tap you on the head.

Activities such as these help the children to establish a meaningful order to the day. This order provides more than an explanation in words can do at this stage of the children's development, for the youngsters must interact with their environment in order to construct mentally the concept of time sequences.

An afternoon circle time is important to help the children internalize these activities, and to help you realize their understanding of the things they have been doing. This is the time to discuss what they liked best about the day. Ask things like "What did you make today that you can tell us about?" "What did you choose to do during free choice in the morning?" Just as the morning circle asked them to look at the daily schedule and make plans for the future, so the afternoon circle asks them to look back at the past and think about what they accomplished. *Checklist* observers need to be present at this group meeting as well in order to determine who really understands the daily schedule and can remember past events.

If You Have Not Checked This Item: Some Helpful Ideas

- *Play a Time Game*

Since children learn best by "doing/playing" and especially by doing something that involves themselves, you might play a time game with them that involves children pretending to be your various activity periods. For instance, you could have one child represent each of the morning periods: arrival, morning circle, free choice, snack, outdoor play, story time, and lunch. Put a sign on the children if you want. The sign could have both words and a symbol: a handshake for arrival, a circle for morning circle, blocks for free choice, a glass of juice for snack, a swing for outdoor play, a book for story time, and a plate for lunch. Then, let the children try to arrange those representing the periods in the order they occur. The children need to talk about it as they do it. Do the same for afternoon activities.

- *Make a Pictorial Daily Schedule*

Draw or paste pictures to illustrate the time blocks of your daily schedule in the sequence they occur. Display this pictorial daily schedule prominently, and discuss it with the children.

- *Play Before and After Games*

Make up brief transition questions that you ask the children while they are waiting for something else to happen. For example, you could ask them "Does lunch come before nap or after nap?" "Does snack come before outdoor play or after outdoor play?" Have them make up similar questions of their own.

- *Read Books with a Time Sequence Theme*

The following stories take place in a nursery school and show children engaged in a sequence of activities. After reading the books, you could discuss the activities in this school that the children are engaged in and the order in which the activities occur.

Cohen, Miriam. *Best Friends.* New York: Collier Books, 1971.
Cohen, Miriam. *Will I Have a Friend?* New York: Collier Books, 1967.
Rockwell, Harlow. *My Nursery School.* New York: Greenwillow Books, 1976, Puffin Books, 1984.

☐ KNOWS WHAT HAPPENED YESTERDAY

One of the problems young children must face in learning time concepts is recognizing the fact that while they are involved in a present event, the memory of preceding events already has disappeared. Thus, the past may exist for a young child only vaguely. We all know that as we grow older, recollections of the distant past fade away and are stored in the recesses of the brain, not to appear again unless tapped by hypnosis or jogged into life by some trigger event. For young children, memories of even the recent past may slip away unless they learn to be aware of it.

Just as all development is interrelated, so the formation of the cognitive concept of time is dependent for young children on the development of both language and memory. Children first of all need to understand the vocabulary of time words: before, after, during, next, today, yesterday, tomorrow, next time, after, while, and soon. This understanding does not occur overnight. Psychologist Margaret Donaldson, in fact, believes, "we have tended both to underestimate children's competence as thinkers and to overestimate their understanding of language" (Donaldson, p. 60).

Recent studies are showing that while children seem astonishingly adept at making original spontaneous utterances, youngsters' understanding of what is said to them is not always that clear. The first words they learn, in fact, are naming words, or nouns, then action words, or verbs. Prepositions and adverbs, which show place, order, and time, are much farther down the scale of words young children understand or use. It takes much longer for these seemingly "less important" words to become a part of the young child's vocabulary.

For children to conceptualize the past, they first must learn what "before," "after," "yesterday," and "tomorrow" mean. Children learn these terms as youngsters learn everything: through actual experiences. Your circle time discussions will help the children to focus on the good experiences they had the day before and the good things they can look forward to tomorrow. As such concepts become meaningful to the children, the youngsters will incorporate these time terms into their vocabularies as well.

Although most of their distant past already may be gone, the children will be able to bring to mind the recent past if it is focused on as a part of their life in your center. In addition, memory and recall, to be discussed later in this chapter, play a part in the children's ability to "know what happened yesterday." (See pp. 212–13.)

If You Have Not Checked This Item: Some Helpful Ideas

• Play Today-Yesterday-Tomorrow Games

Afternoon circle time is a good time to play games that involve events that have happened yesterday and today, or will happen tomorrow. Make three signs, one for each of these days, with a stick figure of a person with hands on hips representing "today," with hand pointing backward (left) representing "yesterday," and with hand pointing forward (right) representing "tomorrow." Then, ask the children questions about activities that actually happened: "On which day did we get new fish?" or "Which day was Bobbie's birthday?" or "On which day will we go to visit the farm?" Let children hold up the proper sign when they guess the correct day.

• *Read Books in Which the Plot Sequence Involves Past Time*

One Bright Monday Morning by Arline and Joseph Baum, New York: Knopf Pantheon, 1962, is a counting book using the days of the week. (See p. 199.) As you read it, you can stop after each page and ask the children, "What happened yesterday?"

The Mysterious Tadpole by Steven Kellogg, New York: The Dial Press, 1977, is a story involving days and the calendar as everyone waits for the mysterious tadpole to turn into a frog. (See p. 146.) Stop and talk about time sequences, what happened yesterday, and what might happen tomorrow as you read this story.

☐ CAN BUILD A BLOCK ENCLOSURE

Understanding Space

Space, like time, is another of the basic organizing dimensions of the young child's experience. Like the other basic dimensions, space has several aspects: 1)enclosure; 2)position of things; 3)closeness of things; 4)distance between things; 5)location of things; 6)order of things; and 7)shapes and sizes, including body in space and body parts. Space answers the question "where?" about things and is one of the three dimensions, along with number and time, that eventually merge to make up the basis for logical thought in later years. (Osborn, p. 115)

Also like time, space is an abstract concept in most respects; young children cannot represent space mentally until they experience "enclosure." As with the other knowledge they create, the idea of space comes from their sensory exploration of things. Children see objects, move across space to touch and play with objects and perceive objects as being close to or far away from other things.

But, in the beginning, the infant's only experience with space involves the nearness of objects. When the object is out of sight, it is literally out of mind for him until he develops so-called "object permanence" at about age eight months. Before that time, he will not continue to search for an object that is out of his range of vision or that has been hidden. He acts as though the object he cannot see is no longer there, as if it has disappeared completely or no longer exists.

With experience and maturity, he comes to understand that objects in his environment are still there even though out of his sight. Yet, even with object permanence, almost every young child cannot perceive objects from any point of view other than his own at first and cannot imagine how an object will look if its position in space is changed, for instance.

Because space is not perceived readily by a youngster unless it is enclosed, *Checklist* observers are asked first to look for this aspect of space perception in assessing a child's cognitive development in this dimension.

Using Block Building

One of the most effective activities for developing cognitive concepts about space involves playing with "unit blocks," those deceptively simple and plain wooden units, half units, double units, quadruple units, cylinders, curves, triangles, ramps, pillars, floorboards, and switches that were invented before World War I by Carolyn Pratt for use by her children in the experimental City and Country School in New York City (Winsor, p. 3).

Today, unit blocks are found in almost every nursery school and in many kindergartens throughout the country. Children learn to sort and categorize during cleanup by putting the blocks back on the shelves having the correct cut out block shape. The block building corner is a favorite area for children's play during free choice period. The youngsters build houses, farms, towers, hospitals, and anything else their imaginations can invent. Adults rarely think of block building as a primary activity that helps children develop such an abstract cognitive concept as space.

Adults often have trouble thinking this way because they have difficulty keeping in mind how children learn: 1)by constructing their own knowledge through sensory interactions with things in their environment, and 2)through free play with such materials. Abstract concepts can come to life in children's minds when such versatile yet defined playthings as unit blocks represent these concepts.

Harriet Johnson, another pioneer early childhood specialist who worked with Carolyn Pratt and later founded the nursery school that still later became the demonstration school for the Bank Street College of Education, spent years observing children's use of building blocks. She eventually published her findings in the 1933 classic study, "The Art of Block Building." (Johnson, pp. 9–24) She found that children go through predictable stages in learning to use blocks based on their maturity and experience when they are given the freedom to use blocks naturally without adult interference. Sound familiar? Her observational data give strong support to much current research on child development.

Her block building stages serve us well today in our observation of children's cognitive development. What better way is there to determine if children understand spatial concepts and relationships than by watching how the youngsters use unit blocks? If the first understanding that children can grasp about space comes only when they can enclose space, then their block creations offer a fine way to witness whether the children have mastered this concept.

The children Johnson worked with ranged from two to six years in age and varied in their experience with blocks. She found that the older children with no experience still progressed through the same stages as the younger ones, but with greater speed. An amended version of her stages include

1. Carrying, filling, dumping
2. Stacking and lining
3. Bridging
4. Enclosures
5. Patterns
6. Representation

Two-year-olds or older children with no block building experience usually begin by massing the blocks together, carrying them around, filling up containers (or toy trucks) with them, and dumping them out—over and over—but not building with them. This block building form is typical of the novice child's approach to most new activities. The approach is all manipulative: getting the feel of the blocks, understanding the heft of them, and realizing the way you can move them around, but not using them for their purpose (which he has not figured out yet), then repeating the activity again and again. The child will use this pattern throughout his natural development of blockbuilding skills if he is given the freedom to proceed on his own.

Then, somewhere between the ages of two and three, real building begins. We all use the same straight, curved, or parallel lines in our doodles, but the results look quite different. Likewise, all children go through the same block building stages, but youngsters' individual buildings also look quite different.

The first real building stage, then, involves either stacking blocks up into a tower or lining them up in a row. Some children do one activity first; some do the other. Some combine the tower and the row. Some learn to straighten their blocks neatly so that their towers will not fall. Others pay little attention to either vertical or horizontal alignment. When they have mastered this first attempt, they tend to repeat it again and again before moving on to the next stage. (Johnson, pp. 11–12)

Eventually, the children are faced with the problem of "bridging," or using a horizontal block to span the space between two upright parallel vertical blocks. If the youngsters are working without the help of a teacher or peers (and they should be), it may take a great deal of time to resolve this building problem. The children's concepts of size and distance are still somewhat hazy at this age, and the youngsters often make many trials and errors before they can get the right sized block. The other solution to the bridging problem, of course, is to move the two upright blocks closer together so that the horizontal bridging block will fit. Some children discover one solution but never the other.

Even when peers at higher levels are building nearby, the novice builder usually does not try to copy their methods. Block building, like art, is a very personal and satisfying expression of a child's creativity, and what someone else is doing matters very little. For that reason, teachers should let children build on their own. The youngsters truly will learn cognitive concepts only by struggling with building problems on their own and by finding their own solutions. Once children have learned to bridge, this skill is incorporated into their own personal building styles, over and over.

Next come enclosures, for some children. Some youngsters master the problem of enclosing or encircling a floor space horizontally with block "walls" or "fences" before learning to bridge.

Adults find it difficult to understand why children have trouble making an enclosure, but the youngsters do have problems with this activity. A child will start out correctly in making two walls to enclose the corral for her toy horse. But, somehow, she will be unable to turn the corner for the third wall, and the wall goes on and on. She seems to know what she wants to do, but she is unable to do it. This experience is frustrating, indeed; it is something like the adult standing before the bathroom mirror trying to cut her own hair! The child needs your support but not your help in arriving at her own solution and her own understanding of space and how to manipulate the objects in it.

Many three- and even four-year-olds make incomplete enclosures for a long time before they perceive how to close the gap. Their enclosures tend to have some rounded corners, as well, because children still have difficulty at this age either constructing or drawing a square. (See Chapter 8, p. 174.) But, once they have mastered the problem of completing an enclosure, children incorporate this skill too into their block building repertory.

A few children begin naming their enclosures when they start to build, but most youngsters do this naming after they have finished the enclosures. An enclosure may be a "garage for the car," a "house for the doll," or a "house for the guinea pig." These objects may not have been in their minds as they started to build, but they know adults and peers want them to name things, so these names sound reasonable.

Whether a name is reasonable depends upon whether the object fits. You will have an additional opportunity to observe the children's conception of space and size when you see whether the object fits its enclosure. Often, it does not. Children sometimes try to force the object into the space without seeming to realize that the object is too big and will not fit. Why can't they see that it doesn't fit, we wonder? The youngsters' mental structures still have gaps, overgeneralize, and are not refined enough to handle such details. The children need more practice as well as maturity. Playing with blocks on their own will help to correct these deficiencies.

With skill in towers, rows, bridging, and enclosures, children are ready to build in patterns—decorative, repetitive, and often geometric—building either horizontally or vertically and incorporating the repertory of building skills they have developed over the years. Four- and five-year-olds use the same building styles they began with at ages two and three, but in a more sophisticated and complex manner. You thought that block building was simple children's play? Now that you know it is neither simple nor play as adults know it, perhaps you will want to record with an instant print camera the children's stages of building over the year or two they are with you.

The final stage, as with art, is representative building. Children start by building a structure and then giving it a name, such as school, playground, house, store, or fire station. But soon, they learn to name the building first and then build it according to their own inner design. Most early efforts at representation do not look much like the building they name. But, practiced builders eventually are able to represent a wide range of structures. The play of these practiced builders also becomes less solitary or parallel and more of a group effort, as discussed in Chapter 4, Social Play. At this point, the children want their structures to remain standing at the end of the period in order to play with the structures later. You may have to enlarge your block building area if you have many of such skilled builders.

Keep pictures of houses, stores, bridges, roads, barns, and office buildings mounted in your block building area. The pictures should be at the child's eye level when the child is seated on the floor. Where can you mount the pictures when block shelves are in the way? Pull the shelves away from the walls, and use the shelves as room dividers for your building area. Then, pictures can be mounted on the walls. Take photos of completed buildings and their creators, and mount the photos attractively in the same area to motivate further building.

If You Have Not Checked This Item: Some Helpful Ideas

▪ *Have a Special Building Day*

If boys tend to dominate the block building area, try having a special building day for girls only. Is this idea too sexist for you? Then, try having a special building day for all the children wearing red (or blue, or sneakers, or some other distinctive feature). If one child never seems to build, perhaps you could choose the feature from that child's clothing to help get him or her interested.

▪ *Build Things Seen on a Field Trip*

Take your instant print camera along on your next field trip, and take photos of structures that children might want to represent in blocks upon returning to the center, structures such as highways, bridges, towers, office buildings, stores, barns, and houses. Mount the pictures in the block area, and watch what happens.

▪ *Read a Story that Features a Building*

Make a photocopy of illustrations from a book that features a building, and mount the copies in the block area to motivate building. The children will not copy the buildings pictured as adults see the structures, but the children will construct buildings according to their own inner view of what buildings similar to the photocopies should look like.

The Trip by Ezra Jack Keats, New York: Scholastic Book Services, 1978, shows the inner city boy Louie taking a fantasy trip through the towers of mid-Manhattan. (See p. 167.)

Anno's Counting Book by Mitsumasa Anno, New York: Philomel Books, 1982, shows an interesting house with cutaway rooms and windows with people appearing and disappearing. The book may be too difficult for preschoolers to use for counting, but perhaps it could motivate their building.

Nothing Ever Happens on My Block by Ellen Raskin, New York: Scholastic Book Services, 1966, shows a little boy sitting on the curb in front of a block of houses in which all kinds of wild things are happening, that he doesn't notice because his back is turned.

If your children like these stories, then those individuals who can may want to try building the structures found in these books.

☐ CAN LOCATE AN OBJECT BEHIND OR BESIDE SOMETHING

A second *Checklist* item that demonstrates the children's understanding of space asks whether they can locate an object that is behind or beside something. To respond accurately, they need to have constructed mental images of the position of things, the closeness of things, and the distance between things, as well as the meaning of the spatial prepositions being used. This item provides an especially good example of the interrelatedness of child development.

Children must have developed physically enough to be able to make sensory explorations of the objects in the environment. Youngsters need the mental maturity to convert this perceptual knowledge into cognitive concepts. Children need language development and experience to put words to these concepts. Preschoolers and kindergartners are only at the beginning of such a synthesis, but your program is in an excellent position to help them create this knowledge.

Here are some of the prepositions children need to be aware of to understand spatial relationships

behind	down	in
back of	under	inside
beside	underneath	into
alongside	below	out
at the side of	over	outside
by the side of	above	out of
next to	up	
in front of	up above	
between	on	
in between	on top of	

It must be an overwhelming chore for youngsters to make sense of so many seemingly "unimportant" words. As mentioned previously, children first learn nouns, naming words. These nouns are much easier to learn because children hear these words over and over in the abbreviated sentences used around the youngsters when they are first learning to speak. Nouns can be seen, touched, and experienced in many ways. Next come verbs, the action words. These words, too, are used frequently in the children's presence to describe what is happening to the noun.

Prepositions, however, are much more abstract. They do not represent a thing, but a location, which means that children must first learn the concept of location in space by experiencing the concept. Then, the youngsters pick up a few of the location words, but the children's understanding of these words during the preschool years is still limited and incomplete. One of the difficulties may be that these words are so much alike. "Behind" and "beside" even sound alike. Children tend to learn one or two words for the same location, but the youngsters do not realize that there are still other words with the same meaning. For instance, under, underneath, and below all can mean the same thing. Most young children have trouble with such synonyms.

An interesting study of preschool children's understanding of the words on, next to, in, underneath, behind, over, outside of, below, between, in front of, above, beside, inside, under, and out of was carried out by Holzman and her students in the form of a game. Each child was asked to put the Cookie Monster doll in a certain location involving a small red box inside a large, one-shelved blue box. Twenty percent of the children made errors on the words underneath, below, over, and under. (Holzman, p. 120)

The concepts of inside and outside evolve from the child's understanding of enclosure or surrounding. Observe how many of your children who can make an enclosure also understand the location of beside. What about the other children?

Because a child's awareness of space and location grows out of his own body in space, he will need to move physically around your classroom in order to determine the locations of behind and beside. The child's perceptual awareness of space develops more rapidly than the more abstract concepts involving space. But, if the child has many meaningful sensory experiences with space in your classroom, then the mental construction of spatial location eventually will be created.

If You Have Not Checked This Item: Some Helpful Ideas

▪ *Play Location Games*

"Where is the fish?" is a cumulative game that children enjoy. Play it during circle time by asking the children "Where is the fish?" Have one child go to the location of the fish (or whatever), point to it, and respond, "The fish is in the fishbowl." Then, ask, "Where is the fishbowl?" Another child must go and touch it and say, "The fishbowl is on the table" (or wherever). This activity can continue as long as interest exists. Be sure the children answer in sentences containing a location preposition.

Unlike the concept of enclosure, which children learn best on their own, youngsters need more help understanding location prepositions. You should take the lead in games and questions.

▪ *Read Locate-the-Animal Books*

Use some of the books already mentioned to help children understand location words.

Use the book *Find the Cat* by Elaine Livermore, Boston: Houghton Mifflin, 1973, with one or two children at a time, since they must look closely at complex line drawings in order to find the cat. (See p. 185.) After the children have put a finger on the cat, ask them to tell you in words where the cat is located. This game is a good whole-part activity as well because some of the pictures show only the cat's tail, or its head.

But Where Is the Green Parrot? by Thomas and Wanda Lacharias, New York: Delacorte Press, 1968, can be used in the same way as the *Find the Cat* book. (See p. 185.)

One Snail and Me by Emilie Warren McLeod, Boston: Little, Brown, and Company, 1961, is another book full of humorous animal antics. (See p. 199.) Children can be asked things like, "Where are the turtles?" (They are on the rim of the tub, not in it.) "Where is the duck?" (Sometimes the duck is in the water, but other times it is on the girl's head, on the whale's back, on top of another duck, etc.)

Children can learn spatial relationships through activities that ask them to locate objects "beside," "behind," or "next to" other objects.

☐ RECALLS WORDS TO SONG, CHANT

Developing Memory

Memory, the last of the cognitive abilities to be discussed, is an integration of all of the others. It is the process of storing information in the brain and of retrieving that information for future use. Memory depends not only upon the child's development of classification and seriation abilities, as well as number, time, and space concepts, but memory also rests upon the child's previous experiences. The more a child experiences, the richer his memory banks become.

Children and adults do not necessarily remember things in a pure form, so to speak, but instead, experiences are enriched by being built upon. In other words, every experience a person has changes every previous experience by building on it. For this reason, it is essential for children to participate in numerous activities of every possible variety in your program.

The most basic experiences in the beginning, as we have reiterated, are perceptual; they are the sensory experiences of seeing, hearing, feeling, tasting, and smelling. The richness of perceptual learning will determine the meaningfulness of future experiences. According to Spitzer, "The most important single determinant of what we remember is the meaningfulness of the information" (Spitzer, p. 64). This statement may be one of the most important ones you will read in this text. Think about how this statement might affect the way you organize your program.

If information has to be meaningful to the child in order to be remembered, then we need to provide all kinds of activities the child will participate in because he or she finds them interesting, enjoyable, exciting, worthwhile, and fun. And, we must give the child the freedom to explore the activity on his or her own. The activities must be experiences the child chooses because he or she wants to try them and not because he or she is directed to them by an adult. It is no wonder that children have made spontaneous play their particular process for learning, and it is no wonder children have difficulty remembering information that has little meaning for them or is dull or boring.

Why haven't adults made play the basis for their own learning? It is because the basis for learning shifts during the later preschool years from perceptual experiencing to language. As language facility increases, verbal functions take over the role of the senses and become the principal basis for learning. We should not forget, though, that the meaningfulness of verbal information is still the most important determinant of our ability to remember.

Due to the cumulative effect of past experiences—that is, even verbal experiences have to be built on the child's earlier perceptual experiences—the child with the richest perceptual experiences can develop the richest language and verbal memory.

Understanding Recognition and Recall

Memory has three different aspects: recognition, recall (discussed here), and recollection (which will be discussed under the next *Checklist* item). Recognition is the most basic of the three processes. It is the simple knowing that an object has been met with previously. The infant uses this form of memory to make sense of his world. As he experiences his environment over and over, he begins to recognize its forms and ingredients. By about age eight months, his recognition of objects has developed to the point that he knows they exist even when he cannot see them. The more experiences he has, the more material his memory has to build on in the future. Recognition seems to be the primary mechanism for remembering until about age two. (Spitzer, p. 65)

Then, recall comes into play more and more. This is the memory process by which pieces of information are retrieved from the memory banks of the brain for use by the child. Recall is more abstract than recognition; recall does not depend upon an outside object, person, or event to trigger memory. Children who show understanding of the time concepts of past and future have the ability to recall. Until this process has developed, youngsters really cannot remember much of the past and have difficulty anticipating the future.

Recall is necessary in order for the child to learn language. Much of his early attempts involve imitating the words of others, which he files in his memory banks and then recalls at the appropriate time in his speaking.

Using Songs and Chants

Observers using the *Child Skills Checklist* are asked to listen to whether children in your program recall the words to a song or a chant. Singing and chanting are excellent methods for practicing recall abilities. Such activities give children perceptual memory cues, making an appropriate bridge between sensory and language learning. For example, songs and chants are rhythmic. Children can tap their toes, clap their hands, or beat a rhythm while they sing in unison or listen to a record. Songs and chants are also usually in rhyme, a good memory cue for later recall of words. Chants are usually done to finger plays or body actions. Thus, sensory experiences provide memory cues for later recall of words.

Children as young as one to two years old may begin to chant using nonsense syllables. These children are usually unable to sing accurately at this age, but they enjoy musical sounds, especially the human voice. Between ages two and three, children often chant or sing to themselves at play—often in a monotone— and try to keep time to the beat of the music they hear. By age three, youngsters can sing simple songs, play simple singing games like "Ring Around the Rosy," and move to the beat. Four- and five-year-olds have improved all around if they have had practice. (Greenberg, pp. 23–26) They still may not pronounce all the words of the songs accurately, but what does it matter? Singing is for enjoyment, not perfection, during the early childhood years.

To teach your children songs and chants, you need to repeat the songs and chants over and over again with the children every day. Sing morning greeting songs; transition songs; finger plays at circle time; singing games in the large motor area; songs for the seasonal holidays of Halloween and Thanksgiving; songs for rainy days, sunny days, and snowy days; songs about animals; and, especially, songs and chants about the children themselves. Use nursery rhyme favorites of your own, and make up words to familiar tunes using the children's names whenever possible; you soon will create an interested group of young singers. Records are fine for occasional use, but give your children a special cognitive memory boost by helping them learn their own words to songs and chants.

You do not need to be a good singer yourself. The children never will know the difference. If you cannot sing, then chant with the children in unison or in a monotone. Research shows that children who have experienced nursery rhymes in the preschool years have fewer problems learning to read in later years than those who have not encountered nursery rhymes.

If You Have Not Checked This Item: Some Helpful Ideas

- *Use Children's Names in Songs*

Make up words to a familiar tune using children's names; for example,

> *Where is Bridget?*
> *Where is Bridget?*
> *Here she is!*
> *Here she is!*
> *How are you this morning?*
> *How are you this morning?*
> *Nice to know,*
> *Nice to know. (Tune: "Are you Sleeping?")*

Some other tunes you can use are the following:

"Here We Go Round the Mulberry Bush"
"Lazy Mary Will You Get Up"
"Row, Row, Row Your Boat"
"Sing a Song of Sixpence"
"This Old Man"
"Three Blind Mice"
"Twinkle, Twinkle Little Star"

▪ *Read a Story about a Song*

There are several good children's books that may motivate your children to sing.

Lizard's Song by George Shannon, New York: Greenwillow Books, 1981, is about a lizard who sings a simple song about his home. The bear tries to remember the song but keeps forgetting. The music is included, so the children soon will learn to sing the song and not forget.

The Banza by Diane Wolkstein, New York: The Dial Press, 1981, is a Haitian folktale about a little goat with a banjo who sings a song that protects her from ten fat tigers. The children soon will be singing this song, as well, and may want to make their own banjos.

▪ *Do Finger Plays*

There are several excellent finger play books you may want to use with your children.

Finger Frolics by Liz Cromwell, and Dixie Hibner, Livonia, Mich.: Partner Press, 1976, contains the words and actions to dozens of finger plays for seasons, holidays, animals, community helpers, and transportation.

Eye Winker, Tom Tinker, Chin Chopper by Tom Glazer, Garden City, N.Y.: Doubleday & Company, 1973, contains fifty musical finger plays with piano arrangements and guitar chords.

☐ CAN RECOLLECT AND ACT ON A SERIES OF DIRECTIONS

Understanding Recollection

Recollection is the most advanced of the three aspects of memory. It is an information-retrieval process in which the brain groups/selects particular information and recalls it for use by the child. It includes recognition and recall but takes them a step further. The child's mind must not only recognize things and recall information, but it must also group information in a meaningful way for use.

To be successful at recollection, the child first must be able to locate things and events in space and time. Researchers involved with programming computers and creating artificial intelligence are very much concerned with information processing and retrieval. These researchers talk in terms of short-term memory, long-term memory, and attention. Short-term memory is the storage of information that is received visually or auditorily by the brain. If the information is understood and useful, then it goes into long-term memory for storage. In order to receive any information at all, the person must attend. Attention refers to what a person selects to process from all of the information available through the senses. (Schickedanz, p. 389)

A young child only has limited attention. During the early years, the child seems able to see only one aspect of objects or situations at a time. Therefore, the child's thinking skills lack the full range of information necessary to provide understanding for many events. His long-term memory, which is called upon when he must recollect and act upon a series of directions, is not capable of holding as much information as a mature mind. You may not be able to check this item for all of your children. Many are only at the beginning of this mature memory process.

You will need to provide many experiences for the children to put their memories to use by following directions. Play direction-following activities with the children every chance you get. Ask the youngsters to look in the cupboard at the end of the room and find the jar of blue paint; or to go to the teacher in the room next door and ask to borrow some yellow construction paper; or to set one table for lunch with plates, forks, and napkins from the cupboard and cartons of milk from the refrigerator.

If You Have Not Checked This Item: Some Helpful Ideas

- *Read Cumulative Tales*

Children love to hear stories in which one event builds on the other in the manner of The House That Jack Built. Once they have heard the story several times, the children will begin to remember the sequences of actions and to want to repeat the sequence aloud.

The Gingerbread Boy, New York: Platt & Munk, 1961, is the classic tale of the gingerbread boy who runs away from a little old woman, a little old man, some men cutting hay, a big red cow, etc., until he is warned by a bird about a hungry cat, and so runs back home again.

Bringing the Rain to Kapiti Plain by Verna Aardema, New York: The Dial Press, 1981, is a rhyming African tale that sounds like *The House That Jack Built*. Children will delight in the pictures of African birds and animals who need the rain so badly, and the youngsters soon should be able to repeat some of the verses.

- *Have a Challenge Table*

Designate one of your morning activity tables as a "challenge table" at which you challenge any of the children interested to solve the problems or follow the directions you pose using three-dimensional materials. For example, one morning, you could use a set of colored table blocks. The challenge could be to build a tower with three red blocks on the bottom, two yellow blocks in the middle, and one blue block on top. Tell the children they must listen carefully because you will give the directions only once. Or, ask the children to make a garage for the red car with yellow blocks on one side, blue blocks on the other side, and a red door. Young children do not need to win prizes if they are successful. They really enjoy this type of learning for its own sake, as long as it is a game and fun for all. If they are unsuccessful, do not make a fuss, and let them try again.

REFERENCES CITED

Cowan, Philip A. *Piaget with Feeling.* New York: Holt, Rinehart, and Winston, 1978.

Donaldson, Margaret. "The Mismatch Between School and Children's Minds." *Human Nature.* March 1979.

Greenberg, Marvin. *Your Children Need Music.* Englewood Cliffs, N.J.: Prentice-Hall, 1979.

Holzman, Mathilda. *The Language of Children.* Englewood Cliffs, N.J.: Prentice-Hall, 1983.

Johnson, Harriet M. "The Art of Block Building." *The Block Book.* Washington, D.C.: National Association for the Education of Young Children, 1974.

Osborn, Janie Dyson, and D. Keith Osborn. *Cognition in Early Childhood.* Athens, Ga.: Education Associates, 1983.

Schickedanz, Judith A., et al. *Toward Understanding Children.* Boston: Little, Brown, and Company, 1982.

Spitzer, Dean R. *Concept Formation and Learning in Early Childhood.* Columbus, Ohio: Charles E. Merrill Publishing Co., 1977.

Winsor, Charlotte B. "Blocks as a Material for Learning Through Play—The Contribution of Caroline Pratt." *The Block Book.* Washington, D.C.: National Association for the Education of Young Children, 1974.

OTHER SOURCES

Beaty, Janice J. *Skills for Preschool Teachers.* Columbus, Ohio: Charles E. Merrill Publishing Co., 1984.

Donaldson, Margaret. *Children's Minds.* New York: W. W. Norton & Company, 1978.

LEARNING ACTIVITIES

1. Use the *Child Skills Checklist*, "8. Cognitive Development," as a screening tool to observe all of the children in your classroom. Which of your children did you check for most of the items? How do these children fare on other areas of the *Checklist?*

2. Make a graphic rating scale for block building, and observe all of the children in this area. How do the results compare with the *Checklist* results in "8. Cognitive Development"? Can you draw any conclusions from this comparison?

3. Try to find out how many of the children whom you have checked on the item "Can build a block enclosure" also can locate an object that is beside something.

4. Set up a "challenge table," and record the results of the children's voluntary activities. How do these results compare with the *Checklist* results?

5. Use one of the activities suggested under each item with a child who needs help in cognitive development, and record the results.

10 Spoken Language

Spoken Language Checklist

☐ Speaks confidently in the classroom
☐ Speaks clearly enough for adults to understand
☐ Speaks in expanded sentences
☐ Takes part in conversations with other children
☐ Asks questions with proper word order
☐ Makes negative responses with proper word order
☐ Uses past tense verbs correctly
☐ Plays with rhyming words

S poken language is one of the important skills that make us human beings. We assume, without much thought, that our children will learn to speak the native tongue before they enter public school. Language acquisition cannot be that difficult, we decide; otherwise, how could a little child accomplish it? After all, the child does not have to be taught; language acquisition just seems to happen. It is nothing to get excited about, we think, unless it does not happen on schedule.

As a matter of fact, the acquisition of a native language is one of the greatest developmental accomplishments and mysteries we ever may encounter involving the young child. It is a great accomplishment because the child starts from scratch with no spoken language at birth and acquires an entire native tongue by age six; sometimes, the child develops more than one language if he is in a bilingual family. The acquisition of this complex skill is a great mystery because we are still not exactly sure how it takes place.

True, we may not show concern while all goes well, but we should learn all we can about the kinds of things that help or hinder the language acquisition process in order to smooth the way. The years from age two to age five are especially crucial in the acquisition process; the child's vocabulary suddenly expands from 250 words to 2,000 words, and he learns the rules of putting words together properly to speak in complex sentences. During these years, the child is often in an early childhood program; thus, the language environment you provide can have a significant effect on his progress.

In order to support your children's language development, you must know at the outset how accomplished they already are as speakers. Using an observation screening device such as the eight *Child Skills Checklist* items under "9. Spoken Language" to assess each of your children at the beginning of the year is a good way to start. Then, follow up with written or tape-recorded language samples of each child.

☐ SPEAKS CONFIDENTLY IN THE CLASSROOM

The first *Checklist* item actually refers more to the child's emotional adjustment to the classroom than to his or her speaking abilities. A child must feel at ease in the

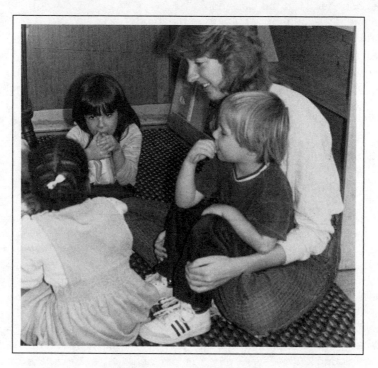

A child must feel at ease in the classroom in order to speak with confidence.

strangeness of the classroom environment and among peers in order to speak at all. The so-called nonverbal child is frequently one who lacks confidence to speak outside the confines of the home. The child may have a shy nature or may come from a family that uses little verbal communication. The child also, of course, may have a physical disability such as a hearing impairment that has interfered with language development.

Spend time assessing this child using the entire *Child Skills Checklist.* The areas of Self-Identity, Emotional Development, and Social Play are especially important. Does the child have trouble separating from her parents when she comes to the center? Can she do things for herself with any confidence? Does she seem happy? Does she play by herself or with others?

Set up a meeting with her parents, and discuss the *Checklist* results with them. If the results point toward some type of disability, then the parents will want to have the child tested further by a specialist. If the parents indicate that the child talks fluently at home, then the nonverbal child may not feel at ease in a strange new environment.

Your principal task with the shy or uncommunicative child will be to help her feel comfortable in the classroom. Using pressure to get her to talk before she is at ease may well produce the opposite results. You and your co-workers will need to take special pains to accept the child as she is and to try to make her welcome in the classroom. You can invite her to join appropriate activities, but if she refuses, then you need to honor her reluctance. It often takes a great deal of patience and forbearance on the part of an early childhood classroom staff to allow the shy child to become at ease in her own good time.

If the nonverbal child seems to feel comfortable with one child, then you may be able to have that child involve her with the others. On the other hand, sometimes the only solution is to leave the nonverbal child alone. If your environment is warm and happy, she eventually should want to participate.

The environment must be stress-free. For many children, speaking in a group of peers is a new and untried experience. To help them feel at ease about speaking, you need to help them feel at ease about themselves by accepting them as they are. Show you accept them with smiles, hugs and words of welcome and praise. Show you are happy to see them everyday and want them to participate.

In addition, you need to accept their language, no matter how poorly pronounced or how ungrammatical it is. Language is a very personal thing. It reflects not only the child's stage of development, but also his family life style. You must be especially careful not to correct a child's language. Telling him he is saying a word wrong or using the wrong word is a personal put-down. He will learn the correct form himself when the time is right by hearing you pronounce the word correctly and by practicing it with his peers.

A stress-free environment means that your classroom is free from stressful situations for the young child. He should not be put on the spot and forced to perform verbally, creatively, or in any other way. Offer him opportunities and encouragement, but do not force the shy or unsure child to speak.

If You Have Not Checked This Item: Some Helpful Ideas

- *Use a Prop for Security*

Many young children feel more secure when they have something in their hands, especially something soft and cuddly that has the quality of a security blanket. You might want to keep several stuffed animals for children to choose from and hold when feeling out of sorts, or when first coming to the classroom and not yet feeling comfortable. Your "nonverbal child" even may end up talking to her stuffed animal; this talking may be the beginning of her verbal integration into the classroom.

- *Use a Puppet*

Almost every child likes the idea of putting a puppet on his hand. Have a box of various kinds of puppets, and let the shy child choose a different one every day if he wants. Preschool children tend to play with puppets as if the puppets are a part of themselves rather than a separate toy like a doll. Because puppets have mouths, children often first experiment by trying to bite with the puppet, in fun, of course. Later, the youngsters get the idea of having the puppet speak, perhaps in a whisper or in a different tone from their own voice. Shy children often are more willing to have a puppet speak for them than they are to speak for themselves. You might find yourself able to talk with a shy child's puppet through a puppet you put on your own hand.

Puppets can be played with alone, but they often lead naturally to involvement with other children. Thus, puppets are an excellent transition material to help integrate the shy child painlessly into the activities of the classroom, and the shy child integrates all on her own. (See *The Magic of Puppetry: A Guide for Those Working with Young Children* by Peggy Davison Jenkins, Englewood Cliffs, N.J.: Prentice-Hall, 1980.)

- *Read a Puppet Book*

Louie by Ezra Jack Keats, New York: Scholastic Book Services, 1975, tells the story of inner city boy Louie who has never been heard to speak a word. When he attends a neighborhood puppet show, he becomes entranced with the doll puppet Gussie, and he says his first word, "Hello."

Maria Teresa by Mary Atkinson, Chapel Hill, N.C.: Lollipop Power, 1979, is about an unhappy little Hispanic girl who moves from her home in New Mexico to a new school where no one can even pronounce her name. She solves her problem by making a sheep puppet who speaks only Spanish and sharing him with the class at show and tell. This book is somewhat advanced for preschoolers, but bilingual classes and kindergartners should enjoy hearing the Spanish spoken by the puppet.

☐ SPEAKS CLEARLY ENOUGH FOR ADULTS TO UNDERSTAND

The pronunciation of the language, or articulation, may be another speech area of concern to the teacher of young children. When children first begin to speak, they try to imitate the speech sounds of those around them, but with limited success. As they listen and practice, their vocal organs become more adept at making the sounds of English consonants, vowels, and blends. At first, children may use only ten basic sounds: nine consonants and a single vowel. By the time they are completely mature speakers—usually by age seven—the children will have mastered forty to forty-four separate sounds. (Eisenson, p. 75)

Most children with normal speech and hearing abilities are able by age four to produce most of these sounds. A few letters or blends, such as "s," "l," "r," "th," and "sk," still give many children problems. Usually, children substitute an easy sound for one they cannot pronounce: for example, "pwease" for "please." By age seven or eight, even these difficulties have disappeared in most children, and the youngsters are able to articulate like mature adults. In fact, some children— and more likely girls—may produce mature speech by age five.

Yet, language development, like the other aspects of growth, is highly individualized. Some children normally will be more advanced than others. Others are normally slow developers. One study showed that about ten percent of three-year-olds were slow language developers, but most of these outgrew their problems within a year (Caplan, p. 40).

Articulation, the way children pronounce words, is difficult for the lay person to evaluate. While mispronouncing words is a common speech disorder, articulation problems with preschoolers tend to be developmental lags rather than disorders. Something may seem to be a disorder to you because you cannot understand the child, but the "disorder" may be merely a delay in the child's development.

If you have doubts, call on a specialist to evaluate the child. All aspects of the child's speaking, hearing, and other areas of development should be taken into account.

In the meantime, you and your co-workers will need to serve as good language models for the child, helping and supporting him in classroom activities, but taking care not to correct his speech. Modern linguists now realize that it is pointless for adults to try to correct a preschooler's speech by making him repeat words according to an adult standard that he is not yet ready to use. Correcting, in fact, is a negative response that tends to reinforce the unwanted behavior and make the child feel there is something wrong with him personally. Instead of improving a child's language, correcting often makes the child avoid speaking at all in the presence of the corrector.

If the other children in your classroom can understand the child speaker, then you should be encouraged. It often takes longer for an adult with set speech patterns to become used to a child's speech idiosyncrasies. Listen carefully, and try to pick up what meaning you can without embarrassing the inarticulate child by making him repeat everything over and over.

Occasionally, a child who has been pronouncing words normally will slip back into a kind of baby talk. He or she also may display other similar signs such as thumb sucking and wetting. Since these signs tend to be an indication of an emotional upset, you should talk with the parents about the pressures in the child's life that may be affecting him or her adversely and causing the temporary regression. Is there a new baby in the family? A new family member? A death or divorce? Someone in the hospital? A move? Young children feel these emotional upheavals in their families as severely as adults. Sometimes, slipping back to earlier speech patterns is the first indication of such stress on a child.

But, because they are in a group of other child speakers, most young children quickly will pick up or revert back to the speech patterns and word pronunciations they hear around them. Their brains are programmed to do this copying at this stage of their lives. Even non-English speaking children soon will join the mainstream of language with continued exposure to mainstream speakers. The common mispronunciations of these preschoolers should be overlooked. As soon as the development of their vocal apparatus allows them to, the youngsters will be pronouncing English words just like everyone else.

If You Have Not Checked This Item: Some Helpful Ideas

- *Do Not Make a Fuss*

Making a fuss about children's mispronunciations may cause more trouble than it solves. As previously pointed out, a person's speech is highly personal. If the child is made aware that he is doing something wrong, then he may stop trying altogether. Or, in the case of children who are going through a period of disequilibrium in their development and begin to stutter, calling attention to their problem tends to make it worse. Have patience and faith. Once through a stressful period, most children will continue their language development normally.

- *Help the Child to Feel Accepted*

Children want to talk like the others around them. A child's pronunciation trouble already may make her feel out of place. You will need to show by your actions and your words that you accept the child as she is, that you are happy to have her in the class, and that you will support and encourage her in all of her endeavors.

- *Help the Child Succeed at Something Else*

All children need to experience success at this stage of their development. If they are having trouble speaking clearly, then help them to be successful in something else. Perhaps they can finger paint or model with clay or play dough. Such art activities are also therapeutic for children under stress.

- *Try Singing*

Sometimes, children who have trouble saying words will be able to sing the words. Do not single out such children, but include them with the others in your singing activities. Give verbal praise to your children for their singing just as you do for their block building. They will be happy you liked what they did, and they may be more inclined to want to do it again another day.

☐ SPEAKS IN EXPANDED SENTENCES

Young children ages three, four, and five are just at the stage when their speaking develops most rapidly. From the simple two-word sentences they uttered before age two, now they suddenly are able to expand the subjects and predicates of their sentences into longer, more complex thoughts. While their early communications included gestures—"want more," they might have said while pointing at the milk bottle—they now speak complete and expanded sentences, such as "I want some more milk," with no necessity for gestures.

How did this expanded language come about? Linguists are searching for answers by audiotaping infants' utterances, videotaping infants' interactions with their caregivers, and comparing infants' development with deaf children, children from other cultures, and children from a variety of backgrounds.

We know that soon after an infant walks, he talks. We also know that all human infants are predisposed to acquire their native language. Their brains are programmed to sort and store the information that will later be used in producing speech. Human infants give their attention to human voices, listening and then responding at first in babbles but as soon as possible in word sounds. Then, sometime between a year and a half and two years of age, the infants realize that everything has a name. Immediately, their vocabulary starts expanding as they begin to absorb the words for everything they see and touch.

This is the crucial time for meaningful caregiver intervention. The parent or caregiver can name objects and actions. The children will listen and try to imitate. The caregivers will listen to the children and respond; all of this interaction takes place in the natural give-and-take manner of parents playing with their children.

This is also the crucial time for an enriched physical environment and the child's freedom to explore it. As children learn names for things, the youngsters need to see, feel, hear, and try out the items. The children will want to see the doggie, pet the doggie, and laugh at the doggie's funny antics with a rubber bone. Young children learn words by interacting with the things that are represented by words in the environment. The more things the child interacts with, the more words the child will learn, we might say, as long as support, encouragement, and good language models are also at hand.

Young children do not learn word meanings by having someone teach the meanings, but, rather, youngsters induce meanings on the basis of hearing the words used in life experiences (Holzman, p. 65). Children hear a word being used and watch carefully what is going on while it is used. Their first words are names, such as "mama;" "daddy;" "doggie;" "ball;" "bottle;" and "bed," or other common words they hear, such as "byebye;" "no-no;" and "drink."

At first, these words are used only in one way to mean one thing, but soon, the infant discovers he can call, direct, demand, point out, play with, and ask things by the way he intones the word. "Ball" comes to mean: "There is the ball." "Where is the ball?" and "Get me the ball." By this time, he is putting two words together to make primitive sentences. "Mama ball," may mean "Mama get me the ball," "Mama see the ball," or "Mama find the ball." He is beginning to learn the rules for producing sentences. In the meantime, mama hopefully is responding not only by giving him the ball but also by repeating the child's sentence back to him, just a bit expanded: "Oh, the ball. Here's the ball. Mama's got ball. See the ball? Baby want ball?"

Children seem to be predisposed to learn language this way. Linguists find it surprising that adults and older children also seem predisposed to "teach" children language this way. Observers watching mother-infant interactions soon picked up this behavior. The language behavior of the infant seemed to elicit language behavior from the mother that was appropriate to the infant's level of development. As the infant's ability improved, the mother's level of response expanded. (Holzman, p. 87) Even more surprising is the fact that anyone playing with an infant seems to be able to adapt intuitively to the infant's language level.

Studies with four-year-old boys who had no younger brothers or sisters showed that the boys were able to adjust their language to a two-year-old with good language ability and another two-year-old with poorer skills in explaining how a toy worked. The boys listened to the toddlers' responses to their own instructions and made adjustments intuitively. (Holzman, pp. 107–8) This result very well may indicate that not only are infants born with the method for acquiring their native language, but also that the speakers around them are endowed with a similar skill for helping them acquire the native language.

By around age two, children are able to use the proper word order consistently in their primitive sentences. As they suddenly blossom into pretend play at this time, a parallel expansion seems to occur in their language. Their sentences grow longer and more complex, and their vocabularies increase. (McCormick, p. 72) Once the children have absorbed the basic rules for forming sentences, they are on their way, for they then will be able to produce sentences they never have heard. For most children, this mastery has occurred by age four.

Obviously it is important for children to be involved with competent speakers of the native language. If youngsters do not hear the language used or do not engage with someone in speaking it during these crucial years, they may have difficulty acquiring it. Language tends to be an activity carried on by the left hemisphere of the brain. The brain is programmed to acquire language during the early years. Recent evidence seems to indicate that if language acquisition has not occurred before puberty (as in the cases of extremely deprived children), then it is too late for the young person ever to learn it, except at a primitive level (Holzman, p. 100).

It is important for you to know which children in your class are speaking in the expanded sentences most three-, four-, and five-year-olds should be able to use. Some who are not speaking in sentences may be the shy or ill-at-ease children who have the ability but not the confidence to speak in the classroom. Others may come from homes where language is not used so extensively. Still others may have physical or mental impairments and need to be tested by a specialist. For these and all of your children, you must provide rich language opportunities that allow the youngsters to hear sentences spoken and to respond.

If You Have Not Checked This Item: Some Helpful Ideas

• *Provide Dramatic Play Opportunities*

Children's imaginative play is one of the best preschool activities to motivate and promote language growth in young children. Youngsters take on roles in which they must produce dialog. Even the shy, nonverbal child will learn by listening to the others. Be sure to schedule enough time for children to become involved in this pretending type of play. Take a role yourself in order to help the shy child join the others. But, once he is involved, you should withdraw.

- *Go on Field Trips*

Children need many real experiences with their world in order to process and use information in thinking and speaking. Give the youngsters many new things to think and talk about by going on field trips. These out-of-class experiences do not have to be elaborate or distant. Have one adult take three children down to the corner store to buy something. Take a small group on a walk around the block to see how many different sounds they can hear. Be sure to take along a tape recorder that can be played and discussed later. Go on a field trip to a tree every week in the spring or fall to see how it changes. You may want to take an instant print camera along to provide pictures to talk about back in the classroom.

Listen to children's own interests about their world. Have the youngsters ever really explored the building they are in? Do they know where the heat is produced? Young children are fascinated by things like furnaces, which adults take for granted. Take the children to see such things, and listen to the sentences produced.

☐ TAKES PART IN CONVERSATIONS WITH OTHER CHILDREN

If children feel comfortable in your classroom and have mastered the skill of speaking in expanded sentences, then they also should be participating in conversations with the other children. As soon as they are able to participate in these conversations with ease, their speaking ability will show even greater improvement from practice with their peers, some of whom may speak at a bit higher level. Once the basic rules of language are mastered, children improve in speaking most rapidly when in the presence of speakers whose abilities are just a bit higher than their own.

For this reason, it is important to have mixed age groups in preschool programs. The younger children learn language skills from the older ones. The older children have an excellent opportunity to practice their skills with someone a bit younger. As noted previously, children seem to be able to adapt their language level intuitively to less mature speakers, thus enabling younger children to improve their speech.

Just as the infant is predisposed to acquire his own language in a particular manner, he also seems to bring with him in life a preprogrammed way to learn the rules of conversation. Researchers have noted that infants as young as ten weeks old are beginning to learn behaviors necessary for later conversation (Holzman, p. 3). For instance, in order to converse, speakers must listen to what someone says, speak one at a time, and then pause for the other speaker to have a turn.

Another interesting finding is that mothers seem to treat their babies' gestures, cries, coos, smiles, and babbling as meaningful contributions to a real conversation. An infant's arm may reach out toward her rattle. The mother responds by picking up and giving the rattle to the child, and at the same time, conducting the following conversation: "Oh, you want your rattle. Here it is. Your

A child improves most rapidly in speaking when in the presence of another child whose speaking ability is just a bit more developed than her own.

rattle.'' The baby takes the rattle and shakes it; the mother replies, ''Yes, your rattle. Your nice rattle.'' The baby pauses to hear the mother say this, shakes the rattle, and smiles. Then, the baby pauses to hear the mother again respond, ''Oh, you like your rattle. Shake your rattle.'' The baby shakes the rattle and pauses for the mother's response. The mother smiles and nods her head in approval, ''shake, shake, shake,'' etc. Thus, the rules for conversation are born long before the child can speak.

We may wonder, who is reinforcing whom? The mother starts the ''conversation,'' but the baby listens and replies with her physical response, which makes the mother say the next thing and the baby respond again. It takes two to talk in conversations. Children learn this from infancy, unless there is no one to talk to or no one who will listen. Parents who do not talk to their children during this preverbal period of development make a great mistake. Children need to hear their native language being addressed to them from the moment they are born if we want to motivate them to become fluent speakers themselves.

You have heard that one of the best things preschool caregivers can do is to read to their children. This statement is true. But, an even greater contribution is to converse with children, to listen and respond to them in conversational speech. Because many mothers intuitively treat preverbal youngsters as real contributors to conversations, the youngsters eventually become such. Caregivers who do not respond in this manner to infants and young children in fact may be causing a delay in the youngsters' language development.

If you have children who do not participate in peer conversations, the youngsters still may not be confident enough. But, an additional reason is the one discussed above: The children may not have learned to converse naturally in their earlier years.

If You Have Not Checked This Item: Some Helpful Ideas

• *Converse with Your Children*

Spend time every day in conversations with small groups of children. One of the best times is at snack or lunch. Be sure an adult sits at each of the children's tables and helps to carry on a conversation. Talk normally about anything that interests you or the children. You do not have to be the "teacher" who is teaching them the names of the fruits on the juice can. Instead, relax, and enjoy your snack or meal with the children. Say the kinds of things you would at your own meal table at home: "Whew, isn't it hot today? I think summer is coming early." "What's that you say, Jamie? You like summertime best of all?" "Me too. I love to swim and picnic." "You like to do that too, Jill?" "Yes, you are lucky to live next to the park."

• *Encourage Dramatic Play*

Children's own conversations often take place in dramatic play situations. Bring in props to encourage imaginative play in the housekeeping area, the block building area, and the water or sand table. Take props outside to encourage dramatic play there, too.

☐ ASKS QUESTIONS WITH PROPER WORD ORDER

Asking questions with the proper word order is another good indication that your children's command of language is developing normally. Most children are able to ask questions as adults do by about age four. Before that, children go through a predictable sequence in learning to ask questions, just as in other areas of development. (McCormick, p. 74)

Children usually do not learn how to ask a question until they have learned how to answer one. Between a year and a half and two years of age when they are putting a few words together to form primitive sentences, children also ask their first questions, if caregivers have been asking them questions first. The word order of these first questions is the same as for statements, but with a rising intonation at the end: "Bobbie drink milk?" meaning, "May Bobbie have a drink of milk?" or "Should Bobbie drink his milk?"

Next, the children begin to learn the use of the "wh" words at the beginning of questions, words like what, where, and who: "Where Mama going?" meaning "Where is Mama going?" This type of question becomes quite popular because the adult generally responds, and suddenly, the child realizes he has stumbled onto another way of controlling an adult: asking a question the adult will answer. This control is not always possible with mere statements. Since a child delights in adult attention and adult responses to things that he originates, he often will burst into a period of questioning. The child not only wants to know the answer, but he also wants the adult's attention.

The next stage in learning to ask questions comes as the child expands his sentences to include auxiliary verbs such as "can" and "will." These questions, though, are often in inverted word order: "Where Daddy will go?" instead of "Where will Daddy go?"

The final stage is the expanded question in proper word order, which most children are able to ask at around age four: "Can I go with you?" "What are you doing?" "Why doesn't the light go on?"

If you discover through your observation that certain children yet have not attained this final level, then what will you do? Will you sit down with them and teach them how to say a sentence correctly? If you have been reading this text carefully, you know that the answer is "no." Young children develop neither language skills nor many other developmental kinds of skills by being taught formally. Then, how do children learn how to say a sentence correctly? Children learn this skill in the same way they develop physical skills: They teach themselves proper word order by hearing the proper language forms spoken around them and by practicing the forms when physical and mental development has progressed to the point where practice is possible.

If You Have Not Checked This Item: Some Helpful Ideas

- *Ask Questions Yourself*

If children do not ask a question correctly until they have learned to answer one, then you need to include questioning in your activities with the children. Circle time is a good time for everyone to hear the proper word order of questions, and to volunteer to answer the inquiries if so inclined. Even the children who are not at the point of answering questions in front of a group will learn by listening.

- *Ask Children to Help You Gather Information*

You can ask a child to ask three or four other children for some information you need. For example, if you are planning a field trip, you might ask several children to go around asking others if their mothers would like to come along. This may not be the most accurate way to gather this information, but it is an excellent practice in questioning skills; you always can check the accuracy of the information with the children later.

- *Read a Question Book*

A number of children's picture books have questions in the title or the text. Read the books with the children, and give the youngsters a chance to answer the questions asked and to make up similar questions of their own.

Where Does the Butterfly Go When It Rains? by May Garelick, New York: Scholastic Book Services, 1961, is a rhyming story about where various animals, birds, and insects go to get out of the rain. The book contains many questions that are asked and answered, with the exception of the question in the title. This format should motivate a discussion of how people find out such answers.

The 2 Ton Canary & Other Nonsense Riddles by Polly Cameron, New York: Coward, McCann & Geoghegan, 1965, is a wonderfully crazy riddle book full of riddle questions on every other page. Most are elephant-joke or animal riddles, such as "What is gray and has four legs and a trunk?" Answer: "A mouse on vacation." Many of the children may not have the cognitive understanding to get the point of the answers, but it really does not matter. The book, with its outlandish gray and red illustrations, is so much fun, and the children love to repeat the riddle questions, which is the real point for reading it to the youngsters at this time.

Hey, Riddle Diddle! by Rodney Peppe, New York: Puffin Books, 1971, is a more traditional riddle book in rhyming verses and questions with clear illustrations that give clues to the answers. Children love to guess: "What has a face but cannot see?" Answer: "A clock."

☐ MAKES NEGATIVE RESPONSES WITH PROPER WORD ORDER

As with questions, making negative responses with the proper word order is another sentence cue that can help you determine whether children are on target in their language development. By about four years of age, children should be producing statements containing negatives, just as adults do.

The child's development of negative sentences parallels that of questions because many questions must be answered in the negative. As soon as he understands the use of "yes" and "no," the young child usually includes them in his utterances. "No" is especially popular when he finds out—probably to his great astonishment—that he can cause adults to respond with vigor when he says it. Using "yes" definitely has a lesser effect, so he delights in saying "no," no matter what he really means.

This acquisition of "yes" and "no" happens around two years of age. Much of the theme song of "the terrible two's" is based on the toddler's use of "no." What would happen if adult caregivers refused to respond as they usually do to such negative declarations? What would happen if adult caregivers just ignored these declarations? Why don't you try it and find out!

Once they understand the use of "no" and "not" at around age two, children begin to tag these negatives onto simple phrases: "No do it," meaning "I won't do it." "Not more milk," meaning "I don't want any more milk."

By age three or three-and-a-half, many children have learned contractions: don't, can't, won't, isn't, ain't. Children often use contractions, though, in sentences with inverted word order: "Why me can't go out?" instead of "Why can't I go out?" (McCormick, p. 75) Through hearing others speak with proper order and by practicing it themselves, children come to learn the mainstream manner of speaking. If they are not exposed to standard English in their homes, though, they will come to your center speaking the language or dialect used at home.

Again, it is not up to you to correct their speech. Instead, you will be providing them with many opportunities to listen to and engage in the speaking of standard English.

If You Have Not Checked This Item: Some Helpful Ideas

- *Have Question-and-Answer Discussions*

At circle time or with a small group, ask "why" questions containing negatives such as: "Why can't cats come down out of trees as easily as cats climb up?" "Why don't we usually see the moon in the daytime?" "Why can't you ride a two-wheel bike as easily as you can ride a trike?" Some of their answers should contain the proper use of negatives. Make up your own questions with negatives based on your children's interests.

- *Read a Book Containing Negative Sentences*

Pierre by Maurice Sendak, New York: Harper & Row Publishers, 1962, is one of the tiny "Nutshell Library" books that has a rhyming story about a little boy, Pierre, who "doesn't care." His parents ask him to do many things, all of which he refuses by saying, "I don't care."

☐ USES PAST TENSE VERBS CORRECTLY

By listening to the particular errors children make at the various stages of development, linguists have learned how children construct knowledge about language. Because the errors are different from those of mature speakers, and because the young child's language is different from any he has heard from an adult, we know that children learn language by methods other than pure imitation.

One common error that young children make is to put "ed" at the end of all past tense verbs, whether the verbs are regular or irregular. A child hears adults in his environment saying "walked," "dressed," "looked," "hoped," "wanted," and "needed," and he somehow absorbs the fact that they are talking about past time, something that happened before. His brain stores this information as a new rule to be applied when talking about something that happened in the past. Then,

TABLE 7. Language development

Age	Articulation	Expanded sentences	Questions	Negative Responses
0–1	Pronounces first word near end of first year or beginning of second year	Uses one word to express different meanings		
1–2	Uses only ten basic sounds at first	Realizes everything has a name; expands vocabulary; speaks in two-word sentences	Asks first questions; uses same word order as for statements (e.g., "Bobby go?")	Uses "no" alone
2–3	Uses only ten basic sounds	Uses telegraphic speech (e.g., "Me go store")	Uses question words "what," "where," and "who"	Uses "no," and "not," tagged onto simple phrases
3–4	Has mastered most sounds but may have problems with a few: "s," "l," "r," "th," and "sk"	Uses proper word order consistently in statements	Uses "can" and "will" in questions, sometimes with inverted word order	Uses negative contractions "don't," "can't," "won't," "isn't," "ain't"; inverts word order sometimes
4–5	Has mastered most sounds but may have problems with a few: "s," "l," "r," "th," and "sk"	Has mastered basic rules for expanding sentences	Asks questions in adult manner	Produces negative statements in adult manner
5–6	Most children of this age speak in a mature adult manner.			

he begins applying this rule to every past tense situation he talks about without realizing there are many exceptions in English to the "ed" for past tense rule.

He says things like "I eated," "I runned," "She goed home," "I seed the man," "My leg hurted" . . . forms he never heard an adult say. From this construction, we learn that children do indeed create their own grammar rules. The children do not create their rules from imitating mature speakers because mature speakers do not talk this way. Because all children make these same errors in the same sequence and at about the same time during their language development period, we realize that the human brain must be preorganized to take in language information and sort it out in this way. Applying a past tense rule like this one to every past verb, even the irregular ones, is called *overgeneralizing*.

Children do the same thing with other general rules their brains have established. Once they learn that plurals are formed by adding "s," they say "boys" and "girls" but then overgeneralize the rule, saying things like "tooths," instead of "teeth," and "foots," instead of "feet."

Children's brains seem to be programmed to absorb information about things, then to extract rules from the way the information seems to work, and then to apply the rules to similar things. This procedure is called *inductive reasoning*. Preschool children who are allowed to play with computers learn to use the computers in the same way. The youngsters induce rules about how a computer works from working with it. They play around with it, making mistakes, trying again, and finally figuring out what to do. This process is an effective method for self-learning. Perhaps this is the reason that adults, who generally think deductively, have trouble learning to use the computer, while children seldom do.

When children are at the overgeneralizing stage in language production, adults cannot—and should not—do much to correct the youngsters. You can ask a child to say "ran" instead of "runned" over and over, but somehow, it always comes out as "I runned home." To learn the proper formation of past tense verbs, the child will need more than just hearing the verbs used correctly at this stage.

Be patient. When the brain matures, the child will discriminate more finely with word forms just as she does with motor coordination. Provide her with a rich language environment where she will hear competent speakers and will participate in all kinds of speaking activities herself.

If You Have Not Checked This Item: Some Helpful Ideas

- *Use Tape Recorders*

Help children learn how to listen to and record tape cassettes on their own. Then, provide the youngsters with some motivation for taping. You could start a story on the tape and ask an interested child to finish it. Have several tapes for all the children who want to record. Play the tapes to a small group later. You might start with something like: "As I was coming to school today, I heard a very strange noise. It sounded a little like a train. It sounded like it was coming around the corner. I felt like running away, but I didn't. Instead, I . . ."

- *Use Toy Telephones*

Have at least two toy telephones in your classroom for children to use for pretend conversations.

- *Read Many Good Books*

Children eventually learn the correct English forms by hearing the forms spoken. Reading books or telling stories aloud is yet another way to fill the environment with the spoken language.

Cloudy with a Chance of Meatballs by Judi Barrett, New York: Atheneum, 1978, is a hilarious tall tale of a world where food falls from the sky. The story very well could motivate your children to make up their own tall tales. The youngsters may want to record their own stories.

☐ PLAYS WITH RHYMING WORDS

Just as they play with blocks, toys, and each other, children also play with words. Youngsters make up nonsense words, repeat word sounds, mix up words, say things backwards, make up chants, and repeat rhyming words. Most people have paid little attention to this activity, as it seems so inconsequential. What we have not seemed to realize is that through this activity, children are once more at work creating their own knowledge through play. This time, the content is language rather than cognitive concepts, and this time, the child is manipulating the medium (words) with his voice rather than his hands or body. Once again, he is structuring his experiences by finding out what words do and what he can do with them. Play is once more the vehicle because of the pleasure it gives him.

All children play with words, especially in the early stages of language development, but of course, there are great individual differences in the amount of language play you will witness among your children. We do know that children who are involved in rhyming activities at an early age carry over this interest in poetry into adult life (Caplan, p. 41), and that children who have had early experience with nursery rhymes are more successful later in reading than children who have not. It behooves us, then, to observe the children's language play and to provide encouragement and support for all youngsters to become more involved with it.

Although mothers often promote language play with their infants by playing word and action games with the infants such as patty-cake and peekaboo, much language play is solitary. Children carry on monologs in which they manipulate sounds, patterns, and meanings of words. These three areas have, in fact, been identified by specialists as common types of word play. (Schwartz, pp. 16–26)

Infants from six to eighteen months old often "talk" to themselves before going to sleep, repeating rhythmic and rhyming sounds. The infants sound almost as if they are really talking, only with nonsense words. With older children, sound play contains more meaningful words, consonants, and blends. The children often repeat these words in nonsensical fashion: "Ham, bam, lamb, Sam, wham, wham, wham."

Pattern play is a common form of play that involves manipulating the structure of the language. The child begins with a pattern and then substitutes a new word each time he says it: "Bobby go out; Mommy go out; Daddy go out; doggie go out." or "Bite it; write it; light it; sight it; night it; fight it."

Meaning play is not as common among younger children, but it is really more interesting. Here, the child interchanges real with nonsensical meanings or makes up words or meanings. An interesting example Schwartz found was children doing water play with floating and sinking objects, and telling the objects to "sink-up," meaning "float," or "sink-down" (Schwartz, pp. 19–20).

Piaget describes much of the talk of three- to five-year-olds as egocentric. It is as if much of their speaking is not directed to anyone in particular, but produced for their own pleasure. Some children go around muttering to themselves most of the day, especially when they are involved in an interesting activity. This muttering seems to disappear by the time they enter public school, but the muttering may become inner speech instead. (Caplan, p. 41)

Are any of the children in your class engaged in word play? They will be if you sponsor or promote it. Do finger plays and body action chants with the children during circle time or for transitions between activities. Read children's poems and nursery rhymes to the youngsters. Use tape recorders to stimulate the children's own made-up rhymes.

If You Have Not Checked This Item: Some Helpful Ideas

• *Do Finger Plays*

There are several good finger play books on the market containing the words, actions, and, in some cases, the music to accompany the chant. You also should consider making up your own chants or listening to the children's word play and incorporating it into a chant for all to say.

Finger Frolics: Fingerplays for Young Children compiled by Liz Cromwell, and Dixie Hibner, Livonia, Mich.: Partner Press, 1976, is one of the best books on finger plays. It contains dozens of finger plays about seasons, holidays, animals, and people.

Eye Winker Tom Tinker Chin Chopper: Fifty Musical Fingerplays by Tom Glazer, New York: Doubleday & Company, 1973, contains many of the traditional rhymes with piano arrangements and guitar chords.

• *Read Books of Rhyme and Verse*

There are many traditional nursery rhyme books on the market. Children still enjoy hearing and repeating nursery rhymes.

Mother Goose illustrated by Aurelius Battaglia, New York: Random House, 1973, is a traditional Mother Goose book with illustrations of medieval people and animals.

The Bedtime Mother Goose pictures by Ron Himler, New York: Golden Press, 1980, has some different rhymes with illustrations of Early American children.

Dogs & Dragons Trees & Dreams by Karla Kuskin, New York: Harper & Row Publishers, 1980, is one of a number of poetry books by this popular author. Long and short, rhyming and nonrhyming, the poems in this collection are full of word plays, questions and answers, and humor. Children will enjoy listening to and repeating the poems.

- *Read Books Containing Funny Words*

Certain children's books are especially attractive to their audience because of one or two hilarious words; at least, the books are funny for the children who go into spasms of laughter upon hearing the words and who want the books read again and again.

Mert the Blurt by Robert Kraus, New York: Simon & Schuster, 1980, is one of these funny books. Little Mert cannot keep anything to himself, but goes around blurting out fanciful family secrets to a colorful host of neighbors.

The Surprise Party by Pat Hutchins, New York: Collier Books, 1969, is a delightfully mixed-up communication muddle like the game, Gossip. Here, rabbit whispers to owl that he is having a party tomorrow and it is a surprise. The message is passed on from one animal to another in such a garbled form that the message truly is a surprise for all in the end. Children love the nonsensical phrases that the animals repeat and the youngsters may want to try the phrases on their own.

REFERENCES CITED

Caplan, Theresa, and Frank Caplan. *The Early Childhood Years: The 2 To 6 Year Old.* New York: The Putnam Publishing Group, 1983.

Eisenson, Jon. *Is Your Child's Speech Normal?* Reading, Mass.: Addison-Wesley Publishing Company, 1976.

Holzman, Mathilda. *The Language of Children.* Englewood Cliffs, N.J.: Prentice-Hall, 1983.

McCormick, Linda, and Richard L. Schiefelbusch. *Early Language Intervention.* Columbus, Ohio: Charles E. Merrill Publishing Company, 1984.

Schwartz, Judith I. "Children's Experiments with Language." *Young Children.* July 1981.

OTHER SOURCES

Beaty, Janice J. *Skills for Preschool Teachers.* Columbus, Ohio: Charles E. Merrill Publishing Company, 1984.

LEARNING ACTIVITIES

1. Use the *Child Skills Checklist,* "9. Spoken Language," as a screening tool to observe all of the children in your classroom. Which children seem to need help in more than one of the items? How do these children fare in the various areas of cognitive development?

2. Choose a child who seems to be having difficulty with spoken language, and observe him or her on three different days, doing a running record of his or her language activities. Compare the results with the *Checklist* results. How do you interpret the evidence you have collected? Are there any pieces of evidence that are still missing about this child's language performance?

3. Choose a child whom you have screened as needing help in several of the *Checklist* items, and carry out one or more of the activities listed. Record the results.

4. Teach the children a finger play or rhyming game. How did the children perform whom you noted as needing help in this area?

5. Do a tape recorder activity with a small group of children. Have them tape record their own words and then play them back. They may want to tell about themselves, tell a story, or say a verse.

11

Written Language

Written Language Checklist

- [ ] Pretends to write by making scribbles in horizontal lines
- [ ] Includes features of real letters in scribbling
- [ ] Identifies own written name
- [ ] Identifies classroom labels
- [ ] Knows some alphabet letters
- [ ] Makes real letters
- [ ] Prints letters of name
- [ ] Prints name correctly in linear manner

W hy should a chapter on children's written language be included in a book on observing the development of young children? Surely, learning to write has little to do with child development, right? Furthermore, teaching children to write should come later when children are in first grade, shouldn't it? The answers to all of these questions are quite different today than they would have been as recently as fifteen years ago.

Enough research about the beginnings of writing and reading, children's perceptual development, and how children make sense of their world through playful exploration has since been completed, and it has changed our minds forever about the way children develop and how we best can support their growth.

We know now that written language is an outgrowth of the same urge that drives children to express themselves orally and even pictorially. We also know that given the proper tools and support, all children everywhere go through the same sequence of stages in teaching themselves to write. Yes, writing is indeed a natural part of a child's development. The fact of the matter is "learning to write is largely an act of discovery," as one specialist puts it (Temple, p. 2).

Thus, writing joins language; thinking; and emotional, social, and motor skills as another aspect of development that the child can arrive at on his own by playfully interacting with the materials in his environment, once his physical and mental maturity have made that playful interaction possible.

This does not mean that writing development always occurs naturally. Many children come from families with few toys, let alone the tools for writing. Children need to practice writing just as they do speaking if we want them to be proficient. Without a tool to write with or something to write on, they can do little more than make marks on steamy windows or scratches in the dirt.

Nor does it mean that we should sit down with the preschool child and formally teach him or her how to write any more than we should formally teach him how to walk and talk. Instead, we should fill his environment with examples of written language; we should serve as models by doing a great deal of writing and reading in the presence of the child, and we should provide him with the tools and encouragement to attempt writing on his own.

Can any of your children print their names? Do any of them pretend to write, perhaps at the easel, by scribbling rows of markings? Make an assessment of the children in your classroom by using the eight items of the *Checklist* under Written Language. Then, set up a writing table or writing area complete with a variety of tools, and watch what happens.

☐ PRETENDS TO WRITE BY MAKING SCRIBBLES IN HORIZONTAL LINES

The first natural attempts by young children to write are usually scribbles. This initial scribbling is also true with art, you may point out. Yet, children as young as three years old seem to recognize the difference between writing and drawing. In fact, some children do drawing scribbles on one part of a paper and writing scribbles that "tell about the picture," on another part (Vukelich, p. 4); the two parts look completely different.

Although it is true that children's first attempts at both art and writing take the form of scribbles, writing scribbles are done in a horizontal, linear manner across the page, something like a line of writing. The children who make the writing scribbles seem to understand that writing is something that can be read, and the youngsters sometimes pretend to read their pretend writing, known also as *linear mock writing.* (Temple, p. 29) This behavior is the first step in the natural acquisition of writing. Once their scribbles have become horizontal lines instead of circular or aimless meanderings, the youngsters are indicating they understand that writing is something different from drawing.

Their first scribbles do not resemble letters at all. The children, in fact, seem to be trying to copy only the broad, general features of the writing system: that it is arranged in rows across a page and that it consists of a series of loops, tall sticks, and connected lines that are repeated. Only later will the children differentiate the finer features of the system: the letters.

Where have the youngsters acquired this knowledge of written language so early in life? Look around you. They, like all of us, are surrounded by written material: in newspapers and magazines, on television advertising, on the labels on food products, in letters in the mail, in the stories read to them, on signs on stores, on bumper stickers on cars, and on mottos on T-shirts. The printed word is everywhere.

Some families, of course, encourage their children to print their own names at an early age, and family members even take time to write out the stories the children make up. Some children have older brothers or sisters who bring written material home from school. These children see family members engaged in writing or reading and want to become involved themselves.

Observe to see which children do pretend writing, this first step in the writing process; which ones have progressed beyond this beginning; and which ones have not started. Of course, if children have moved beyond this first stage, you will not need to check this item; you should indicate with a "+" mark that they have advanced to a higher level.

If You Have Not Checked This Item: Some Helpful Ideas

▪ *Set Up a Writing Area*

Most children will not ask to become involved in writing if there is no sign of it in their environment. Set up a special writing table with all of the implements, and you soon will have a group of budding writers.

For paper, it is best to use unlined sheets. Children will be placing their scribbles and pretend letters all over the page, and lined paper may inhibit this free form exploration of how writing works. Use typing paper or stationery as well as tablets and pads of different sizes and colors. You may want to have an individual notebook for each child with his or her name on the front.

For writing tools, you need to include a variety. We sometimes think of pencils first, but research with beginning writers shows that pencils are the most difficult of all writing implements to manipulate effectively (Lamme, p. 22). Children, themselves, choose colored felt tip markers as their favorites. You also should include colored chalk and a small chalkboard, crayons, and a few pencils in addition to the markers. It is not necessary to have only the large primary-size pencils. Some preschoolers have great difficulty handling these large pencils and

Preschool children teach themselves to write most easily with felt tip markers and unlined paper.

much prefer to use regular pencils. Put out a variety of writing tools, and the children will find out on their own what is best for them.

Some children choose pencils from the beginning and seem to be able to handle these implements well. These children may well be ready for some direction on how to hold the pencil properly. If they grip it too tightly or bear down too hard, they probably will tire easily and may lose interest. (Lamme, p. 23)

Voluntary and not forced participation in writing activities, of course, should be the rule in your program. Some children need to develop better eye-hand coordination before they engage in it. They might do better painting at the easel or playing with the utensils you have put out at the water or sand tables, instead. If the youngsters can build a tall block tower without its toppling over, can drive a nail straight into a piece of wood, or can use a pair of scissors with ease, then their eye-hand coordination is probably developed enough for them to use a writing implement.

☐ INCLUDES FEATURES OF REAL LETTERS IN SCRIBBLING

Just as an infant's babbling finally begins to take the sound of real talking, so a child's first linear scribblings eventually begin to look like real writing. For many children, the lines of their scribbles become somewhat jagged and then finally take on features of real letters such as straight, curved, or intersecting lines, although no real letters are formed (Schickedanz, p. 243). This advanced scribbling happens as a natural developmental sequence when children have the freedom and opportunity to experiment with writing on their own. Teaching, in fact, has no effect whatsoever at this point.

Children extract the elements of writing from the environment and play around with these elements using markers and paper. The children once again are "manipulating the medium" (writing), and they manipulate it until they have learned how to handle it, what it can do, and what they are able to do with it. Just as they do when they first learn to climb stairs, put together a puzzle, or ride a trike, they want to practice over and over. Many children will fill pages with this pretend writing, and the youngsters will take great satisfaction in doing so. This activity provides wonderful practice for them in learning to control the writing tool as well.

The children sometimes think their scribbling is something much more meaningful. If this is writing, as some reason that it must be, then someone who knows how to read should be able to read it. Often, they will take a piece of pretend writing to an adult and ask her to read it. How should you respond? Be honest about it: "Oh, Sharon, your writing is beginning to look almost real. Can you tell me what it says?" Some children really have a story in mind when they do their pretend writing, and they will be able to tell it to you. Others think that since they do not know what their "words" say, their "words" must speak only to someone who can read.

Observe to see which of your children are at this stage in their experimental writing. What can you do to help them progress further?

If You Have Not Checked This Item: Some Helpful Ideas

- *Support the Children's Efforts*

You need to praise the children for their efforts in all the writing they do, just as you do for their art. You may want to save samples of this stage of their writing and to keep the samples in a folder or the scrapbook you are making to show each child's accomplishments. Be sure to date these samples so that you will be able to compare them with later samples.

- *Use Sand or Salt Trays or Finger Painting*

Put out small trays of sand or salt in your writing area so that children can practice "writing" with their fingers. It is easy to "erase" this "writing" by simply shaking the tray. Finger painting on tabletops or paper also gives the children practice doing linear pretend writing with their fingers.

☐ IDENTIFIES OWN WRITTEN NAME

If we want children to become involved with written language on their own, then we must provide many examples of it throughout the preschool classroom. Because the principal focus of children this age is themselves, a good place to begin written language is with their own names. Children may not be ready to recognize written names at the beginning of the year, so it may be better to start with pictorial symbols at first.

Mount a different symbol on each child's cubby. The symbols can be various single-colored geometric shapes: stars, circles, squares, and triangles. Or, you can use peel-off labels with pictures of animals, birds, or flowers as symbols. Once each child is familiar with his or her own particular symbol, you should include his or her printed name on the same sign. Use both upper and lowercase letters and not just capitals. The children will be using both forms later on in school, and the youngsters should learn how their names look printed the proper way.

At this point, the children may be identifying their name signs by either or both the symbol and the written name. Eventually, you should remove the symbol altogether, so that the children will become familiar with the look of their names. This familiarity does not mean the youngsters identify the individual letters at first. Children tend to look for whole configurations. Youngsters often are able to identify their own names and those of several others just by "the way they look."

Use children's name labels and tags to mark the youngsters' cubbies, toothbrushes, cots, table places at meal time, science collections, block building structures, and the tags they use to hang in their free choice activity areas. Print individual names on artwork, personal scrapbooks, puzzles made of the children's photos, and other personal possessions or products created in your class.

Talk about the children's names. Encourage the youngsters to identify their own. Mix up the place cards at your lunch tables so that children will have to search for their seats. Put name tags on the chairs or floor space at circle time so that children will have the fun and practice of searching out their places again.

How many of your children can identify their names? This is the important first step before the youngsters actually print their names.

If You Have Not Checked This Item: Some Helpful Ideas

- *Use Alphabet Blocks, Magnetic Letters*

Let children play as they want with alphabet blocks and magnetic letters at first. Then, you can start a game called "Whose letter (or name) is this?" Pick out the first letter of someone's name. Then, spell the entire name with alphabet blocks or magnetic letters, and see if anyone can recognize the whole name.

- *Read a Name Book*

With *Andy, That's My Name* by Tomi de Paola, Englewood Cliffs, N.J.: Prentice-Hall, 1973, children may be motivated to make their names from alphabet blocks just as Andy does.

- *Use Computer Software*

If you have a computer in your classroom that children are allowed to "play" with, then a commercial "name" program might be appropriate. (See pp. 256–57.)

☐ IDENTIFIES CLASSROOM LABELS

Children may learn to write their names but still know very little about the concept of symbolization, i.e., that words are symbols that represent things. Children need to have many meaningful experiences with print in their everyday lives. Printed signs, labels, and charts in your classroom can give the children this experience.

In addition to labeling the children's cubbies and seats with their names, you should have each activity area labeled with its name, as well as job, attendance, experience, weather, and recipe charts; animal and fish pets; pictures of community helpers; homes and buildings in the block area; the first aid kit and emergency directions; records of children's height, of how much their plants have grown, of how far children can jump, and of which children have pets at home; stories the children have made up; favorite songs and finger plays; and sections of the play supermarket. There are many opportunities for using printed material in your classroom. Be sure these labels and signs are mounted at the children's eye level.

From this exposure, children will learn several things

1. Written words convey messages that can be read.
2. Writing is arranged in horizontal rows. (Be sure you do not use vertical labels.)
3. Writing is made up of letters.
4. Some letters are repeated, but never more than two together.

(Temple, p. 51)

Obviously, such concepts are internalized subconsciously, and you should not point them out. Your role is to fill the environment with printed material. The children's interaction with it will make certain impressions on their minds. Some youngsters will realize, just as they did when they first learned to talk, that everything has a name and that this name can be written.

To find out which of your children understand that written words convey meaning, ask them to point to the part of the story you are reading that tells what is happening. Some still may point to the picture on the page instead of the words. You may want to run your finger under the words you are reading to a small group from time to time so that the children will see that you are using the words to tell the story and not the pictures.

If You Have Not Checked This Item: Some Helpful Ideas

- *Write Down What Children Are Doing*

Encourage children to tell you about the art work they are doing, the block buildings they are constructing, and the dramatic play situations they are involved with. You can write their explanations down for them to keep in a scrapbook of their own. Take instant print pictures of children engaged in activities, and mount the pictures in an album with labels or words the children use to describe what they are doing.

- *Make Group Experience Charts*

When some of the children have done something together, ask them to dictate it to you, and write the dictation for all to see on an experience chart. Telling about a field trip, a holiday, or a special class occasion could prompt such written dictations, as could the dramatic play roles that the children play in the dress-up area.

- *Be a Writing Model Yourself*

Do a lot of writing in the presence of the children. If they see that it is important to you, they will want to do it too. If you are doing *Checklist* recording or running records in their presence, they often will want to use your pen and paper to do some pretend writing themselves. Do not give it up, but, instead, be sure you have a well-equipped writing table to which they can be directed. Serving as a writing model almost always will stimulate certain children to try their own hand at writing.

- *Read Many Stories*

You should read at least one story daily to small groups or individuals. Reading to the total group is not as satisfactory because not everyone gets to sit close to the teacher and see the pictures and words of the story.

- *Have a Class Mailbox*

Put your written communications to children or their parents in a class mailbox. You can have a child take the mail out every day and, with your help, distribute it. You may want to make a field trip to the post office or have a mail carrier visit and talk to your class.

You should plan on writing one note to each child on a weekly basis. It should be simple and nice: "Rob, I love your new sneakers!" or "Shirl, thanks for helping Carol today." When the note is delivered to the child, one of the adults in the class can help him or her to read it. This modeling behavior on your part should stimulate children to want to write notes to classmates or to answer your notes on their own. The children will need help, which your co-workers can provide.

☐ KNOWS SOME ALPHABET LETTERS

This *Checklist* item, like the previous ones, refers to children's natural development of writing, and not to their formal learning of the alphabet by being taught by an adult. Children do learn alphabet letters on their own just by being surrounded by the letters. The youngsters' own names are often the first source. Children may learn to say the letters in their names soon after the youngsters recognize their name sign. Many children then will be able to identify those particular letters wherever the letters are seen.

Reciting or chanting the ABC's is not the same. Just as children can chant the numbers from one to ten, but not understand what any of the numbers mean, so preschoolers often chant the alphabet without the slightest idea of what they are saying. Programs like Sesame Street, of course, teach children the letter names, and some youngsters may have learned from this technique, although it is a much more passive and formal method.

Other children may have learned alphabet letters from a personal computer at home or in the classroom. A number of software programs feature alphabet games for children two to six years of age. In many ways, computers are superior to television as a learning tool because with computers, children are actively and playfully involved in their own learning. Computers should be used this way with young children, rather than in formal lessons. Children should be free to use a classroom computer during free choice period in the same way as they use blocks, dolls, or the water table.

Have alphabet games on the shelves of your manipulative area; alphabet letters mounted on the wall at children's eye level; alphabet books in the book area; and wooden, plastic, sandpaper, or magnetic letters available for the children to choose to play with. But, do not teach the alphabet formally. You will find if you have filled the children's environment with writing, there will be no need to teach the alphabet formally.

In recognizing alphabet letters, children progress through a particular sequence just as they do in learning to make speech sounds naturally. The first distinctive features children seem to recognize is whether the line that makes the letter is straight or curved. Letters that are round such as O and C are distinguished first. Then, letters with curved lines, such as P and S, are noted. Next, curved letters with intersections, such as B and R, are distinguished from curved letters without intersections like S and J. Letters with diagonal lines, such as K and X, are among the last to be recognized. (Schickedanz, p. 311) We noted earlier in Chapter 8 that young children have difficulty distinguishing shapes with diagonal lines as well.

This is the natural progression. Your children, of course, may learn some letters out of sequence because the letters occur in the children's names. The youngsters still, however, may have difficulty when it comes to writing certain letters.

If You Have Not Checked This Item: Some Helpful Ideas

- *Read an Appropriate Alphabet Book*

There are many good alphabet books on the market, but you first will need to review any you plan to use with your children to see if the books are appropriate to the youngsters' age level. Some alphabet books are for very young children. Looking at the simplicity of the pictures may help you to determine the appropriate age level. If there are pictures of children in the book, are the children in the book the age of yours?

Some alphabet books are too sophisticated for young children. These books display the talent of the artist, but they do not teach the letters. Other alphabet books are confusing because of the unfamiliar objects used as illustrations. Alphabet books are most effective if they

1. Use both upper and lowercase letters
2. Have simple illustrations that children can recognize
3. Use illustrations with only one common name (not cat/kitten or rabbit/bunny, for instance)
4. Use words starting with a single consonant (such as cow, sail, or ball) rather than a blend (such as church, ship, or brown)
5. Have a theme, a simple story, or rhyming verses

These books are more effective if read to one or two children at a time rather than to a group. The children need to sit close to the teacher to identify the objects being named and to see the shapes of the letters. Have the books on your bookshelves so children can use the books by themselves as well. Chall's extensive study on learning to read in America found that children's ability to identify letters was an important predictor of reading achievement in first and second grades (Chall, p. 141).

A new book following all of these guidelines is *An Edward Lear Alphabet* illustrated by Carol Newsom, New York: Lothrop, Lee & Shepard Books, 1983, which uses Lear's classic rhyming verses for each letter with Newsom's lovely yet humorous animal illustrations. Children will enjoy the word play for each letter: "Pumpy, shumpy, flumpy, pumpy, dumpy, thumpy little pump."

▪ *Use Alphabet Software in Your Computer*

(See pp. 256–57 in this chapter.)

▪ *Have Alphabet Soup*

Serve alphabet soup for lunch, and see if the children can identify any of the letters.

▪ *Have Fun with Pretzels*

Have pretzels for snack sometime, and see what letters your children can make by breaking off pieces before eating the pretzels.

☐ MAKES REAL LETTERS

Young children may begin making a few real letters even before the youngsters can name them. Often, these letters are from the children's own names. The youngsters may have seen the teacher or their mother write their names on their art products or other possessions. If children have the opportunity and materials, they may try to imitate an adult's writing of their names.

The children's first attempts are usually flawed. The youngsters make the same mistakes in writing letters that they do in recognizing letters; that is, the children often overlook the letters' distinguishing features. Development of children's written language, just as their other aspects of development, progresses from the general to the particular. Until their visual perception becomes fine-tuned enough, they will have difficulty making letters that are accurate in all the details.

Let the children practice on their own. Pointing out errors is not really productive, just as it was not in their development of spoken language. In time, their errors will become less frequent as the children refine their perception of individual letters and gain control over writing tools.

One of the children's problems in printing letters has to do with their orientation in space. Children often are able to get the features of the letters accurate, but not the direction of the letters. The youngsters reverse some letters and even write some upside down. Occasionally, their letters are facing the right direction, but just as often, their printing may be a complete mirror image of the real thing. We often wonder if children really see the letters like that.

Part of the answer may lie in the fact that the orientation of other kinds of things, that is, the direction they face, makes no difference in identifying them.

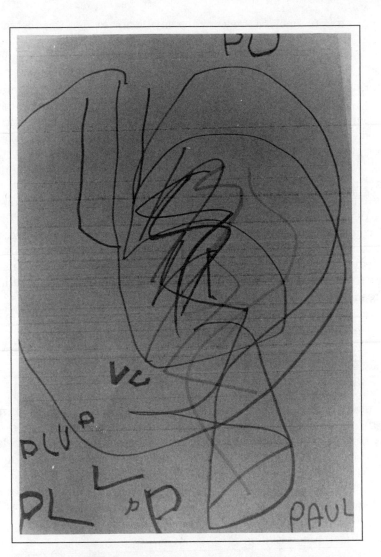

A child who has seen the teacher write his name on his art products often tries to imitate the letters.

For instance, a cup is a cup, no matter whether the handle is pointing toward a person or away from her. A flashlight may be lying horizontally or standing on end, but it is still a flashlight. Objects, in other words, do not change their identity because they face a different direction.

But, letters do. Letters made with the same features are completely different depending on the direction their curved lines face and whether their straight lines are at the top or bottom. If children are not used to paying attention to the direction certain features face, imagine the trouble they will have identifying and printing the letters "d," "b," "p," and "q." All four are made with the same curved and straight lines. It may take many years to get this detail straight. Children often reverse letters even into the elementary grades.

One of the problems in children's playing with three-dimensional letters is the fact that these letters can be reversed or turned upside down. If you have such letters in your writing area, be sure to have real alphabet letters mounted on the nearby wall at the children's eye level so that the youngsters easily can see the proper orientation. Magnetic letters are better than letter blocks or plastic letters in this respect. At least the magnetic letters cannot be reversed when placed on a metal backing.

Another detail children sometimes overlook when they first print letters is whether the letters are open or closed: the difference between ''O'' and ''C.'' This distinction problem may have to do with the children's perception of space and their difficulty in making enclosures, as discussed in Chapter 9. The young-sters, in fact, may not really see this detail at first. With practice and maturity, these problems resolve themselves unless a child has a learning impairment. Your best strategy is to fill the environment with words, letters, and occasions to write, as well as to support and encourage the children's own attempts at writing. But, do not ''teach'' the children.

If You Have Not Checked This Item: Some Helpful Ideas

- *Make Letters Personal*

Children always learn in a more meaningful way if the subject somehow is connected to them. Help children to recognize the first letter in their own first names by playing games with it. You can have letter cards on string necklaces that the youngsters can hang around their necks. Let the children find their own letters. Then, let the youngsters see if they can find any other child with a letter like theirs. Be sure to have enough similar letters, and make them big enough so that everyone can see them easily.

- *Have Many Writing Practice Activities*

Trays with sand or salt on the bottom are fun to ''write'' in and easy to erase by shaking the tray. The Etch a Sketch picture board can be used by mature children with good eye-hand coordination to make letters. Some computer programs allow children to draw letters. Can children form letters out of cooked spaghetti?

Children also like to trace around cardboard cut out letters. Be sure that the face of the letters is distinctive from the underside, so that the children will have the proper orientation.

- *Have Alphabet Cards*

Let children play with alphabet cards that contain a picture of an object. In that way, the youngsters will be seeing the letter in the proper orientation. The object on the card also will give them a clue to the name of the letter. It is best to have cards that show both upper and lowercase letters. Then, children will see that each letter can be written in two different ways. It is not helpful for children to use only capital letters, since the youngsters will need to write in lowercase as well in the elementary grades.

- *Use a Primary Typewriter or a Computer*

If you have access to either a primary typewriter or a computer, then consider yourself fortunate. Children love to play with letters and eventually words that they can type. Do not give the youngsters formal lessons on either instrument. The instruments should be used by children in a natural and spontaneous way, just as all of your writing tools are. In other words, children will teach themselves.

☐ PRINTS LETTERS OF NAME

Children may start printing their names before they make other letters. These last two *Checklist* items sometimes, in fact, appear out of sequence with some children who show evidence of learning written language in the natural process described here.

Let the children learn to print their names on their own. You may be surprised at the youngsters' initial production. Their names may contain all of the proper letters, but written in different sizes, pointed in different directions (both backward and upside down), ordered in no particular sequence, and scattered around the paper as if they are dangling in three-dimensional space instead of lying flat on a two-dimensional surface.

Watch how the children print the letters of their names naturally. Children experiment with writing just as they do with block building to find which way works best for them. They may print the first letter of their names in the middle of the paper, then turn the paper half-way around and print the next letter. They may turn the paper again for the following letters or keep it straight and print the remaining letters on the parts of the paper with the most space. If you find your children from the outset printing their names in a linear manner with the letters in the proper sequence, you will know they probably have had practice at home.

The example of initial word writing described here points up the concepts that children need to acquire before the youngsters can write successfully

1. Words start at the left side of the paper and go right.
2. Words are written in a linear manner with all of the letters in a row.
3. The letters in words follow one another in sequence.

You understand that the children eventually will learn these concepts spontaneously without being "taught" formally, just by being surrounded by writing and by trying it out on their own. Do not expect your beginning children to learn to write properly all at once. When they first write their names, they concentrate on making the letters and have little concern for the placement of the letters.

Correct orientation and placement may not come until their cognitive concept of position in space is more developed.

Let them explore writing their names any way they want. If they come to you and ask you to write their names as a model for them to follow, you, of course, can print their names in a linear manner in upper and lowercase letters at the top of a sheet of paper. The children still may be unable to copy this model, but it gives them another opportunity to see the proper form for writing. Follow the children's lead. Do not impose your own timetable on "teaching children to write their names." Some children may learn it quickly on their own because of their maturity and practice. Others may not learn it at all for another year or so.

It is better for children to learn to write their names with a beginning capital letter and the rest in lowercase. Words appear in print this way, and the children will be required to write like this in elementary school. It is no more difficult for the youngsters to learn lowercase than uppercase. The three-dimensional letters they use in play, the alphabet books, cards, and letters on the wall also should contain both upper and lowercase letters. Too often, children are taught to write their names in capital letters only. This orientation makes writing very confusing when the children reach the elementary grades and have to "unlearn" this incorrect method.

Have the children who can write their names or even the first letter of their names sign their paintings and other classroom products. Youngsters are used to having an adult do this signing. They will get great satisfaction from doing it for themselves. Be sure, however, to write the names of those who cannot yet write their names themselves; be certain to write their names with a capital and lowercase letters so that the youngsters will have an accurate model to follow. The children even may want to try writing the first letter of their names on their artwork after you have written their names out completely.

If You Have Not Checked This Item: Some Helpful Ideas

- *Write Greeting Cards*

Make large greeting cards on newsprint at least once a week to send to various people on all sorts of occasions. You might send a thank you note to the mail carrier for visiting your class, a congratulations card to one of your families that has a new baby, a Halloween card to the grandmother who volunteers in your program, or a "have a nice day" card to your bus driver. Have the class help you to make up the message, which you can write at the top of the paper with colored felt tip markers. Then, let the children sign their names underneath. Those who have not yet learned to write letters can sign with scribbles, and you can print their names underneath. Fold up your giant "cards," and send them in manila envelopes.

- *Use Computer Name Games*

Several companies put out computer software for children two to six years of age that includes name games. *Kindercomp* by Spinnaker has a set of games that includes names, drawing, matching, letters, and numbers. *Stickybear ABC, Numbers, Shapes,* and *Opposites* are four learning game programs by Weekly Reader. *Nine Learning Games* and *Early Games* by Counterpoint Software, Inc. include letters, names, drawing, colors, shapes, and sizes.

These games and others are found on the shelves of computer stores. Try the games out before you purchase any to make sure they are appropriate for your children. As mentioned previously, you should allow children to experiment and learn on their own with the computer, just as you let them learn on their own how to build with unit blocks.

☐ PRINTS NAME CORRECTLY IN LINEAR MANNER

The last of the *Checklist* items is also the last to appear in children's written language. Not all of your children will progress to this stage until kindergarten. They may not be able to print words in a linear manner from left to right until a horizontal baseline shows up in their paintings. Some five- and six-year-olds continue to have difficulty in reaching this stage.

Directionality is also a problem in the words of beginning writers, just as it is with their letters. Adults take for granted that words start at the left and go to the right. Young children have not established that directional perspective at first. They may print a word such as "book" by starting with a "b" in the middle of the page and going either way: "ꞔoobook." They merely may be "manipulating the medium" (letters) as they do with paint and unit blocks to find out how it works.

We know, however, that young children do not start out with a Euclidean or plain geometry frame of reference, knowing that there is a single horizon or baseline and that things are located along straight lines or formed into shapes with angular corners. Instead, the children seem to operate from the viewpoint of "topology," a fluid point of view that sees various shapes as being the same as long as their boundaries are not broken. A square can be a circle and a triangle if the perimeter is considered fluid like that of a rubber band. For this reason, three- and four-year-olds find it next to impossible to "line up in a straight line." Where is the line? It is in whatever direction each child happens to be facing at the moment. One wonders if nine months of "floating" in a mother's womb could have created this frame of reference!

Children may write words from top to bottom or from right to left as easily as from left to right. Most youngsters go through a stage of writing their names backward in a perfect mirror image. The children seem to see things from a number of different perspectives, in fact, before the youngsters finally learn a single linear orientation.

You may think that lined paper would help them to establish this baseline. During these early formative years, however, the children's experiments with letters and words just do not fit between lines, and the youngsters are better off with unlined paper. Later in elementary school as they learn to control their pencil movements and refine their perceptions of letters and words, a line can be very helpful to the children.

There are three common processes children use when they begin writing words: tracing, copying, or generating their own words (Temple, p. 47). When they are exploring writing on their own, the youngsters may use any or all of these methods. Tracing is the easiest method, and some children seem to do it spontaneously. When a teacher or parent writes these children's names on a piece of paper, the youngsters trace over the names again and again. Then, the children try writing the same thing on another part of the paper.

Other children copy their names from a paper or words from a classroom label onto another sheet of paper or a chalkboard. The farther away the words are, the more difficult it is for the children to copy the letters. If you see children trying to copy words from a distant part of the room, suggest that the youngsters move closer.

No matter how the children do it, we should applaud their beginning efforts at writing just as we do their initial attempts at block building, painting, or riding a trike. We should provide many opportunities for them to practice on their own, and we should serve as writing models ourselves. Every time children see you writing in the classroom, they will want to write too. If you have a writing table available, then they can join you in this important communication skill, which we now know is possible for them to acquire naturally.

If You Have Not Checked This Item: Some Helpful Ideas

- *Play Linear Games*

Have children try to line up objects in a row: dominoes, toy cars or people, blocks, or Lego building blocks. If the children have magnetic letters, then let the youngsters see how many rows they can make.

- *Make Place Cards*

Have the children who are able to, make their own place cards for mealtime. Perhaps the youngsters can help other children to do theirs.

REFERENCES CITED

Chall, Jeanne. *Learning to Read: The Great Debate.* New York: McGraw-Hill Book Company, 1967.

Lamme, Linda Leonard. "Handwriting In An Early Childhood Curriculum." *Young Children.* November, 1979.

Schickedanz, Judith A., "The Acquisition of Written Language in Young Children." in *Handbook of Research in Early Childhood Education.* Edited by Bernard Spodek. New York: The Free Press, 1982.

Temple, Charles A., et al. *The Beginnings of Writing.* Boston: Allyn and Bacon, 1982.

Vukelich, Carol, and Joanne Golden. "Early Writing: Development and Teaching Strategies." *Young Children.* January, 1984.

OTHER SOURCES

Schickedanz, Judith A., et al. *Toward Understanding Children.* Boston: Little, Brown, and Company, 1982.

LEARNING ACTIVITIES

1. Use the *Child Skills Checklist,* "10. Written Language," as a screening tool to observe all of the children in your classroom. Compare the children with checks at the higher levels of Written Language with their results in Spoken Language. Can you draw any conclusions?

2. Set up a writing table with paper and writing tools, and make a running record of how children use it on three different days.

3. Observe and make a running record of children using a typewriter or computer on three different days. How do they go about teaching themselves how to use the instrument? Do you see them changing what they are doing on the basis of their learning something about how the instrument works? Do they learn from their mistakes?

4. Read an appropriate alphabet book to an individual or small group of children. Let them try to match the letters in the book with letters from a set of magnetic or plastic letters.

5. Find out what other words the children who write their names can identify or write. What other activities might you plan for these children?

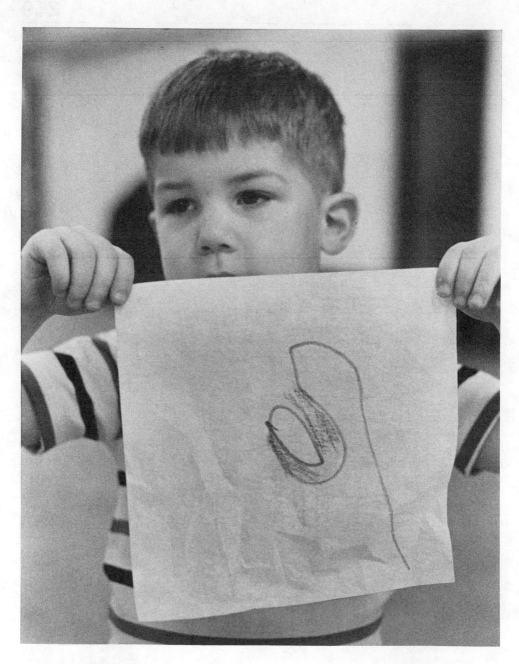

12 Art Skills

Art Skills Checklist

- ☐ Makes random marks or covers paper with color
- ☐ Scribbles on paper
- ☐ Forms basic shapes
- ☐ Makes mandalas
- ☐ Makes suns
- ☐ Draws human as circle with arms and legs attached
- ☐ Draws animals, trees
- ☐ Makes pictorial drawings

T his chapter on the development of children's art skills and the following one on the development of imagination focus on the growth of creativity in young children. Too often, creativity is not included when the major aspects of children's development—emotional, social, physical, cognitive, and language—are discussed. Yet, creativity is as notable a drive in the development of the young human being as thinking or speaking.

The unfolding of the creative urge in the young child is a joy to behold for most sensitive early childhood caregivers. To help foster and not suppress such development is just as important here as it is for speaking and thinking skills. Yet, somehow we equate creativity with special talent that not everyone displays; therefore, we downplay or ignore the development of creativity as more of a frill than a necessity for getting along in life.

In downplaying or ignoring creativity, we deprive the developing human of a basic aspect of his expressional capacities. Every child, surprising as it may seem, has the capacity to become an artist, a musician, a writer, or an inventor, if his interests carry him in that direction and if his caregivers and teachers give support and not control for his urge. The fact that not many people become artists is evidence of society's low priority for creativity and high priority for conformity.

Creativity connotes originality and novelty. To create, one brings into existence a new form of some kind. Creative people have original ideas, do things in new and different ways, see things from unique and novel perspectives. Creative people do not imitate; they do not follow the crowd. In a word, they are nonconformists.

Who are they? Artists, inventors, poets, writers, actors, musicians, interior decorators, chefs, architects, clothing designers, to name a few, and young children. They all are people who follow their own bent and who use their ingenuity to design something new. Young children are naturally creative because everything they do, make, or say is completely new to them. They explore, experiment, put things together, take things apart, and manipulate things in ways no adult would ever think of, and youngsters behave this way because they do not know any better.

Children come into the world uninhibited and with an entirely fresh point of view, their own. They continue to follow its bent until "they learn better," until they learn how society expects them to behave. Only those youngsters with strong enough psyches or strong enough outside support to resist society's inhibitions become the artists or creators whom we value as adults.

Could the children in your classroom become such creative adults? If the youngsters' natural-born creativity is supported and valued by the adults around them and if it is given an opportunity to blossom and grow, then the children have the chance to escape the smothering pressure to conform and to be able to enrich their own lives and those of others with the products of their talent.

This chapter on creative development deals with art skills, not only because art is an important curriculum area in most early childhood programs, but also because many early childhood caregivers need help in restructuring their art programs. Too many activities in such programs suppress rather than support creativity.

The chapter just as well could deal with the development of science skills, which are also dependent on children's natural exploratory bent. Yet, science at the preschool level has somehow escaped the controlled approach that many teachers take with art. It seems good for children to explore plants and animals in all sorts of ways. But, drawings should be done only in the manner prescribed by adults, because, of course, "adults know better."

This traditional point of view needs to be challenged. We need to step back and take a good look at the development of creativity. When does creativity appear in human beings? What are its characteristics? What can we do to help it grow? How can we keep from suppressing it?

This chapter looks at an eight-step developmental sequence in drawing skills, which appear in all children everywhere in the world in the same order. Even blind children exhibit the beginning steps of the sequence until the youngsters' lack of visual feedback discourages them from continuing. You will note that this sequence is similar to the steps children take in developing physical, cognitive, and even writing skills.

It is obvious that the brain is programmed to accomplish all kinds of development in this particular order, from the general to the specific, as youngsters have the opportunity and materials to interact with the environment in a playful manner and thus discover what it and they are able to do.

As you observe each child in the *Checklist* area of Art Skills, if you find that a child has progressed beyond the behavior described in the item, be sure to mark the item with a + instead of leaving it blank. A blank indicates that a child has not accomplished the behavior. An *N* indicates you had no opportunity to observe the behavior, and a + indicates the child has advanced beyond it.

☐ MAKES RANDOM MARKS OR COVERS PAPER WITH COLOR

During their first year of life, children really do not draw. If they have access to a crayon, they are more apt to put it in their mouths than to put a mark on a paper.

Around the age of thirteen months, according to Piaget, children's first scribbling begins (Lasky, p. 9). The first marks they make are usually random. The marks have more to do with movement, in fact, than with art. The toddler is surprised to find that a crayon, a pencil, or a paintbrush will make marks. The youngsters often are captivated by watching the lines that their movements can make on a surface. The surface is not always paper, much to their caregiver's dismay. Children will mark on walls, tabletops, or anything else that will take a mark.

We need to be careful about scolding the child for her mistake. She only was investigating the properties of a strange new implement; she had no idea she was damaging anything. We want her to understand that the exploring and the marking were all right to do, but not on the walls and table. Harsh punishment at this stage may abort the budding creator's continued exploration of art. Have her help you clean off the marks with a child-size sponge; give her a tablet to mark on, and put a newspaper under it to control slips.

This first stage of art skill development is purely mechanical and manipulative. The child is gaining control over the art tool, whether it is a crayon, paintbrush, pencil, felt tip marker, or chalk. The child makes random marks or covers the paper with color without using eye control. Even blind children make the same kind of random marks. The urge to draw seems to be inborn because young children with no art materials will make marks anyway on frosty windows or in the dirt.

Older children in your program who have had no access to art supplies or who have been suppressed in their art attempts at home still go through these same *Checklist* stages, but more quickly. It will take these children far less time to learn manipulation of materials, for instance. The youngsters soon will be into scribbling. For children who have passed beyond the "random marks" stage, mark this item with a " + "

If You Have Not Checked This Item: Some Helpful Ideas

- *Have Art Materials Available during Free Choice Period*

Creativity blooms only when children have the freedom to try things on their own. Have paints available at one or two easels all the time. Have colored chalk and a small chalkboard, sets of watercolor felt tip pens, sets of primary crayons, soft pencils, and various kinds of drawing paper available on low shelves next to art tables. Let children select and use their own materials in a spontaneous manner.

- *Make Only Positive Comments about Children's Art Efforts*

Beginning drawers often will produce art that is smudgy and uninteresting from an adult point of view. Refrain from negative comments. You need to know that the children are not trying to draw a picture, but only to manipulate the medium. Your comments should reflect this: "You really worked hard in art this morning, Jeff. I'm glad you enjoy it so much."

☐ SCRIBBLES ON PAPER

From about two years of age on through age three, four, and sometimes later, depending on the child, an individual will mark on paper in a scribbling manner. At first, the scribbles may be endless lines done in a rhythmic, manipulative manner. Eventually, the child will use eye control as well as hand/arm movement to make the scribbles and to direct their placement on the paper. One scribble often is placed on top of another until the paper is a hodgepodge of lines and circles. Painters may cover over scribbles with layers and layers of paint before they are finished. These scribbles are different from the writing scribbles noted in Chapter 11.

The product she has produced has little meaning to the child at first, for she is not trying to create something, but merely experimenting by moving colors around on a paper. The process is important to her, not the product. Adults, however, think of art mainly in terms of creating a product. Their response to scribbling is often either to dismiss it as unimportant and worthless or to ask children to tell what they have drawn. Once children learn that adults expect this sort of information, the youngsters often begin naming their scribbles. This behavior does not mean that the children really had anything in mind when they began moving the brush or crayon around on the paper. Our comments should focus on their efforts in the process of drawing, not on the imperfect products they create in the beginning.

Scribbling is hardly worthless. It is the first step in the self-taught process of learning to draw. In many respects, scribbling is the equivalent of babbling in the child's learning to speak. We support children in their babbling and congratulate them when they finally make sounds that seem to be words. Think what might happen to their language development if we forced them to stop making such worthless sounds, just as some adults force children to stop wasting time by making "worthless" scribbles.

Children work hard at scribbling. Only they know when a scribbled "drawing" is finished. Actually, not the drawing, but the process, is finished. Some youngsters go over and over the lines they have made, almost as if they are practicing the way to make a straight or curved line. Their early products seem to show a greater proportion of vertical lines, especially in easel paintings (Smith, p. 301). But, the children are able to make multiple horizontal lines, diagonal lines, and curved lines as well. Back and forth the youngsters work, sometimes changing their hand direction when they get tired and sometimes even changing their hands. While two-year-olds place one scribble on top of another, three- and four-year-olds frequently put a single scribble on one paper (Kellogg, p. 18).

Rhoda Kellogg, who has collected and analyzed hundreds of thousands of children's drawings from around the world, has identified twenty scribbles that children make. Not all children make all twenty. Individuals tend to concentrate on a few "favorites" and to repeat them in many variations. The fact that all children everywhere produce the same twenty scribbles spontaneously—and no others—seems to indicate that this early form of art somehow must be inborn in the human species.

Kellogg considers these scribbles to be "the building blocks of art." (Kellogg, p. 15) The individual's scribble "vocabulary" most easily can be read in his finger painting. He will draw his "designs" with one or more fingers and then will "erase" them before starting over. Because the designs do not pile up one on top of the other as with opaque paint or crayons, it is easier to see which of the twenty basic scribbles the child favors.

It is not necessary for the early childhood teacher to identify a child's scribbles, only that he or she understands the importance of scribbles in the sequence of art skills development. If your children have passed beyond the scribble stage, then you should mark this item with a +. Many children, however, continue to go back to scribbles even when the youngsters have progressed beyond scribbles to shape drawings. This behavior is a perfectly natural progression. All child development tends to occur in a spiral rather than in a straight line. We can expect children to slip back even while they are moving forward.

If You Have Not Checked This Item: Some Helpful Ideas

■ *Provide Controllable Materials*

Beginners will not be able to progress much beyond scribbling unless they can control the materials. Be sure to provide fat, kindergarten-size crayons for children to grip well. Children can use thin crayons, too, but sometimes, the youngsters bear down so hard that they break the thin implements. Mix your tempera paints with just enough water to make them creamy but not drippy. Cut off the ends of long easel paintbrushes so that youngsters can manipulate the brushes easily. Wrap ends of colored chalk with masking tape to help gripping and prevent smearing.

Provide easel painters with contrasting colors rather than complementary colors in the beginning in order to prevent muddy results. Children have more control when they start with only two contrasting colors instead of several different kinds. Avoid putting out red and green together, yellow and purple together, or blue and orange together. Haskell recommends any of the following combinations instead:

1. Yellow with blue or red or green or brown
2. Orange with green or purple or brown or red
3. White with blue or red or green or purple

(Haskell, p. 74)

■ *Be Nondirective*

Allow children to explore and experiment with paint and chalk, finger paint and crayons, and felt tip markers and pencils completely on their own. Put the materials out for the children's use during free play, or have the materials invitingly placed on low shelves near art tables for the youngsters' own selection.

☐ FORMS BASIC SHAPES

As children's physical and mental development progresses and they are able to control the brush and paint more easily, their scribbles begin to take on the configuration of shapes. Kellogg has identified six basic shapes in children's early art: rectangle (including square), oval (including circle), triangle, Greek cross (+), diagonal cross (X), and odd shape (a catchall) (Kellogg, p. 45). These shapes do not necessarily appear separately but rather mixed up with scribbles or with one another.

If children have had the freedom to experiment with art as toddlers, they usually begin to make basic shapes spontaneously by age three. The children's perceptual and memory skills help them to form, store, and retrieve concepts about shapes quite early if the youngsters have had appropriate experiences. (See Chapter 8, Cognitive Development.) The particular shapes a child favors seem to evolve from his own scribbles. Attempts at making ovals and circles usually appear early. This form seems innately appealing to young humans everywhere, perhaps because of their preferred attention to the human face.

Circular movements in their scribbling eventually lead the children to form an oval. Then, the youngsters often repeat it, going round and round over the same shape. Visual discrimination of the shape and muscle control of the brush or crayon finally allow them to form the shape by itself instead of intertwining it within a mass of scribbles. Memory comes into play as well, allowing the children to retrieve the oval from their repertory of marks and to repeat it another day.

Thus, the child's capacity to draw shapes seems to emerge from his capacity to control the lines he makes in his scribbling. In other words, he makes one of the basic shapes because he remembers it from creating it spontaneously in his scribbling, not because he is copying the shape from his environment. As he experiments, he stumbles onto new ways to make new shapes. But, certain ones seem more appealing, and individual children return to them again and again.

Three- and four-year-olds first create rectangles by drawing a set of parallel vertical lines and then later adding horizontal lines at the top and bottom, rather than drawing a continuous line for a perimeter (Smith, p. 301). We understand why when we remember the problem children first have trying to make an enclosure with blocks. (See Chapter 9.) Thus, we see why it is important to give youngsters many opportunities and much time to practice. The children are teaching themselves to draw, just as they did to block build, walk, talk, think, speak, and write.

If You Have Not Checked This Item: Some Helpful Ideas

• *Provide Materials Children Can Use on Their Own*

Easels always should be available. They are one of the best motivators for spontaneous drawing that you can have available. Children soon find out that all they need to do to paint is to put on a painting smock and go to the easel. There is no need to get out paints, for they already are mixed and waiting. There is no need to ask for help or direction from the teacher. If an easel is free during free choice time, then the children can go and paint at it.

For children who are experienced easel painters, it is always good to challenge them with a new activity. Perhaps they would like to try flat table painting with paints in a muffin tin. Or, you might make a table easel with two sections of cardboard taped together to form an inverted "V" over a table. Paper can be fastened to it with tacks or masking tape. Paint can be mixed and waiting in muffin tins or jars that are taped to the table so they will not tip over.

☐ MAKES MANDALAS

The next step in the sequence of children's self-taught art skills involves combining two of the shapes the youngsters have made. Kellogg has observed and written a great deal about this behavior. The Greek cross and the diagonal cross are favorite shapes. These are often combined with an oval or rectangle to make what is called a *mandala*. Mandalas do not necessarily stand alone on a sheet of paper but usually are repeated in a balanced way. Groups of these shapes or others form the bulk of art for three- and four-year-olds.

Pictorial drawing eventually evolves out of particular combinations of shapes. One of the first representations to occur in children's art is the human being. This representation seems to evolve naturally from the child's first experiments with an oval shape combined with a cross inside it (the mandala), which leads to an oval with lines radiating from its rim (the sun), which evolves into an oval with two lines for arms, two for legs, and small circles inside the large head/body oval for eyes (the human).

From mandalas to suns to humans is the natural sequence found in much of children's spontaneous art. Watch for this development in the children in your classroom. Talk to parents about the spontaneous way art skills develop in children if the youngsters are given the freedom to explore on their own. Both you and the parents may want to save the children's scribbling and early shape drawings to see if you can identify the sequence of their development. Be sure to date the art.

Because the shape combination called the mandala is a key part of this sequence, it is treated as a separate *Checklist* item for observers to look for. The circle with the cross inside is a symbol found throughout the world. In Oriental religions, the symbol represents the cosmos. Obviously, young children are producing it spontaneously without any notion of its symbolic meaning. But, there must be an inborn appeal for such a shape for it to appear as a natural sequence in children's art. Kellogg feels that its overall balance is what makes the shape so appealing to the human species (Kellogg, p. 68).

Early scribblings show many examples of crossed lines as well as ovals and rectangles. It seems only natural that children eventually would experiment by trying to put the two together. Many scribbles show early attempts at placing a cross over a circle, possibly because children make all scribbles this way, putting one scribble on top of the other. As children gain control of their implements

As children scribble, they often combine shapes such as the circle and the cross to form a natural "mandala."

and remember how to make the shapes they like, a shape like the mandala easily should emerge. If the shape is something appealing to them, they then will repeat it endlessly.

Perhaps this method reveals how early man came to include the mandala in his repertory of symbols. Circles and squares with crosses inside them are found throughout the world in the rock writing petroglyphs and pictographs of ancient man.

If your children have gone beyond this stage in their natural evolution of art skills, mark this item with a +. Remember, however, that development occurs in a spiral fashion which may bring the youngsters back to this more abstract form even after they have developed pictorial skills. Not all children make mandalas, but most of them do. These basic shape combinations are never really lost once they have become a part of a person's art vocabulary. Take a look at the doodles adults make in a non-thinking, spontaneous fashion. You, yourself, still may draw the mandalas you first discovered as a child!

If You Have Not Checked This Item: Some Helpful Ideas

- *Provide Variety in Your Art Materials*

Not all children may enjoy painting at an easel. You should include other possibilities as often as possible. Finger painting is one. It can be done on a smooth paper, a tabletop, or a cookie sheet. Paper finger painting can be hung to dry and thus is preserved if the child wants to save it. Tabletop finger painting also can be preserved before the table is cleaned, by pressing a paper onto the finger painting and rubbing the paper.

The finger paint, itself, can be made from liquid starch that is poured on paper that has powder paint shaken into it, from wallpaper paste that is mixed with water and poster paint to the proper consistency, or from soap powder mixed with a little water and paint powder. Soap powder also can be whipped until it is stiff and used as white paint against colored construction paper.

☐ MAKES SUNS

A combination of an oval with lines radiating from its rim is often the next step in the child's natural sequence of drawing a pictorial representation. We call this shape combination a "sun" because it looks like the symbol adults use to represent the sun. Children do not call their sun shape a sun unless adults or more experienced peers first give it the name. The youngsters are not drawing a sun; they merely are experimenting with shapes. If this combination appeals to the children, they will repeat it many times. When they finally do begin to draw pictorially, they sometimes will call this figure a "spider."

Although the figure seems quite simple to draw, the sun does not appear spontaneously in children's drawings in the beginning. Two-year-olds can make curved and straight lines, but children rarely produce suns before age three. (Kellogg, p. 74)

The sun figure may well emerge from the children's experimentations with the mandala figure. Most of children's early attempts at sun figures include some kind of marks in the center of the figure, either lines, dots, or ovals. Once the children have begun to make a sun with a clear center, they have progressed beyond the mandala to something new. These early suns with center marks are not forgotten, however. When children begin to draw "sun faces," their first humans, they include center marks for eyes, nose, and mouth.

We see sun figures in primitive rock art as well. Early man must have followed the same sequence in his progression to artistic representation.

If You Have Not Checked This Item: Some Helpful Ideas

• *Draw with Chalk*

Colored chalk is very appealing to children if they can grip it and control its smeariness. Wrap the upper end of the chalk with foil or masking tape to make gripping easier. Soft, thick-size chalk is preferred. Regular-size chalk breaks too easily with the pressure some children apply. Chalk first should be used dry for children to become used to its properties. Then, you can wet either the paper or the chalk for a richer effect. Use either a water-sugar solution (4 parts warm water to 1 part sugar) or liquid starch, and apply it to the paper for children to draw on with dry chalk. Or, use the liquid as a dip for children to wet the chalk but draw on a dry surface. Many children like the rhythm of dipping and drawing. (Haskell, p. 45) Dry chalk marks on paper also can be smeared around to create different effects.

• *Draw with Felt Tip Pens*

Water soluble felt tip pens are always favorites with children. Youngsters seem to be able to control these more easily than paintbrushes or crayons. The pens' thick size and smooth marking ability makes them especially well suited to preschool art. Some marking pens have brush tip rather than felt tip points. These pens have the spreading capacity of water color paint, and preschoolers easily use the implements. It is not necessary or even desirable to give each child an entire set of pens in all colors. Give the youngsters only a few colors at a time until the children express the need for more.

• *Keep Art Activities Spontaneous*

Do not use pictures, figure drawings, or models for your children to copy. Spontaneous art does not develop this way. Even those children who have reached the pictorial stage do not need to copy. You will find that they draw what they know rather than what they see.

☐ DRAWS HUMAN AS CIRCLE WITH ARMS AND LEGS ATTACHED

One of the first pictorial figures that the young child draws is a person. He draws it as an oval or circle with two lines coming out of the bottom for legs, a line from either side for arms (sometimes these are omitted), circles or dots inside the head circle for eyes and sometimes a nose and mouth. All children everywhere seem to draw their first humans in this spontaneous manner. These drawings are known in the art world as "tadpole" drawings because of the resemblance.

To adults unfamiliar with the child's sequence of development, these are strange humans indeed: all head and no body, with arms and legs attached to the head. Surely, children age three and four can see that a person's arms and legs are attached to the body and not the head. Adult concepts about art, however, are entirely different from those of the young child. All along, adults have felt that the product of children's art, that is the drawing or painting, is the most important thing. As a matter of fact, to the young child, the process is more important. In the beginning, children are not drawing a picture; they are developing a skill.

Their production of a human is the transition to pictorial drawing for most young children. The method they apply is the same one they used for making shapes and symbols. They draw *what they know how to make, and not what they see*. Out of their practice with mandalas and suns comes this sun-face human with a few of the "sun's rays" for arms and legs.

It is not surprising, in fact, that the children's first people are all face. We remember that even infants attend to this image most of all. The human brain seems to be programmed to take in details about faces. This, after all, is the most important part of the human being.

As children first create their circle humans, they do not always repeat their drawings exactly the same. All children make armless humans at one time or another, even though the youngsters may have drawn arm lines earlier. This behavior does not indicate the children are regressing or are cognitively immature. It may appear only because the proportion of two parallel legs to head is more appealing alone than with arms sticking out at the sides. Children rarely draw legless humans. (Kellogg, p. 101) Or, the behavior may result from the brain's tendency to overgeneralize in early categories. Later, details will be more discriminating.

Without a great many examples of a single child's drawings, it is risky to try to determine where he or she stands in this developmental sequence. Schools or psychologists who try to evaluate a child's intelligence on the basis of only one drawing of a person (such as the Draw-a-Person Test) are basing their findings on extremely sketchy information. Kellogg found that one-third of 2,500 public school children who were asked to "draw a man" each day for five days drew such different humans that their scores on the Draw-a-Man Test varied by as much as fifty percent. (Kellogg, p. 191)

As the child has more practice drawing her early people, she often adds hair or hats, hands or fingers, and feet or toes. The additions may be lines, circles, or scribbles. The child may identify her person as being herself or anyone else. The actual size of the person named in the drawing usually is not considered by the young child. Instead, she often draws the most important person in the picture as the biggest. The so-called "stick figure" is not a part of spontaneous children's art; the figure seems to be learned by children at age five or six by copying the work of adults or older peers (Kellogg, p. 108).

Eventually, children will add a body to their head drawings. They often do this by drawing two extremely long legs and putting a horizontal line part way up between them. You may remember that this is the common method they used earlier to draw rectangles. The youngsters often will draw a belly button in the middle of the body. By this time, they frequently are drawing other pictorial representations, as well. These representations, as you will note, are based on the children's previous experience, showing once again how development proceeds in a continuous sequence from the general to the specific as long as children have the freedom to learn naturally.

If You Have Not Checked This Item: Some Helpful Ideas

- *Record Children's Stories about Their Drawings*

Some children verbalize a great deal about their drawings. Others do not. You should take your lead from the child. If he or she likes to tell you stories about the people in the drawings, then you may want to record these stories. Children may want to have their stories displayed along with their art on the classroom walls. On the other hand, they may want to make a scrapbook of their art or to take their art home. If children do not want to talk about their art products, then you can support them best by comments like, "You surely put a lot of effort into your drawing today, Sheila."

Keep in mind that much early children's art is not pictorial, so there really are not any stories to tell about it unless, of course, adults press children to make up something.

☐ DRAWS ANIMALS, TREES

Animals

Once children have discovered the way to draw a person, they often will begin drawing animals as well. Youngsters' first animals are hard to distinguish from humans. It is obvious the animals are based on the same practiced form: a head with eyes, nose, and mouth and a body with arms sticking out from the sides and legs coming out the bottom. Often, the animal is facing front like a person and seems to be standing on two legs. The two ears sticking up straight from the top of the head usually make the drawing an animal. Sometimes, these ears are pointed like cat ears, and sometimes, these ears are circular like mouse ears. This is a transition animal.

Eventually, the young artist will find a way to make his animal horizontal with an elongated body parallel to the bottom of the paper, four legs in a row from the bottom of the body, a head at one end, and often a tail at the other end. The features of the face are still positioned in a frontal pose and not a profile. Most animal head profiles do not appear in children's drawings until around age five or later.

In fact, many children do not draw animals until they go to kindergarten at age five. This behavior—or lack of it—may be due to their progress in their own developmental sequence, but drawing animals also is influenced by the kindergarten curriculum. Often, kindergarten teachers give children outline animals to copy that may, in fact, short-circuit the youngsters' spontaneous development. Kellogg believes many teachers seem to feel that a child's self-taught system differs too widely from adult drawing, and, therefore, the child needs to be taken in hand and taught how to draw correctly (Kellogg, p. 114). Children often abandon art in elementary school because of a lack of teacher approval for their natural art.

Trees

The first trees are also transitional drawings based on the human figure children have taught themselves to draw. The first trees look like armless humans with two long legs for the trunk and a circular head for the treetop, which often contains small circles or dots that may be leaves but look more like fruit. The trees are not drawn to size. They may be similar in height to the humans in the picture or even smaller. A few four-year-olds may draw trees, but most children are five-years-old and older before they begin drawing trees.

As children have practice, more details evolve on trees. The tops of some trees resemble the sun with the rays being branches and balls at the end of the branches being leaves. Other children make branches coming out from the trunk like arms on a human. The first flowers also are drawn to a familiar model: a sun with a stem.

The children in your classroom may not have advanced to this level. In this case, you should leave the *Checklist* item blank. Given the freedom to develop art skills spontaneously, children will make their own progress as individuals. It is not your role to push the youngsters ahead, but to provide materials, time, and support so that the children may make their own progress according to their own biological timetables.

If You Have Not Checked This Item: Some Helpful Ideas

• *Add New Art Activities*

Your children may want to try drawing with liquid glue from a plastic squeeze bottle. They may want to draw with a pencil or other marker first and then follow the lines with glue. Or, they can try the glue without guidelines. Because glue is transparent when it dries, you may want to add food coloring to the bottles. This liquid glue is a much more free-flowing medium; the children will need to play with it for awhile to see how it works and how to control it. They will need to squeeze and move the bottle at the same time, a trick of coordination that may be difficult for some. Do not expect pictorial designs from glue drawing.

☐ MAKES PICTORIAL DRAWINGS

A few of the children in your classroom may begin doing pictorial drawings at age three and a few more at age four. Do not expect all of the youngsters to. Let them progress through their own sequences of development at their own individual rates. Those that do draw pictorially will be using the previously discussed repertory of figures that they have developed. Their drawings will be representations and not reproductions, for the young child draws what he knows, not what he sees. This principle is especially apparent in children's spontaneous drawings at age six when many youngsters go through a stage of so-called "X-ray drawings," which show both the inside and outside of objects at the same time. The children's drawings show things as the youngsters know them, rather than just what can be seen. People are shown inside drawings of houses that are seen from the outside, for example.

The children in your classroom neither will have reached this stage or will have developed a baseline in their drawings much before age five. Objects are still free-floating on their art papers, just as their first spontaneous letters are. (See Chapter 11.) This different perspective used by children sometimes is used by adult artists as well.

Children also interpret their pictorial drawings differently from adults. Often, youngsters do not start out to draw a particular thing. Instead, they describe their art more by the way it turns out than by what they had in mind. The way it turns out may have more to do with the materials the children are using than anything else. Runny paint in easel drawings may remind the youngsters of smoke, rain, or fire, for instance.

On the other hand, the children purposefully may make a picture of the post office that the class visited on a field trip. The picture will look, of course, just like the building shape they have learned to do spontaneously, and not at all like the post office, itself. Children first draw buildings by combining mostly rectangular shapes in various ways and not by looking at buildings. The drawing often has a door in the middle and at least two square windows above it. Roofs may be flat or pointed and often have a chimney with smoke coming out. The drawing catches the essence of the building, not the reality. Some four-year-olds also draw cars and trucks, as well as boats and planes. Often, it is hard to tell the difference between early cars and trucks.

Once children have a repertory of figures that the adults around them seem to accept, children will begin to put the figures together into scenes. The size and color of their objects will not be realistic. The more important the object or person, the larger the child will make it. Colors will have little relation to the object being depicted. They depend more upon the particular brush the child happens to pick up, or a color the child happens to favor at the moment. Objects will be free-floating, as mentioned, and not anchored to a baseline. But, the effect will be balanced and pleasing, nevertheless.

Those children who verbalize about their art may tell you things about their drawings that have little to do with what your eyes seem to show you. The youngsters must be speaking about an inner vision of their world, you decide. You are right, of course. And, from inner visions come creative ideas, you remember. Let's support this beginning urge toward creativity in all of the children by giving it the freedom to grow spontaneously.

If You Have Not Checked This Item: Some Helpful Ideas

- *Encourage Children to Draw about Field Trips*

Not all of your children can or want to draw pictorially. But, for those who do, you can suggest they draw a picture about a trip you have taken together. Children find it satisfying to be able to represent things they know about. They can tell about the things in words, have you write down their words, or record their words on tape. But, it is also good to make a drawing or build a block structure about new things they have encountered. Their products help you as a teacher to find out what is important to them and how they conceptualize the new ideas they have gained.

- *Have The Children Draw about Things in Their Repertory*

If you know the children can draw people, houses, trees, and animals, they may want to draw a picture of their house and family. Those who want to can have you write down their story about the drawing.

TABLE 8. Development of art skills

Age	Art Skill
1–2	Makes random marks on paper Begins scribbling
2–3	Makes scribbles one on top of the other May cover paper with layers of color
3–4	May put a single scribble on a paper Makes basic shapes
4–5	Combines two shapes, often the circle and the cross to make "mandala" Draws "suns" Draws human as circle with arms and legs
5–6	Draws heads of animals in profile Draws trees Makes pictorial drawings Includes baseline in pictures

REFERENCES CITED

Haskell, Lendall L. *Art in the Early Childhood Years*. Columbus, Ohio: Charles E. Merrill Publishing Company, 1979.

Kellogg, Rhoda. *Analyzing Children's Art*. Palo Alto, Calif.: National Press Books, 1970.

Lasky, Lila, and Rose Mukerji. *Art: Basic for Young Children*. Washington, D.C.: National Association for the Education of Young Children, 1980.

Smith, Nancy. R. "The Visual Arts in Early Childhood Education: Development and the Creation of Meaning," in *Handbook of Research in Early Childhood Education*. Edited by Bernard Spodek. New York: The Free Press, 1982.

OTHER SOURCES

Beaty, Janice J. *Skills for Preschool Teachers*. Columbus, Ohio: Charles E. Merrill Publishing Company, 1984.

Jenkins, Peggy Davison. *Art for the Fun of It: A Guide for Teaching Young Children*. Englewood Cliffs, N.J.: Prentice-Hall, 1980.

LEARNING ACTIVITIES

1. Use the *Child Skills Checklist*, "11. Art Skills," as a screening tool to observe all the children in your classroom. Compare the children with checks at the higher levels in the sequence of art skill development with their checks in cognitive development, Chapter 8, especially in the items, "Recognizes basic geometric shapes," "Recognizes colors," and "Recognizes differences in size." Also compare these children's checks in cognitive development, Chapter 9, especially in the areas of space ("Can build a block enclosure" and "Can locate an object behind or beside something") and memory ("Recalls words to song, chant" and "Can recollect and act on a series of directions"). Can you draw any conclusions from this comparison?

2. Based on your screening survey, choose one or two children who have not shown much interest or development in art, and try to involve them in an art activity. Use one of the other *Checklist* areas in which they have shown interest and skill as the basis for the art activity. Record the results.

3. Set up your art area so that children can use it without adult help or direction. Record by running record what happens in this area on three different days.

4. Carry out one of the suggested art activities from the chapter with a group of children who show interest. Compare their results with their *Checklist* standings in art skills. What can you conclude from this?

5. Save the art products of one of the children over a six month period. Be sure to date the art. How do the art products compare with the sequence of art skill development discussed here?

13 Imagination

Imagination Checklist

- ☐ Pretends by replaying familiar routines
- ☐ Needs particular props to do pretend play
- ☐ Assigns roles or takes assigned roles
- ☐ May switch roles without warning
- ☐ Uses language for creating and sustaining plot
- ☐ Uses exciting, danger-packed themes
- ☐ Takes on characteristics and actions related to role
- ☐ Uses elaborate and creative themes, ideas, details

A second important aspect of creativity in young children is their development of imagination. For young children, imagination is the ability to pretend or make believe, to take a role other than their own, to create fanciful situations, and to act out a fantasy of their making. It is an activity that most children seem to engage in a great deal of time before the age of seven. It is a type of play that many adults fail to see as significant in the development of the child because they do not understand it. But early childhood specialists have come to recognize imagination as one of the most effective means for promoting the development of the young child's intellectual skills, social skills, language, and, most especially, creativity (Smilansky, p. 12).

One of the basic tools for creating is "imagery," the ability to see a picture in our mind's eye, to imagine something we already have experienced or something we would like to do. This ability allows us to tap into memories of the past and reform them as possibilities for the present or future. Children's make-believe relies heavily on this capacity to draw on such internal images and to create new ones. The Singers, who have done extensive research and writing on children's imaginative play, believe that imagery is essential to the development of intellectual and language skills as well. Children remember ideas and words they actually have experienced because the youngsters can associate the ideas and words with pictures in their minds. (Singer 1977, p. 6) This association reveals why it is so important for children to have many real experiences. Otherwise, there are few images stored in the youngsters' brains for them to draw on.

A number of adults who have been identified as creative report that they engaged in a great deal of daydreaming and fantasy play as children (Singer 1977, p. 228). This finding is not surprising when we realize that imaginative play relies heavily on the creative skills of the young child. She must utilize previous experiences in new and different ways. She extracts the essence of a familiar experience such as getting ready for bed and applies it creatively to a pretend activity such as putting to bed her doll who does not want to go. Or, she may take the role of the doll as well as that of the mother, who is losing her patience with the stubborn dollie.

The child experiments with the situation, playing it this way one time and that another. If a peer joins in, then there is another point of view to reckon with. If the original player strays too far from her role, she may lose it to a player with more definite ideas on how a mother should act. Or, she may switch to a different role herself and try on yet another set of characteristics. She learns to recall fragments of past experiences and to combine them in novel ways, adding original dialog, fresh nuances to her characterizations, and new directions to her plots. No playwright ever had better practice.

In addition to being her own creative playwright, she is also the actor, the director, the audience for other actors, and an interactor with the others, whether she plays her role or steps out of it to make "aside" comments on the progress of the spontaneous play. Just as with every other aspect of her development, she is creating her own knowledge when she has the freedom to participate in imaginative play.

This time, the knowledge is about real life and the other actors in it: how they behave, how they respond to stressful situations, how they carry out their work roles, how they speak, and how they interact with one another. Adult observers of imaginative play find that most of the make-believe play of children is centered around "the social problems of adults with whom children have close contacts." (Smilansky, p. 21) Common themes include the family and home, doctors and hospitals, work and professions, school, and dramatizations of escape, rescue, and superheroes.

Playing at life is not the inconsequential activity many adults seem to think it is. Children who have had extensive practice doing imaginative play are often those who are most successful in life as adults. Many disadvantaged children who have not been allowed or encouraged to engage in such play are also at a disadvantage as adults, for they have missed an important grounding in social, intellectual, and creative skills.

Chapter 4 discusses imaginative play as it applies to the development of children's social skills in solitary, parallel, and group play. This chapter will look at the same phenomenon in relation to the development of creativity in young children. To discover where the children in your classroom stand in the sequence of their development, make an assessment of each of them using the eight items of the *Checklist* as you observe the children pretending in the dramatic play area, at the water table, in the block corner, at the wood bench, with science materials, at the easels, or on the playground.

You will find that young children pretend about everything they do, both alone and with others. Tap into this rich vein of creativity in young children, yourself, and you may see life and the world from a completely new and fresh perspective, the "what if" point of view. This "what if" perspective is the true "magic of childhood": the belief that children can make life anything they want it to be.

Adults know from the hard facts of reality that life is just not so, or is it? What if we also believed we really could make life anything we wanted it to be? Does believing make it so? Children act as if this idea were true. Is there a way we can help them develop into adults who actually will be able to make their adult lives the way they want them to be? Is there a way we can preserve the "child" in ourselves so that we can do the same? Take a hard look at the developmental sequence in imaginative play that follows to see what you need to do to keep this spark alive in children and to rekindle its essence in your own life.

☐ PRETENDS BY REPLAYING FAMILIAR ROUTINES

This *Checklist* item describes the earliest of the imaginative play behaviors in young children. Incredibly enough, pretending by replaying familiar routines appears as early as when children are one year of age (Smilansky, p. 10). By age eighteen months, infants may go through the imaginary routine of feeding themselves with an empty spoon and cup and even saying "Yummy!" The Singers believe that this tendency to play or replay past events through imagery is one of the basic capacities of the human brain (Singer 1977, p. 3).

Two-Year-Olds

By two years of age, most normal children spend a great deal of time at home or in a toddler program replaying fragments of everyday experience if given the chance. Pieces of familiar routines are repeated over and over with little change or little effort to expand them into a longer sequence. The toddler will put the baby to bed by putting the doll in the cradle, covering it, and saying "Nite-nite." Then, the toddler will pick up the doll and begin the routine all over again. Once a particular routine is established with a two-year-old, it seems to become quite rigid, almost like a ritual. (Segal, p. 92)

Words are not all that important in the pretending of two-year-olds, however. The youngsters use words sparingly, mainly to accompany actions or for sound effects. Actions are the main ingredients of the imaginative play of two-year-olds. Once the youngsters get an idea for pretend play, they try to put it into action immediately. They do not set the stage with words or search for appropriate props.

Props may be used, though, if they are available. Two-year-olds use props realistically, for the most part. Dishes are used for eating, not usually as a steering wheel or a flying saucer. Because two-year-olds are also impulsive in their behavior, props can influence the type of pretend play the youngsters engage in. A toy broom can inspire the children to sweep, for instance, even though they had no previous plans for cleaning. They do not need props to pretend, however. Some two-year-olds even may carry on their play with invisible props.

The imaginative play of two-year-olds mainly is centered around chores and routines, such as eating, going to bed, caring for the baby, getting their hair washed, turning on television, shopping, visiting grandma, driving the car, and getting gas for the car. Two-year-olds are very serious about their imaginative play and take offense if adults make fun of their sometimes comical mode of pretending.

Doll play is also a frequent activity for both boys and girls of this age. Dolls are usually undressed, laid in a box or bed, and covered completely over with a piece of cloth in a very ritualized routine. (Caplan, p. 143)

The play of two-year-olds is frequently solitary and rarely with more than one other player. They and their agemates have not yet developed the social skills for coming together in a common endeavor. When two children this age play

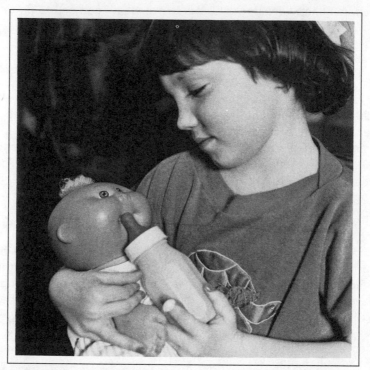

Both three- and four-year-old girls engage in doll play, but older children often depend more on their imaginations than on props.

together, one child usually imitates the other. However, others will join in if they see one child doing something; sometimes, a wild melee ensues. The pretend play of children this young is brief at best, and it suddenly may disintegrate into running and squealing if other children are around.

Older children who have not done much imaginative play may start in this manner in your center. Their maturity usually carries them on quickly to a more advanced level. If you note that children have advanced beyond this level, do not leave the item blank, but mark it with a +.

If You Have Not Checked This Item: Some Helpful Ideas

- *Read Imaginative Books*

Books with talking animal characters or human characters who use their imaginations to behave in unusual ways may stimulate your children to do likewise.

Bubble, Bubble by Mercer Mayer, New York: Four Winds Press, 1973 is a small-format, wordless picture book that features a little boy who buys a magic bubble maker and then goes off to blow a wild assortment of bubble figures until his creatures begin to turn on him and he has to blow new creatures to scare away the old. Children must make up their own story to go along with the pictures. Two-year-olds will enjoy having the adult first make up the story and then trying to make a story themselves. Because it is a small book in which every picture must be seen, you should read it only to one or two children at a time.

If you use *Bubble, Bubble* in your program, be sure to have a bubble pipe and soap available for children to create their own inventions afterwards.

- *Have Appropriate Props Available*

Knowing that the youngest children pretend mainly about familiar household routines, have eating, cleaning, and sleeping props available in your dramatic play area. Put out all kinds of baby dolls and their beds as well.

☐ NEEDS PARTICULAR PROPS TO DO PRETEND PLAY

Three-Year-Olds

If three-year-olds have had a chance to pretend when they were age two, then they gradually develop new skills and interests in their imaginative play. The fragments of familiar routines that occupied the children earlier become more extended and less rigid as the youngsters mature. Three-year-olds begin to think a bit about the pretending they are about to do, rather than acting on a sudden impulse. This thinking ahead leads them to preplanning the play by finding or gathering certain props. In fact, some three-year-olds cannot proceed with the play until the right prop is found.

The rigidity expressed by many two-year-olds in their ritualistic manner of pretending thus is carried on by many three-year-olds in their insistence on particular props in order to play. Three-year-olds may feel they need a particular hat, costume, doll, or steering wheel in order to begin or carry out a role. Many times, the object is the basis for the play, but not so much on impulse as with two-year-olds. Three-year-olds very much enjoy dressing up and playing a role, and they have a much broader concept of how to do it.

Props very well may serve the children as an instrument for getting out of themselves. Because three-year-olds are still strongly self-centered, they may need a prop in order to break away from their own point of view. Just as shy children can lose themselves in speaking through a hand puppet or from behind a mask, three-year-olds may need the extra impetus of an object that is outside of themselves to get them started in pretending to be someone else.

Some three-year-olds are very much into imaginary play of a different sort, at home. They have an imaginary playmate or invisible friend. This is the most common age for children to invent such a friend. Research finds that first-born children who do not have many playmates may use their imaginations to create such a companion (Segal, p. 10). This research seems to be another evidence that pretending is an innate activity with young humans.

Such invisible companions, however, serve a different purpose from the pretend play in nursery school. They are invented companions for children who

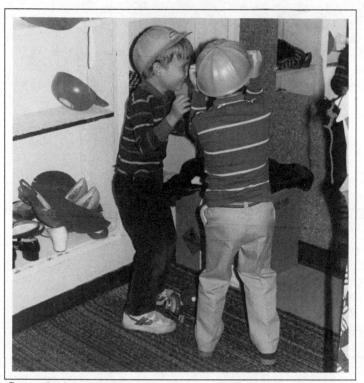

Some children need a particular hat or costume in order to carry out a role.

have none, or loving friends for children who do not receive love from those around them, or protectors for children who need someone to support them. When children come to a preschool program, they usually leave their imaginary friends behind, often permanently. Once the children are occupied with real peers, the youngsters have little need for a made-up friend.

Family activities are still a large part of three-year-olds' pretend play in preschool programs, with dress-up in the housekeeping area, doll play, hospital play, and community helpers play included. Three-year-olds also enjoy driving cars and trains, flying jet planes, and being firefighters. These themes are carried out in dramatic play, block building, table block games, clay and paint creations, water table and woodworking bench activities, singing, creative movement, puppet play, and toy telephone activities, and these themes are carried out anywhere and everywhere children gather.

If you have not checked this item for certain children because they do not need a particular prop in order to engage in imaginative play, then you should mark the item with a +, meaning they have advanced beyond this level of the sequence. If, however, they are not using props or even engaging in pretend play, then leaving a blank here is appropriate.

If You Have Not Checked This Item: Some Helpful Ideas

- *Have a Variety of Props Available*

In the large motor area, have large wooden riding trucks, wagons, and wheelbarrows as well as large hollow blocks and floorboards for building child-size structures. Put out a full-length mirror in the dress-up area. Include costume jewelry, scarves, handbags, wallets, belts, vests, shoes, aprons, all kinds of hats, doctor's equipment, goggles, binoculars, badges, umbrella, and canes. An assortment of men's and women's clothes in teenage size is often easier for young children to handle.

- *Make Your Own Special Props*

There is no need to spend a great deal of money equipping your dramatic play area when you can make your own props as needed. The excellent book, *Be What You Want To Be! The Complete Dress-Up and Pretend Craft Book* by Phyllis and Noel Fiarotta, New York: Workman Publishing Company, 1977, gives directions for making from discarded materials such props as telephones; cash registers; typewriters; wigs; mustaches; hats; magnifying glasses; screwdrivers; gas pumps; musical instruments; cameras; ships' helms; barber shop poles and supplies; restaurant supplies, including fake food; florist shop supplies, including potted plants; bakery supplies, including fake cakes; plumbing, shoe repair, and firefighting equipment; and more. Obviously, it is beyond the capabilities of many three-year-olds to make these props on their own. However, the youngsters can assist adults in preparing the props, and the children will love it.

- *Read Books That Will Motivate Pretending*

A whole series of books that three-year-olds may relate to tells the adventures of three-year-old Anthony and his "invisible" friend, Blackboard Bear. *We're in Big Trouble Blackboard Bear* by Martha Alexander, New York: The Dial Press, 1980, is a recent addition to the series, in which the bear goes out at night when Anthony is sleeping, causing all sorts of mischief at the neighbors' house. The bear, like Anthony, is able to make things right with his drawing skill on the blackboard. Children also will enjoy, *Blackboard Bear; And My Mean Old Mother Will Be Sorry, Blackboard Bear*; and *I Sure Am Glad To See You Blackboard Bear*.

☐ ASSIGNS ROLES OR TAKES ASSIGNED ROLES

Three-year-olds usually find it is more fun when several children play together. You will have checked on this behavior previously in your observations concerning, "3. Social Play." This item signals the beginning of peer play for most children. Pretend episodes usually do not last long in the beginning because most children of this age are not yet flexible when it comes to differences of opinions. This inflexibility sometimes shows up when the children try to decide who will play what role.

Many three-year-olds try to control imaginative play by assigning the roles. The dominant child takes the role he or she wants and assigns roles to the others, who may or may not agree. Most children this age want their own role. As their creativity blossoms through this type of play, their solutions to role assignment problems are often highly creative and something an adult would not have thought of. Listen to the children in your classroom to see how they resolve such problems.

The role of mother is a favorite one for girls of this age. What would you have done when all four of the girls playing together wanted to be the mother, and no one would give in? After a few minutes of discussion—or rather argument—when it became clear to the four that Janie who spoke up first about being the mother would not change, nor would the other three, then a different solution needed to be found. The girls accepted the fact that there could be only one mother in the household, but they could not agree that the other girls would be sisters, babies, or grandmothers. Suddenly, one of the girls said, "We'll all be other mothers who are visiting Janie this morning," and they were.

Three-year-olds who are playing pretend roles at home often will act the same way in assigning roles, even to adults. "I'll be the mother, and you be the baby," is a role reversal commonly proposed by a child to her mother. Go along with the role reversal if you are the adult, and you will enjoy observing how your child plays your role.

Here is a typical role assignment situation played by three-year-olds and recorded in a running record

> *Sherry is in the play grocery store holding a box of cereal. She hands the box to the child playing the role of cashier, walks back to grocery shelves, picks up box, and puts it in grocery cart. "Here's our groceries, Mother," she says to Ann who is standing nearby. Sherry picks up bag filled with groceries and carries it to play house. She walks back to grocery store. "I'm gonna be mother," she says loudly to herself. She picks up several boxes off shelf, walks to cashier, and puts groceries in bag. "Mother, it's time to go home," she says to Ann. Ann gives no response but pays for her groceries. "There are no more groceries. We have to leave now," says Sherry. She still gets no response from Ann. "I'm the mother, and you're the grandmother. I'm not a little kid," she says to Ann. No response. They walk to house together. She puts her bag down and helps Ann with hers. "We have to unload everything now." They start to unpack all the groceries. "Oh, no, daughter," she says to Ann, "when it's cleanup time, we have to pick all this up." Both girls laugh.*

Since Ann was originally the director of this play episode and Sherry evidently had agreed to the role of daughter by taking that role, it is interesting to see what strategy Sherry now uses to get out of an unwanted role. First, she states loudly but to herself that she is going to be the mother. Since she receives no response, she retains her daughter role at first but then states outright to Ann that she is the mother and Ann can be the grandmother. Sherry still gets no response.

Silence does not necessarily give consent among young children. Silence only may mean that the challenged child does not want to engage in an argument, not that she agrees to give up her role. Sherry tries calling Ann daughter, but Ann refuses to get involved verbally, so the role problem is still unresolved before cleanup time ends the play.

Another imaginative play episode previously recorded in Chapter 1 shows children who are late three- and four-year-olds engaged in the type of role assignment problem being discussed here

> *Katy is playing by herself with plastic blocks, making guns; she walks into other room.*
>
> K: "Lisa, would you play with me? I'm tired of playing by myself."
>
> *They walk into other room to slide and climbing area.*
>
> K: "I am Wonder Woman."
>
> L: "So am I."
>
> K: "No, there is only one Wonder Woman. You are Robin."
>
> L: "Robin needs a Batman because Batman and Robin are friends."
>
> *All this takes place under slides and climber. Lisa shoots block gun that Katy has given her. Katy falls on floor.*
>
> L: (to teacher) "We're playing superfriends, and Wonder Woman keeps falling down."
>
> *Katy opens eyes, gets up, and says: "Let's get out our bat mobile and go help the world." She runs to other room and back making noises like a car.*
>
> L: "Wonder Woman is died. She fell out of the car." *She falls down.*
>
> K: "It's only a game, wake up. Lisa, you be Wonder Woman, I'll be ..."
>
> L: Let's play house now."
>
> *Katy begins sliding down the slide.* K: "We have a lot of super friends to do," *she says while sliding.* "Robin is coming after you!" *She shouts to Lisa, running from the slide and into other room.*
>
> *Lisa has gone into the housekeeping area and says to Katy: "Katy, here is your doll's dress." (Lost yesterday)*
>
> *John joins the girls.*
>
> L: "I'm Wonder Woman."
>
> K: "I'm Robin."
>
> J: "I'm Batman. Where is the bat mobile?"
>
> K: "It's in here."

*They run into the other room, and Katy points under the slide
telling John what the bat mobile can do. Then, they all run to the
other room and back again.*

K: "John, we are not playing superfriends any more."

This typical pretending episode illustrates perfectly the kind of role
assignment and switching so characteristic of children this age. It is obvious from
the children's easy agreement that they have played together before and therefore
accept certain conditions. Katy is the director here and assigns the roles. She takes
the role of Wonder Woman and assigns Lisa the role of Robin. Lisa really does not
agree (we soon see), but she accepts her assignment. She probably has gone
through this with Katy before and knows that if she plays along without making a
fuss, her turn will come. It comes quite soon, in fact, when she notes that Katy
seems to have abandoned the Wonder Woman role by suddenly getting out the bat
mobile and "going to help the world."

Here, Lisa announces that she is Wonder Woman and has fallen out of
the car and died. Katy agrees to her new role by saying: "It's only a game, wake
up. Lisa, you be Wonder Woman." When John joins the game and takes the role of
Batman, the girls do not object at first. But, obviously, they know how to get rid of
unwanted players by announcing: "John, we are not playing superfriends any
more."

Observe to discover what other creative ploys your children use to get
peers to take role assignments or to get out of assigned roles they do not want and
into ones they really want.

If your children are engaged in this kind of dramatic play, you probably
will be checking this item. Leaving it blank means either that the child is not
playing because he has not reached this level of group imaginative play, or that he
does not assign roles or accept assignments. If this is the case, he probably has not
reached the group play level because children who play together like this soon
come to an understanding about role assignments. The use of a + here probably is
not appropriate because this type of role assignment, although stressed by three-
year-olds, also is continued through the more mature levels of imaginative play.

If You Have Not Checked This Item: Some Helpful Ideas

• *Read Books That Will Motivate Role Playing*

A Lion for Lewis by Rosemary Wells, New York: The Dial Press, 1982, is the story of
dress-up play in the attic by two older children (five-year-olds) and little Lewis (age
three) who always gets assigned to play the inferior roles and never a main
character. He is baby to the older children's mother and father, sick child to their
doctor and nurse, and maid to their king and princess. Lewis eventually gets his
way, however, and much in the manner of real children, by finding something
better that the older children really respect: Lewis finds a lion suit into which he

climbs to turn the play upside down. Lewis uses the same kind of creative solution that real children use when they are blocked by their peers.

The development of creativity, as you can see, means much more than becoming an artist or writer. Perhaps the most valuable lesson that children learn from imaginative play, in fact, is how to develop creative solutions to life's sticky interpersonal problems. What an exceptionally strong inducement that is for our promoting of imaginative play in early childhood!

Much Bigger than Martin by Steven Kellogg, New York: The Dial Press, 1976, relates the typical younger sibling/older sibling problem in a highly imaginative way. The young narrator imagines in humorous detail all the things he will do to his older brother Martin when the younger sibling makes himself much bigger. Nothing that the young narrator tries seems to work, however, until he uses his creativity to make a pair of stilts.

☐ MAY SWITCH ROLES WITHOUT WARNING

The pretend play of three-year-olds is obviously more elaborate than that of two-year-olds. But, because of their free-floating nature, the plots three-year-olds make up often shift from one event to another without much advance warning. We have witnessed this characteristic before in these children. They write the letters of their names or of words here and there on a sheet of paper, sometimes starting in the middle and working both forward and backward. And a teacher finds that when preschoolers are asked to line up in a straight line, he has fifteen different versions of straightness.

Three-year-olds are not grounded on a common baseline as in Euclidean geometry, we remember. Thus, their imaginative play also reflects their free-form thinking. They may start out playing superfriends, but soon, the activity becomes house with hardly the blink of an eye. They seem to accept these abrupt shifts as a matter of course since the shifts are part of their nature.

Adults have more trouble trying to follow such thinking patterns. Our only current experience is with nighttime dreams that may start out with one sequence but evolve into something entirely different when we subconsciously play around with a particular detail.

This type of easy shifting is characteristic of divergent thinking, the process in which individuals generate a variety of novel responses to a situation, in a word, creative thinking. It is the opposite of what usually occurs: convergent thinking, in which individuals move toward a uniform response. Obviously, many more solutions to a problem are generated when we practice divergent thinking. For adults, practicing divergent thinking is not all that easy when we have been conditioned for so long to think in a stereotyped format acceptable to all.

The development of creativity calls on us to promote divergent thinking in young children and rekindle its use in our own lives. Divergent thinking is nonconformist in nature and, therefore, somewhat threatening to adults' usual response of going along with the crowd. Most young children have not yet been conditioned to behave in an inhibited manner. Thus, they are more open to novel solutions in their imaginative play. If these solutions could be carried over into adult life, what creative possibilities for resolving interpersonal problems might ensue!

Three-year-olds not only move from one episode to another in their pretend play without much concern, but they also switch from one role to another without warning. Although adults are somewhat disconcerted by such illogical moves, peers seem to accept such switches as normal. "If you want to be someone else, that's your privilege" seems to be the unspoken rule. "However, you must work out what you want in an appropriate manner if you want others to continue playing with you" seems to be the rest of the agreement.

The previous *Checklist* item discussed the assignment of roles by one child and the taking of them by others. Children seem to learn early how to get out of roles they do not want and into roles they do want without disrupting the play.

This behavior may be an illustration of the interesting findings by Gottman and Parkhurst. The researchers' study found that the friendships of three- and four-year-olds were characterized by the playing of extended fantasy roles and that a child this age took particular care to avoid disagreements. When squabbling broke out among them, the children had great difficulty de-escalating it. Therefore, they seemed to create a "climate of agreement" for one another in which they explained or played away disagreements immediately because of their awareness that disagreements had "unmanageable, adverse consequences for their friendships." (Damon, p. 141)

If we look back at the pretend play episode with Katy, Lisa, and John, it is evident that all three know who is who and what is going on even though they are sliding down the slide and running back and forth from one room to the other, and even though the roles have been switched three times. Katy is Wonder Woman, then Robin, then someone unnamed. Lisa is Robin and then Wonder Woman. John is Batman and then excluded from the play.

This format is so typical of the play of three- and four-year-olds. Their ability to handle such role assignments and switches with a nonchalance, or perhaps sensitivity, that prevents squabbles is a positive result of imaginative play that seldom has been pointed out. Not all children are able to play this way. Neither are all three- and four-year-olds able to participate in group play at this level. But, those who have been allowed the freedom and given the support to engage in such play can reach this level. Are they eventually the adults in our society who know "instinctively" how to get along with others? We would like to think so.

If You Have Not Checked This Item: Some Helpful Ideas

- *Allow Children to Settle Their Own Play Problems*

Unless the players physically are hurting one another, it is better to allow them to settle their own problems. For them to experience a squabble that gets out of hand is even important in their learning how to play with one another, as Gottman and Parkhurst discovered.

• *Read a Book That Motivates Turn-Taking in Roles*

Your Turn, Doctor by Carla Perez, and Deborah Robison, New York: Dial Books for Young Readers, 1982, is a marvelously illustrated, hilarious story about a turn-about for the little girl Gloria and her doctor who is about to give her a physical exam. Gloria refuses and instead gives the exam to her doctor. Your children, who are forever engaged in playing doctor, will love the story, and it is a book that every doctor who deals with a young child should know by heart!

☐ USES LANGUAGE FOR CREATING AND SUSTAINING PLOT

While two-year-olds do most of their pretending without much language, three-year-olds depend upon language to set the scene and sustain the action. If three-year-olds are playing by themselves, they often will talk to themselves about what is happening. They also will speak for the characters . . . all of them. If the youngsters are playing with others, they often use a great deal of dialog to carry out their ideas. Obviously, this behavior promotes the children's improved use of language and dialog with others. In addition, it provides yet another opportunity for them to express creativity: in the fresh and novel way they use words.

Words direct what the children do, the way the youngsters act, who the characters are, the unfolding of the plot, and the way the children resolve conflict. Children involved in pretending who do not have the language skills of the more advanced players are able to listen to and eventually imitate the advanced players' use of language. Everyone involved gets excellent practice in improving speaking skills, trying out new words, and using familiar language in new ways.

One of the new ways that some children use language is to express feelings. The characters in these spontaneous, make-believe situations need to express how they feel about what is happening to themselves and others. Many children have trouble putting their feelings into words. Younger children prefer to "act out" rather than speak out. This type of imaginative play gives the children the opportunity to learn how to express feelings.

The youngsters, in fact, are projecting their feelings by expressing what a character feels. If the character is a doll, a puppet, or an inanimate figure of a person or animal, the children have yet another opportunity to speak. Three-year-olds are often more comfortable expressing the feelings of toy people than their own. The youngsters like to take their dolls or stuffed animals to the doctor's, to listen to these pretend people express their fears, and to comfort them. In doing so, the children sort out their own impressions about the situation and try out their own, sometimes novel, ideas for resolving their problems.

Smilansky has found three main functions of language in this sort of dramatic play: for imitating adult speech, for imagining the make-believe situation (mainly dialog), and for managing the play. In this regard, language serves to explain, command, and direct the action. (Smilansky, p. 27)

If you listen carefully to the actors in imaginative play, you will note that they carry out all three of these functions. They definitely imitate adult speech. You practically can hear yourself speaking if you are the parent or the teacher of the child. Children also bring imagery to life in the characterizations that they express through dialog. Finally, someone in the group, usually the self-assigned director, is forever stepping outside her role to explain or reaffirm what is going on.

If inner imagery allows the child to pretend in the first place, then talking aloud allows him to expand the meaning of what he visualizes. He not only hears himself speaking, but he also receives feedback from the reactions of others. This feedback helps him to revise and refine ideas and word use. Until he arrives at the point where he can create and sustain the action of pretend situations through language, he will miss the value of using his imagination in this manner. For eventually, he must use mainly language and not just imagery in thinking. Thus, imaginative play serves as a sort of transition activity for the preschool child to learn spoken words for his internal images.

Creative adults, especially writers, need to be able to express their imagery in words like this. Mental pictures are not enough. Many admit to experiencing rich fantasy lives as children. Providing a variety of opportunities for pretending in the preschool setting may help the children in your classroom to become such creative adults.

If You Have Not Checked This Item: Some Helpful Ideas

• *Have the Children Read Wordless Picture Books*

Most wordless books illustrate their plots in a clear sequence of pictures. Although the pictures tell the story, the child needs to express the action and dialog in words as she "reads" the book. This "book practice" gives her excellent experience for doing the same activity in imaginative play. Wordless books are designed for children of various ages and developmental levels. Some of these books are simple; others are extremely complex and sophisticated. Be sure to go through a book ahead of time to see if it is suitable for a particular child.

The Midnight Adventures of Kelly, Dot, and Esmeralda by John S. Goodall, New York: Atheneum, 1972, is a small-format book containing full-page color illustrations with half-page illustrations between them. The reader turns the half page to reveal a surprising aspect of both whole pages. For instance, the half page facing the child is often a door. He turns it to reveal a double-page spread of the interior of a house. This book is an excellent device to encourage anticipation and imagining of what is hidden behind the half page. Goodall has written many books using this same format. (See his *Porky Pig* series.)

In *The Midnight Adventures of Kelly, Dot, and Esmeralda*, the plot revolves around the adventures of a teddy bear Kelly, a doll Dot and a mouse Esmeralda who come to life when the clock strikes midnight. They then enter a picture hanging on the wall and begin their trip through a fantasy land of talking animals, carnival people, and a cat animal tamer who kidnaps Esmeralda. An exciting and danger-filled escape episode brings the book to a satisfying conclusion.

Children can try out dialog to express the feelings of the adventuresome trio as well as descriptive words to set the scene and follow the action.

- *Use Hand Puppets*

Have a variety of hand puppets available for the children, puppets of animals, characters from books, community helpers, adults, and children figures. A puppet theater made from a cardboard carton can help to motivate the children's use of puppets as play actors. You may need to put on a puppet show yourself to set the stage, so to speak, for your children's dramas. Younger children tend to use puppets as an extension of their arms, using the puppets' mouths for pretend biting rather than speaking, as mentioned previously. Your modeling behavior can show the children a better way to use puppets. It is not necessary to have a puppet theater in the beginning, but your more advanced pretenders may expand their repertory of imaginative play if a puppet theater is available.

☐ USES EXCITING, DANGER-PACKED THEMES

Four-Year-Olds

Most four-year-olds do everything in a more exuberant, out-of-bounds manner than three-year-olds, including pretending. Four-year-olds are more noisy, more active, and more aware of things outside of themselves. They are fascinated with matters of life and death and begin to use such themes more and more in their imaginative play. Superheroes and other television characters show up in their pretending. Bad guys are captured. Good guys are rewarded. People get shot and killed.

Adults look askance and blame television for this behavior. They feel that TV watching surely must be bad for young children. By the age of four, many children are viewing an average of four hours of television a day. Surely, this television viewing must affect the children's pretending and imagination. Research carried on by the Singers, however, resulted in findings contrary to what they had expected. The Singers found no relationship of statistical significance between watching television and imaginary play. Pretending neither increased nor decreased as a result of watching television.

The strongest correlation the Singers found was between the amount of TV watched and overt aggression in the classroom. How true, agree nursery school teachers without perhaps realizing that four-year-olds always have exhibited aggression in their play. The real reason for the increased aggression well may be that sitting and watching television like this for long periods of time does not help young children discharge their aggressive feelings. (Segal, p. 138)

Four-year-olds are extremely active and must have daily opportunities to discharge this pent-up energy. It is only natural for this pent-up energy to take the form of aggressive character roles from the TV the children watch. Ask adults who were reared before the days of television what form their wildest pretending took, and you will hear tales of cowboys and Indians, cops and robbers, and American soldiers and Nazis.

Group play comes into its own when children reach age four. But, when they first get together, it often degenerates into a wild sort of play without plot or dialog, almost a regression from their previous role playing. (Segal, p. 98) This wild sort of play seems to be a natural progression in their learning to get along with one another. The establishment and recognition of dominance is dealt with in such rough and tumble play. Children also develop coping skills as they focus on the sometimes aggressive actions and reactions of peers. Out of this interaction comes a sense of common group purpose that sets the stage for the more organized play to follow.

Teachers can help, not by preventing wild play but by redirecting its energy into the exciting, danger-packed themes that four-year-olds favor. Doctor play, always a favorite, can involve taking sick or injured patients to the hospital in an ambulance. One teacher found that her children needed help organizing and elaborating on their ambulance plot. They had built an ambulance out of large blocks. Now what could they do? This time, the teacher decided to play a role herself. A running record of an observation of four-year-old Jessica includes the following:

> Jessica runs to climber. She climbs up and sits on top. Teacher, who is trying to involve children in dramatic play, suggests they use the climber as their hospital. They are building an ambulance out of large blocks. Jessica climbs down and begins stacking blocks one on top of the other. She sits and watches others finish by putting on paper plates to use as headlights. Jessica picks up plate and tapes it to rear of ambulance. She runs to table to get felt tip marker. "I want the yellow marker. Lots of yellow." She gets the marker. "What am I gonna write on? I want to color something. I'll color the wheels black." Jessica drops yellow marker and picks up black one. She colors in back wheel with marker. "I want to color something yellow." Teacher suggests steering wheel. She does it. She then runs and climbs in block ambulance. "I'm the driver." She uses her plate as a steering wheel. "I wanna be the patient." She gets up and lies down in middle of ambulance. She gets carried to "the hospital" by teacher and other children. She lies by the climber and pretends to be sick, moaning and groaning. The other children leave, but she stays. Then, she gets up and runs to table where teacher is helping children to make doctor bags. Teacher asks her what name she wants on her bag. Jessica answers, "I want to be a nurse, not a doctor." Teacher asks what tools a nurse uses. Jessica answers, "Nurses help, they don't use tools. Doctors use tools." Teacher asks, "What does your mother use when you are sick?" Jessica answers, "I don't know." She takes bag and runs back to ambulance with bag on arm, smiling. She yells, "Lisa, lay down, you're the patient." Jessica sits in front seat and drives ambulance using paper plate steering wheel. She hops up again and runs to teacher, asking teacher to be the doc-

tor. Jessica jumps up and down urging teacher to hurry. "Hurry,
we're ready," she repeats. Teacher comes and helps carry Lisa to
the hospital.

The teacher noted more children participated in this particular role play than any she had witnessed. An ambulance had gone by on the street outside earlier in the morning, siren blaring, and the children who saw it were excited but alarmed. This event prompted their building of the block ambulance. But, the teacher's own participation in the play certainly stimulated the extra number of children to become involved. The teacher's idea for extending the play by helping the children make doctor bags added immensely to the drama. The running record, however, caught four-year-old Jessica just as she normally acted: always on the run.

Her rather stereotyped answers about doctors is also typical of this age. Gender roles seem to become more rigid, with girls insisting on playing the mother, waitress, or teacher, while boys often want to play father, driver, or policeman. Same-gender groups form about this time, with girls' play becoming more relaxed and verbal and boys' play becoming faster-paced and more aggressive. (Segal, p. 101)

Block play, for instance, may get out of hand with four-year-olds. It sometimes disintegrates into throwing when adults are not around, or even when they are. Try to change the direction of the block play by giving the players a new task involving excitement or mystery: "Where is the mysterious tunnel I saw on the floor this morning, boys? What, you didn't see it? I'm surprised. I thought you had X-ray vision like I have. I could see it right through the rug. You don't believe me? Well, maybe if you make your own tunnel, you'll be able to see the mystery tunnel, too. Jeff, you and Lennie know how to build tunnels. Maybe you could make a mystery tunnel at one end of the rug and Rod and Kennie could make a mystery tunnel at the other end. If the tunnels came together in the middle, you all would be able to run your cars through the one tunnel. What do you think?"

If you observe that individual children who are age four have not started playing with exciting and danger-packed themes such as this, the youngsters may be less mature than the others or may need more practice. How do they compare with other four-year-olds in motor skills, for instance? Obviously, it is not appropriate to push these children into something they are not interested in. Provide them with many opportunities to engage in play themes of their own interests. You will know what some of these themes are from your observations and conversations with the youngsters.

If You Have Not Checked This Item: Some Helpful Ideas

▪ *Read Books with Imaginative Adventures*

Come Away from the Water, Shirley by John Burningham, New York: Thomas Y. Crowell, 1977, is a marvelous example of the imaginative life of a four- or five-year-old girl who accompanies her mother and father to the beach. While they sit in their beach chairs and give her directions on the left side of the book's double spread pages, Shirley and her dog engage in an imaginary pirate ship adventure on all of the right-hand pages. While her mother is telling her not to stroke the dog, saying, "Shirley, you don't know where he's been," the opposite page shows Shirley being forced to "walk the plank" on the pirate ship while her dog bites the pirate's leg. Shirley's imaginary adventures are wordless, giving the children a chance to make up their own dialog and descriptions.

• *Have Big Building Supplies*

Four- and five-year-olds like to build big structures to play in. Have the youngsters use hollow wooden blocks if possible. Or, bring in wooden packaging crates you get from a wholesaler. Cardboard cartons, plastic milk carton carriers, scrap boards, and lumber can be used for building huts, forts, houses, boats, race cars, and fire engines. Play houses also can be purchased commercially, made out of pup tents, created by covering a card table with a blanket, or produced by hanging sheets over lines strung in a corner of the room.

☐ TAKES ON CHARACTERISTICS AND ACTIONS RELATED TO ROLE

Four-year-olds have more experience than three-year-olds when it comes to creating a role in their pretend play. Because they desperately want to participate in the adult world, four-year-olds try out all sorts of adult roles: mother at work, father at work, doctor, nurse, bus driver, astronaut, waiter, fast food cook, gas station attendant, mail deliverer, firefighter, truck driver, train conductor, and crane operator. In addition, four-year-olds play their roles with many more realistic details. They select props more carefully, dress up more elaborately, and carry out roles with more appropriate dialog and actions.

If you listen carefully to four-year-olds when you are observing them doing imaginative play, you will be able to learn a great deal about their understanding of the people and situations in their world. In addition, you may gain quite a respect for their use of creativity in developing their roles. Even the mundane roles of mother, father, brother, and baby are played with new twists and novel solutions to problems. Dialog is expanded, and the players even express emotions quite eloquently where appropriate.

Language is used more than ever before to set the scene and create the mood. Because the players are beginning to make greater distinctions between real and pretend, they often make "aside" comments about things that are not real, just pretend, just so you, their peers, and, yes, they, themselves, understand what is real and what is pretend.

Four-year-olds are also more flexible about taking different roles. Children who would not take a "bad guy's" role at age three may play it to the hilt at age four.

Observe your children carefully as they pretend in the dramatic play area, in the block corner, at the water table, and on the playground. Are they playing roles with greater realism than before, using expanded dialog, showing more emotion, and almost becoming the character? If yes, then you should check this item on the *Checklist*.

If You Have Not Checked This Item: Some Helpful Ideas

- *Have Many Sets of Flannelboard Characters*

Children can use cut out characters from their favorite storybooks to play with on a flannelboard. Obtain an extra paperback copy of the book, cut out the characters, and mount them on cardboard with sandpaper backing. Keep the characters in a manila envelope with a copy of the book inside. Then, children can look at pictures from the story, as well, when playing. The youngsters can act out scenes from the book if they want or have the characters participate in brand new adventures. This activity is good practice in role playing with characters the children already know. A child can play by herself or with another child. More than two children at the same flannelboard is a bit crowded. Keep more than one small-size flannelboard in the book area, if you want this to be a popular activity. Flannelboards can be made by mounting flannel or felt to a piece of cardboard that is folded in two with a hinge at the top so that it stands easily on a table.

Some favorite storybooks in paperback from which you may want to cut out characters include

Corduroy by Don Freeman, New York: Viking Press, 1968. Characters include girl, her mother, and teddy bear named Corduroy.

Strega Nona by Tomie de Paola, Englewood Cliffs, N.J.: Prentice-Hall, 1975. Characters include Strega Nona, the Grandma Witch; Big Anthony; the Magic Pot; and the townspeople.

The Three Billy Goats Gruff by Paul Galdone, New York: Clarion Books, 1973. Characters include the little Billy Goat Gruff, the middle Billy Goat Gruff, the big Billy Goat Gruff, and the troll.

Where the Wild Things Are by Maurice Sendak, New York: Scholastic Book Services, 1963. Characters include little boy Max and the wild things.

Whistle for Willie by Ezra Jack Keats, New York: Puffin, 1977. Characters include Peter, his mother, his father, and his dog Willie.

Will I Have A Friend? by Miriam Cohen, New York: Collier Books, 1967. Characters include Jim and his preschool friends.

☐ USES ELABORATE AND CREATIVE THEMES, IDEAS, DETAILS

The themes that four-year-olds use in their pretending are many of the same ones they used at age three, only much expanded. The youngsters still enjoy playing house. Both boys and girls play with dolls as well as take roles in the housekeeping corner. Doll play now includes dressing as well as undressing, but the central action usually involves putting the doll to bed. Many girls of this age prefer playing with little girl dolls rather than baby dolls. Play with dollhouses, however, is still too detailed to hold the interest of most four-year-olds. The youngsters like the dolls more than the houses. Even block structures are not played with as much as they will be played with at age five. The pretending takes place during the process of building, rather than afterwards.

Doctor play is at its peak at age four, and it seldom will be as popular again. All kinds of themes involving community helpers are used, especially after a visit by a community helper or a field trip to a work site. Superheroes are popular, as we have seen, especially TV characters. Monsters sometimes appear, but they are still a bit scary for four-year-olds to handle.

Five-Year-Olds

The pretend play of older four-year-olds and of five-year-olds is characterized by the elaborate nature of the drama, no matter whether the theme is a common one or an invented adventure. Five-year-olds add all kinds of details through their dialog, dress-up, props, and imaginations. Their play gets so involved, in fact, that it even can be carried over from one day to the next. The players remember where they left off the day before and can start right in again.

There is much more talk during pretend play, as well, for five-year-olds have a better command of the language. With this better command of the language, they clarify ideas and talk out problems. Concerns about sickness, accidents, and death are dealt with more realistically in the imaginative play of five-year-olds. Although the youngsters like to use props, those with a high level of fantasy can pretend without props.

Boys and girls begin playing more in groups of the same gender by this time. This structure changes the nature of the play somewhat, with girls' play becoming more calm and boys' play becoming more active. Groups are often larger than before as friendships expand and children learn how to get along with more than one or two peers.

Five-year-olds like to build big buildings and then play inside the structures. Imaginative play is at its height during and just before this period. After children enter first grade and games with rules become the norm, make-believe play begins to wane. It is not at all prevalent among children much after age seven.

By this time, a cognitive change that allows more abstract thinking has taken place within the child. What happens to pretending? We speculate that it does not disappear at all but becomes a part of the inner-self, to be tapped by adults in their daydreaming as well as in their generation of creative ideas. Those adults who experienced a rich fantasy life as children may be the fortunate possessors of the skill to play around with ideas in their heads as adults, just as they did with props and toys as children.

As you observe the children in your classroom on the last of the *Checklist* items, you may want to make a list of the themes the children are using in their play. What can you do to add to this list? Put out more props? Read more stories? Help the children make more costumes? Take children on more field trips so that the youngsters will have additional real experiences to draw from? All of these activities are good ideas. Try them, and see how your children respond.

If You Have Not Checked This Item: Some Helpful Ideas

▪ *Read a Book to Motivate Ideas*

Children love to hear about *Owliver*, the little owl who liked to pretend, in *Owliver* by Robert Kraus, New York: Windmill & Dutton, 1974. Owliver first pretends he is an orphan, but when his mother and father object, he then pretends to be an actor. This time, his father objects and gives him doctor and lawyer toys to encourage more serious interests. His mother, however, gives him acting lessons, including tap dancing. He fools them both, of course, by growing up to become . . . a fireman!

TABLE 9. Development of imagination

Age	Child's Pretend Play Behavior
1–2	Goes through pretend routines of eating or other brief actions, in some cases
2–3	Replays fragments of everyday experience (e.g. putting baby to bed) Repeats routine over and over in ritualistic manner Uses realistic props (if uses props at all)
3–4	Insists often on particular props in order to play May have imaginary playmate at home Uses family, doll-play, hospital, cars, trains, planes, and firefighting themes Assigns roles or takes assigned roles May switch roles without warning
4–5	Uses exciting, danger-packed themes (e.g., superheroes, shooting, and running) Is more flexible about taking assigned roles during play Uses more rigid gender roles (e.g., girls as mother, waitress, or teacher; boys as father, doctor, or policeman)
5–6	Plays more with doll house, block structure Includes many more details, much dialog Carries play over from one day to next sometimes Plays more in groups of same gender

REFERENCES CITED

Caplan, Theresa, and Frank Caplan. *The Early Childhood Years: The 2 to 6 Year Old.* New York: The Putnam Publishing Group, 1983.

Damon, William. *Social and Personality Development.* New York: W.W. Norton & Company, 1983.

Segal, Marilyn, and Don Adcock. *Just Pretending: Ways to Help Children Grow through Imaginative Play.* Englewood Cliffs, N.J.: Prentice-Hall, 1981.

Singer, Dorothy G., and Jerome L. Singer. *Partners in Play: A Step-by-Step Guide to Imaginative Play in Children.* New York: Harper & Row, Publishers, 1977.

Singer, Jerome L. *The Child's World of Make-Believe: Experimental Studies of Imaginative Play.* New York: Academic Press, 1973.

Smilansky, Sara. *The Effects of Sociodramatic Play on Disadvantaged Preschool Children.* New York: John Wiley & Son, 1968.

OTHER SOURCES

Beaty, Janice J. *Skills for Preschool Teachers.* Columbus, Ohio: Charles E. Merrill Publishing Company, 1984.

LEARNING ACTIVITIES

1. Use the *Child Skills Checklist,* "12. Imagination," as a screening tool to observe all of the children in your classroom. Compare the children with checks at the higher levels in the sequence of imagination development with their checks in social play and language development. Can you draw any conclusions from this comparison?

2. Choose a child who has displayed high level skills in imagination, and make a running record of him or her on three different days. What new details did you learn about the child's pretending?

3. Look over the activities suggested, and choose one for use with one of the children whom you have screened as needing help in this area. Carry out the activity you have prescribed for the child. Record the results.

4. Take a field trip with your children to a site of interest where they can see and meet people at work in a special field. Put out appropriate props in your dramatic play area after you return, and record what kinds of pretend play takes place. Is the play any different from what went on previously? If so, how do you account for this?

5. Carry out one of the book activities from this chapter with one child or a small group, and see if it stimulates any pretending on his or her/their part. How could you extend this pretending?

14 Observation of the Whole Child

A s you have studied the twelve separate areas of child development included in this observational program, you may have noted that each of the aspects followed a similar pattern in the growth of the child: from the general to the specific. Children learn to control large muscles before the youngsters develop small motor control. Children recognize overall patterns of cognitive discrimination before the details become clear, speak single words to include whole categories of things before they learn the names for each item, draw a circle to represent a person before they learn to add the details, and pretend in stereotyped roles about mothers and fathers before they add the personal touches identifying specific family members.

This book has proceeded in the opposite direction: specific categories of development were detailed first. We have looked in some depth at self-identity, emotional development, social play, prosocial behavior, large motor development, small motor development, cognitive development (classification and seriation), cognitive development (number, time, space, and memory), spoken language, written language, art skills, and imagination.

Now, it is time to look at the whole picture. The child is, of course, a whole being whose development in these areas is proceeding simultaneously. Once you understand the details of this growth, it is possible to make an overall assessment of the developmental skills that each of your children possesses by using the *Child Skills Checklist* as a whole. From such an assessment, it is then possible to draw a total picture of the child in order to make individual plans that will promote continued development.

TEACHER OR STUDENT TEACHER AS OBSERVER

In order to draw a total picture of the child, you must step out of your role of caregiver and into the role of objective observer. Do this role changing as unobtrusively as possible. Have another staff member take over your duties for a particular period while you observe a single child using the *Checklist* as your guide. Many teachers find that using a clipboard or notebook for backing, with a pencil or pen attached on a string, is a convenient way to record while sitting or standing. Keep away from the activities but as close as possible to the child whom you are observing. Try not to become involved with the children.

If the children ask what you are doing, you can reply that you are busy writing this morning. If they want you to join their activity, you can refuse politely, saying that you have things to write and that you will join them later. If a child wants to use your pencil, you can show him that it is attached to the clipboard and suggest that he use one in the writing area. Children will soon try to imitate you, you're sure to note. (You had better attach a pencil to a notebook in the writing area, as well, for children will want theirs to be just like yours.)

How long should you spend observing? It is a good idea to observe using the *Checklist* for at least half an hour at a time. You should be familiar with

In order to step out of your role as teacher and into the role of observer, you need to ask another staff member to take over your duties while you observe, using the Child Skills Checklist *as a guide.*

the various items by now and not have to spend too much time flipping the pages back and forth to locate something. You may find, as many observers do, that it is difficult to step back in a busy classroom and keep your concentration for much longer than half an hour at a time. Yet, it is important for you to see as much of the child's involvement in all aspects of the program as possible. The solution is to make a number of observations at different times during the day on different days.

Making a reliable overall assessment of a single child is not possible based on only one observation. You should have as much information as you can gather from as many different days, different activities, and different points of view as possible. The best overall records are a compilation made by all of the classroom staff. Have each person put a date by the items she has observed. She may want to indicate her checkmarks with a symbol or her initials if you are using the same *Checklist* for all your observations.

Try to avoid making eye contact with the child you are observing. If he or she looks your way, you can look around at the other children. Children are much more observant than we often give them credit for. In spite of your best efforts, the child you are observing often will pick up the fact that you are watching him or her, if you keep watching long enough. Most children soon forget about the scrutiny they are undergoing and continue their participation in their activity. If you find, however, that your child seems uncomfortable by your presence and even may try to get away, then you should break off your observation. Try again another day, or let another staff member or another student observe that particular child.

How should you begin? You may want to learn something about a particular child in a certain area of development to start. Perhaps he has difficulty getting involved with the others in the pretend play during free choice period. Plan to begin your observation during this period. You will want to look at the items under "3. Social Play." Other *Checklist* areas that often can be seen at the same time as social play include the items under "1. Self-Identity," items under "2. Emotional Development," items under "4. Prosocial Behavior," items under "9. Spoken Language," and items under "12. Imagination."

Circle the *Checklist* area you are observing, and then, place a check-mark beside each item you see the child performing, an *N* beside the items you have no opportunity to observe, or a + beside the item if the child has progressed beyond it and is performing at a more advanced level. Leave the item blank if none of the above conditions apply. This blank means that the child has the opportunity to perform the item but does not do it.

Many observers also like to make notes after each item, jotting down the action the child performs (or does not perform) that prompted them to check the item (or leave it blank). If you use the *Checklist* on more than one day in a cumulative manner, be sure to put the date after each item, as well.

The time of your next observation may be determined by the areas you have not had the opportunity to observe. For "1. Self-Identity," for instance, you will want to observe the child when she arrives in the morning, especially at the beginning of the year. Area "2. Emotional Development," needs to be observed during lunch or snack time, toileting, and nap time.

The *Checklist* is not a test. You should not need to ask children questions about whether they recognize certain colors, for instance. The young-sters' performance on the items should become evident as you observe the children in their natural play over time. Set up activities that will engage the children in the areas you are interested in observing. Be sure these activities are spontaneous and not forced. If a child does not get involved in Art Skills although art activities are available every day, you should circle this area and leave the items blank. Do not use *N*, no opportunity to observe, when, in fact, the child has the opportunity to participate in art activities but chooses not to. You will want to note, though, after the items that "Easel painting and table activities of cutting and pasting are available, but Robbie does not get involved in art."

SAMPLE USE OF THE CHILD SKILLS CHECKLIST

The following *Checklist* was used to observe a four-year-old boy Robbie, whom the teacher was concerned about because he seldom joined the others in their play. She observed Robbie on three different days. Here are her results

Child Skills Checklist

Name: **Robbie**   Observer: **Carol J.**

Program: **Riverside Head Start**   Date: **10/5, 10/7, 10/8**

Directions: Put a √ for items you see child perform regularly.
Put *N* for items where there is no opportunity to observe.
Put + for items where child has progressed to advanced level.
Leave all other items blank.

1. Self-Identity *10/5, 10/7, 10/8*

√	Separates from parents without difficulty **Upset when mother leaves**
√	Does not cling to adults excessively **Plays by himself**
√	Makes eye contact with adults
√	Makes activity choices without teacher's help **Knows what he wants**
___	Seeks other children to play with
___	Plays roles confidently in dramatic play
√	Stands up for own rights **Will not let others take his toys; Shows anger**
√	Displays enthusiasm in regard to doing things for self **Hums a happy tune**

2. Emotional Development *10/5*

√	Allows self to be comforted during stressful time **Lets teacher hold him**
√	Eats, sleeps, toilets without fuss away from home
N	Handles sudden changes/startling situations with control
___	Can express anger in words rather than actions **Sometimes hits when angry; no words**
√	Allows aggressive behavior to be redirected
√	Does not withdraw from others excessively
√	Shows interest/attention in classroom activities **Likes blocks especially**
√	Smiles, seems happy much of the time **Seems happy**

3. Social Play *10/5*

+	Plays by self with or without objects
√	Plays by self constructing or creating something **Likes to build**
√	Plays by self in pretending-type activity **Pretends with small cars, people**
+	Plays parallel to others with or without objects
√	Plays parallel to others constructing or creating something
√	Plays parallel to others in pretending-type activity
___	Plays with a group with or without objects
___	Plays with a group constructing or creating something
___	Plays with a group in pretending-type activity

4. Prosocial Behavior *10/5, 10/7, 10/8*

√	Shows concern for someone in distress **Comes over to child who is crying**
N	Shows delight for someone experiencing pleasure
___	Shares something with another
N	Gives something of his/her own to another

_____ Takes turns with toys or activities *Has trouble with favorite*
⌄ Waits for turn without a fuss *toys*
⌄ Helps another do a task *Helped Nat with his building; helps*
N Helps another in need *with cleanup 10/8*

5. Large Motor Development *10/7*
⌄ Walks down steps alternating feet
⌄ Runs with control over speed and direction *Likes to run*
⌄ Jumps over obstacle, landing on two feet
⌄ Hops forward on one foot
⌄ Pedals and steers tricycle
⌄ Climbs up and down climbing equipment with ease *Very good*
control
⌄ Throws object overhand to target *Throws beanbag well*
⌄ Catches thrown object with hands *(when teacher plays)*

6. Small Motor Development *10/5, 10/7, 10/8*
⌄ Shows hand preference (which is *right*)
⌄ Turns with hand easily (knobs, lids, eggbeaters) *Likes water play*
_____ Pours liquid into glass without spilling
_____ Unfastens and fastens zippers, buttons, Velcro tabs
⌄ Picks up and inserts objects with ease *Puzzles*
_____ Uses drawing/writing tools with control *Does not engage in art*
_____ Uses scissors with control
N Pounds in nails with control *Not available*

7. Cognitive Development: Classification and Seriation *10/8*
N Recognizes basic geometric shapes
⌄ Recognizes colors *Tells colors of clothes*
⌄ Recognizes differences in size
⌄ Sorts objects by appearance *Plays table games well*
⌄ Discriminates things that are alike from those that are different
⌄ Puts parts together to make a whole *Does puzzles easily*
N Arranges events in sequence from first to last
N Arranges objects in series according to a certain rule

8. Cognitive Development: Number, Time, Space, Memory *10/8*
⌄ Counts by rote to ten
⌄ Counts objects to ten
⌄ Knows the daily schedule in sequence
⌄ Knows what happened yesterday
⌄ Can build a block enclosure *Very good with blocks*
⌄ Can locate an object behind or beside something
⌄ Recalls words to song, chant
⌄ Can recollect and act on a series of directions

9. Spoken Language _10/5_

_____ Speaks confidently in the classroom **Speaks very softly**
__✓__ Speaks clearly enough for adults to understand **I need to listen**
__✓__ Speaks in expanded sentences **closely**
_____ Takes part in conversations with other children **Not usually**
_____ Asks questions with proper word order
_____ Makes negative responses with proper word order
_____ Uses past tense verbs correctly
__N__ Plays with rhyming words

10. Written Language _10/5_

_____ Pretends to write by making scribbles in horizontal lines
_____ Includes features of real letters in scribbling
__✓__ Identifies own written name
__✓__ Identifies classroom labels
__✓__ Knows some alphabet letters **Letters of his name**
_____ Makes real letters
_____ Prints letters of name
_____ Prints name correctly in linear manner

11. Art Skills _10/5_

__✓__ Makes random marks or covers paper with color **(not often)**
_____ Scribbles on paper
_____ Forms basic shapes **Art available but Robbie**
_____ Makes mandalas **does not get involved**
_____ Makes suns
_____ Draws human as circle with arms and legs attached
_____ Draws animals, trees
_____ Makes pictorial drawings

12. Imagination _10/5_

__+__ Pretends by replaying familiar routines
__+__ Needs particular props to do pretend play
_____ Assigns roles or takes assigned roles **Doesn't often play with**
_____ May switch roles without warning **others**
__✓__ Uses language for creating and sustaining plot **Talks to himself**
__✓__ Uses exciting, danger-packed themes **With cars & people**
__✓__ Takes on characteristics and actions related to role **Motorcycle**
__N__ Uses elaborate and creative themes, ideas, details **driver Hard to tell**

☐ INTERPRETATION OF CHECKLIST RESULTS

When the teacher, Carol J., had finished observing Robbie on three different days for about half an hour each time, she had a much better idea of Robbie's strengths as well as areas needing strengthening. Her observation confirmed for her that Robbie usually did not play with other children, but seemed to prefer to do things on his own. He seemed to be quite independent, making choices on his own, defending his rights, being enthusiastic about the things he chose to do, and smiling much of the time. She chuckled about his characteristic tuneless humming as he busily engaged himself in block building or racing little cars. She always could tell where Robbie was by his humming.

Being happy and smiling were especially important clues to Carol about the overall status of any child in her class. Robbie demonstrated few negative behaviors, in fact, except for his quick temper when other children tried to interfere with his activities. Carol had tried to get him to express his feelings in words, but without success. Now, she noted that he really did not speak all that much. Somehow, she had missed that important aspect of his behavior because he seemed content, and possibly because he did vocalize . . . if only to hum.

Now, she noted that although she could understand him if she listened closely, his speaking skills were not at the level of the other four-year-olds. She began to wonder if this might be the reason he did not get involved in playing with the others. Because dialog and conversation are so much a part of make-believe play, a child without the verbal skills might feel out of place, she reasoned.

She had a strong hunch that Robbie was highly creative. Watching him build elaborate roads for his race car and talk to himself as he played alone or parallel to the others, he seemed to invent all kinds of situations for the miniature people he played with. She noted that creativity certainly did not show up in his arts skills, but she reasoned that his difficulty with small motor skills may have caused him to avoid painting, drawing, and cutting.

In looking for areas of strength, Carol picked out his enthusiasm and good self-concept, his large motor skills, his cognitive skills, and his imaginative play. His special interests seemed to be block building, water play, and all kinds of outdoor play. She felt he was a bright boy who used his cognitive ability in playing by himself, rather than joining others. Areas needing strengthening included language; small motor skills; use of writing, drawing, and painting tools; control of his temper; and, especially, playing with the other children.

SHARING CHECKLIST RESULTS

In order to confirm her interpretation of the *Child Skills Checklist* observation, Carol shared the results with the two other classroom workers. They also were surprised about how little Robbie verbalized, and that they, too, had not picked up this fact previously. What had they missed about the other children, they wondered. One of them decided to observe Robbie on her own, using the *Checklist* to see how her results compared with Carol's. The teacher assistants were fascinated by the details Carol had gleaned in a very short time and by the way she had interpreted Robbie's inability to join in group play.

Carol decided to set up a meeting with Robbie's mother to share her findings and talk about how Robbie behaved at home. As always, she featured the positive aspects of Robbie's development and behavior, hoping to use them in helping Robbie improve in the areas where he needed strengthening. Robbie's mother was very interested in Carol's observation. She told Carol that Robbie was the youngest of three brothers and did not seem to have the language skills at age four that his older brothers had shown. She also noted that Robbie preferred to play alone, but she had never considered that his speaking skills might be the cause.

She told how all three boys invented their own games because they had few toys at home. As a single working parent, she had all she could do to provide for their food and clothing needs. When Carol suggested that Robbie might like to continue water play at home in the sink with empty containers, his mother thought this was a fine idea and also a way that he might help her with the dishes! She was especially pleased that Carol felt Robbie was bright on the basis of his water play games and block building in the center. She asked Carol for other ideas for making up games with household throwaway items. Carol offered to lend her a booklet full of ideas. When Carol also mentioned that the center liked to send home picture books for parents to read to their children, Robbie's mother said she thought Robbie would like this a lot. She wanted to come back in a few weeks and see how Robbie was doing, to which Carol agreed with pleasure.

PLANNING FOR INDIVIDUALS BASED ON CHECKLIST RESULTS

Once the observation has been completed, the classroom staff can make plans for the individual child by using his areas of strength to help build on his areas needing strengthening. These can be listed on a learning prescription along with particular activities to help the child. Activities to help children improve in each *Checklist* item are described at the end of discussion about the item. (See the following learning prescription that Carol formulated to help Robbie.)

After Carol and her staff had agreed upon Robbie's most important strengths and areas needing strengthening, they then discussed what activities they could set up to involve Robbie in helping himself improve in the three areas listed. They decided to ask him to help a new boy Russ to learn to use the outside climber because Robbie was so good at it. Talking and helping one other child should not be as difficult for Robbie in the beginning as playing with a larger group.

They looked at the activities listed in Chapter 10, Spoken Language, and decided to use puppets as a possible way for Robbie to get more involved in speaking with others. Carol would read the book *Louie* to Robbie and a small group of children and then give each of them a puppet that the staff had prepared from paper bags. The staff decided to name Robbie's puppet, Ron the Race Car Driver. Carol then would use her own puppet to engage the children in talking through

Learning Prescription For: **Robbie** ___ Date: **10/12**

Areas of Strength and Confidence

1. Good self-concept, happy, helpful
2. Creative in blockbuilding, water play
3. Good large motor skills, esp. outside on play equipment

Areas Needing Strengthening

1. Learn to play with others
2. Develop better speaking, conversational skills
3. Improve small motor coordination

Activities to Help

1. Ask Robbie to help new boy learn to use climber
2. Read "Louie" & give him puppet to play with
3. Do medicine droppers/water/food colors in muffin tin

their puppets. Once they got the idea, she would extract herself from the pretending and let them play on their own.

She decided to do this during the activity period every day with small groups of children, always trying to include Robbie. She hoped Robbie and the others would like the activity enough to make other puppets on their own. This also would involve Robbie with small motor and art skills. She also decided to work on Robbie's problem of learning to control his temper through the puppet play . . . by having her own puppet get angry and hit her and by asking the others to help her puppet express anger differently.

In case Robbie did not get involved in making his own puppet, she thought the medicine dropper activity with colored water in a muffin tin should interest him because of his fascination with water play. The staff decided to try these activities for a week and then discuss the results at their planning session the following week. They also decided to do a similar observation for each of the children as time permitted and to make a similar learning prescription.

USE OF THE CHECKLIST BY PRESERVICE TEACHERS AND STUDENT TEACHERS

Preservice and student teachers should use the *Child Skills Checklist* in a similar manner, making a series of observations of a single child until all of the items have been noted. In order to interpret the checked items or blanks, the observer then should read the particular chapters that discuss these areas.

It is especially helpful for the preservice teacher to make a written report or case study that includes an interpretation of the child's development in each of the twelve principal *Checklist* areas. Such a report should include not only specific information from the observations, but also whatever inferences and conclusions the observer can draw from the observational data collected based on her knowledge of child development.

In Robbie's case, the observer will want to read Chapter 2 on Self-Identity, for example, to find out what it could mean when the child has difficulty separating from the mother and why a child seems happy but still does not play with other children. Without a great deal of information, an outside observer often is not able to interpret child observations with the confidence of the classroom staff. However, certain inferences and conclusions can be offered based on the data collected, and the outside observer even may make an important contribution to the understanding of a particular child because of her fresh perspective.

In addition to the written interpretation of each of the twelve *Checklist* areas, the observer needs to summarize the overall development of the child in some detail. A Learning Prescription, similar to Carol's learning prescription for Robbie, should be done and should be followed by an explanation for the activities prescribed.

Case studies such as this can be helpful not only to the preservice or student teacher, but also to the supervising classroom teacher and the parent of the child observed. Supervising teachers need to set up case conferences with individual parents (to which student observers are invited) to discuss their reports.

OBSERVATION OF EACH CHILD

It is important to observe each of your children in this kind of detail during the year. Teachers report that they were able to learn more about each child by stepping back and making a focused observation like this, than by simply having the child in their program for an entire year. It is an eye-opening experience to look at one child in-depth from an observer's point of view, rather than from the perspective of a busy teacher involved with the activities of many other lively youngsters.

Child development college students report that this type of in-depth look at a real child makes textbooks and courses come alive, as well. Parents, too, benefit from the information gained by objective observations. Not only do the parents learn new activities to use with their children at home, but they also often become involved in the fascinating drama of how their own children develop, why their children act the way they do, and how they, as parents, best can help their children to realize their full potential.

Observing the development of young children is thus a teaching as well as a learning technique that should benefit all of its participants—teachers, students, children, and parents—because it outlines each aspect of child development, carefully, objectively, and positively. Promoting development in young children works best when it is focused on an assessment of their strengths. When you know the strengths of each child in every aspect of development, you will be able to design your program to meet individual needs as the children in your classroom work and play together creating their own unique selves.

GENERAL INDEX

INDEX OF CHILDREN'S BOOKS

INDEX OF ACTIVITIES

Activities to help children improve in each of the *Checklist* items can be found on the following pages:

THE
AUTHOR

Janice J. Beaty teaches early childhood education and children's literature courses at Elmira College in upstate New York. She is an author of children's books (*Nufu and the Turkeyfish; Plants in his Pack; Seeker of Seaways*) as well as other preschool teacher-training textbooks (*Skills for Preschool Teachers*). Dr. Beaty has developed training materials and films for the Child Development Associate (CDA) program and has travelled around the country to make presentations at CDA Training Institutes and workshops. Her interest in teaching people of other cultures has lured her to such diverse locations as the island of Guam in the western Pacific and San Salvador Island in the Bahamas. Her present studies focus on young children's learning through self-involvement with materials in their environment.